*To my boys: Nicolas, Léo, and Emmanuel*

# Contents at a Glance

# Contents

# About the Author

**Carol Hamer** has a doctorate degree in mathematics from Rutgers University. She currently works as a software engineer at In-Fusio Mobile Game Connections.

# Acknowledgments

I'D LIKE TO THANK my technical reviewer, William Swaney, for many helpful suggestions and corrections.

Additionally, I'd like to recognize the contribution of my husband Emmanuel Kowalski, who acted as my systems and network administrator throughout this project. Not only did he keep my development environment running smoothly, but he also figured out how to write the scripts and perform the Web server configuration described in Chapter 1.

# Introduction

THE JAVA 2 MICRO EDITION (J2ME) is the version of the Java 2 platform that's designed for use with smaller, less-powerful devices such as mobile phones, Personal Digital Assistants (PDAs), TV set-top boxes (for Web browsing and e-mail without a whole computer), and embedded devices. Since these devices vary quite a bit in their capabilities, the J2ME platform has two different *configurations*, each with its own choice of *profiles*. The Connected Limited Device Configuration (CLDC) is the configuration you'll be working with in this book. It's designed for mobile phones and low-level PDAs. More precisely, CLDC is intended for devices with a 16-bit or 32-bit processor, at least 160 kilobytes (KB) of nonvolatile memory, at least 32KB of volatile memory, and some network connectivity, possibly wireless and intermittent. CLDC's unique profile is the Mobile Information Device Profile (MIDP). This book is specifically concerned with the 2.0 version of MIDP (although I'll explain what changes and restrictions you need to make to write a program that's compatible with the 1.0 version of MIDP). The other configuration associated with J2ME is the Connected Device Configuration (CDC), which isn't covered in this book.

The configuration specifies the type of Java Virtual Machine (JVM) that's used and what will be in the minimal class libraries (the java.* packages and the javax.microedition.io package in the case of CLDC). CDC specifies a complete JVM, but the JVM of CLDC has some limitations compared to the standard JVM. A profile is added on top of the configuration to define a standard set of libraries (the other javax.microedition.* packages in this case). MIDP contains packages for a user interface, media control, input/output, data storage, and security.

## How the CLDC Differs from the Rest of the Java Universe

The designers of the CLDC specification have made an effort to make CLDC resemble the standard platform as closely as possible, and they've done a pretty good job of it. Nothing critical to small applications appears to be missing. I'll give a general outline of the changes here, and I'll refer you to later chapters in this book for a more in-depth discussion of the aspects that have changed the most dramatically.

### Differences in the JVM

The JVM specified in CLDC is mostly the same as the standard JVM. Unsurprisingly, a few of the costlier noncritical features have been eliminated. One example is the method `Object.finalize()`. According to the Javadoc, the `Object.finalize()` method is called on an object when the JVM determines that it's time to garbage collect that object. The actions the object can take in its `finalize()` method aren't restricted, so in particular it can make itself available again to currently active threads! The garbage collection algorithm is already expensive, and this method clearly undermines its efficiency by obligating the JVM to recheck objects that had already been marked as garbage. It's no wonder this method was eliminated in CLDC since it's not hard at all to keep track of the objects that you're still using without requiring the JVM to check with you before throwing anything away.

Some of the other areas where the JVM's set of features have been reduced are in security, threads, and exceptions/errors. See the "Understanding the Differences Between MIDP Security and Security in Other Java Versions" section in Chapter 7 for a discussion of the differences in the security model. See the "Differences Between CLDC Threads and Threads in Standard Java" section in Chapter 4 for information about threads. The changes in the error-handling system are that CLDC doesn't allow asynchronous exceptions and that the set of error classes has been greatly reduced. Instead of 22 possible errors, you now have only `OutOfMemoryError`, `VirtualMachineError`, and `Error`. On the other hand, almost all the exceptions in the java.lang.* package have been retained.

You may not notice a few changes to the JVM just by looking at the Application Programming Interface (API). In CLDC the JVM is allowed to perform some optimizations (such as prelinking classes) that were disallowed to the standard JVM. Such changes shouldn't concern the application programmer in general. The one exception is that an additional preverification stage has been added after compilation. The preverification process adds extra information to the classfile to make the bytecode verification algorithm easier at run time when the device checks that your classfile is valid before using it. You easily accomplish the preverification step with standard tools (see the "Using KToolbar" section in Chapter 1 and the "Compiling and Running from the Command Line" section in Chapter 1). Preverification isn't technically required 100 percent of the time, but it aids in compatibility, and there's no reason not to do it.

One more general item to be aware of is that although a CLDC-compliant platform is required to support Unicode characters, it's required to support only the International Organization for Standardization (ISO) Latin 1 range of characters from the Unicode standard, version 3.0. For more information about character encoding in Java, see `http://java.sun.com/products/jdk/1.3/docs/guide/intl/encoding.doc.html`.

## Differences in the Libraries

As you may guess, the standard libraries have been drastically reduced. It's unfortunate in many cases, but doing without some helpful tools is one of your challenges as a J2ME developer, just as you need to place more of a priority on writing tight, efficient code than a Java 2 Standard Edition (J2SE) or Java 2

Enterprise Edition (J2EE) developer would. The only java.* packages that you have available to you are java.lang.*, java.util.*, and java.io.*. That means you have to do without java.lang.reflect.*, java.math.*, java.security.*, and many others. Many of the missing packages have been replaced by MIDP packages that are more appropriate for small devices, as you'll see throughout this book.

Although the three remaining java.* packages have been greatly reduced, it's clear that the designers of the CLDC have tried to keep as much as possible and create familiar replacements for classes and methods that had to be removed. The java.lang.* package has been pared down to just the classes that correspond to data types (Integer, and so on) and a few necessary items: Math, Object, Runnable, String, StringBuffer, System, Thread, and Throwable (plus the exceptions and errors discussed previously). The java.util.* and java.io.* packages have been similarly reduced to their essentials. For examples of how to use the MIDP versions of the java.io.* classes, see the "Serializing More Complex Data Using Streams" section in Chapter 5. For a discussion of the changes to the java.util.* package, see the "Using the java.util Package" section in Chapter 2.

## What's New in MIDP 2.0

It's possible to write some fun basic games using the earlier (1.0) version of MIDP. I wrote the example game in Chapter 2 to be compatible with MIDP 1.0 so you can see what's available there. But MIDP 2.0 is loaded with additional features that allow you to create a much richer gaming environment. The most obvious new tool you get in MIDP 2.0 is the package javax.microedition.lcdui.game, which is a special package to help you optimize game graphics and controls (see Chapter 3). Also, now you can add music to your game (see the "Adding Music" section in Chapter 4), which was impossible in MIDP 1.0. Plus, a MIDP 2.0 device is more likely than a MIDP 1.0 device to support socket connections in addition to the standard Hypertext Transfer Protocol (HTTP)/secure HTTP (HTTPS) connections (although socket connections are optional in both MIDP 1.0 and MIDP 2.0). Sockets can simplify programming multiplayer network games (see the "Using Plain Sockets" section in Chapter 6). Additionally, a security system has been added to allow the device to regulate which applications can have access to protected resources such as sockets (see Chapter 7).

So many new, powerful features for games exist in the new MIDP 2.0 API that there's a good chance you won't even want to bother making special versions of your games for MIDP 1.0 devices. As I'm writing this (April 2004), almost all the Java-enabled small devices on the market are capable of running only MIDP 1.0. But MIDP 2.0 devices are already appearing on the market, and small devices have fast turnover. The cost of a Java-enabled cell phone is generally reduced when the customer purchases it along with a yearlong phone-service contract. Consequently, a typical user will reason that since the phone wasn't too expensive to begin with, he might as well buy a new one the next year. It probably won't be long before the MIDP 1.0 devices are the ones that are rare.

# CHAPTER 1

# Getting Started

IN THIS CHAPTER, I cover what you need to do to set up your computer for Java 2 Micro Edition (J2ME) game development and how to get your games running on an actual target device. Once you have your development environment running, you can start by building and modifying the examples from this book. You can download all the source code for the examples from the Downloads section of the Apress Web site (http://www.apress.com). This includes all the image files, descriptor files, and optional scripts.

## Downloading and Installing the Toolkit

If you haven't already downloaded and installed a development toolkit, you can get the standard one at http://java.sun.com/j2me/download.html. Look for the J2ME Wireless Toolkit 2.0. If you're planning to develop some games that will also run with Mobile Internet Device Profile (MIDP) 1.0, you may also want to download the J2ME Wireless Toolkit 1.0.4 for backward-compatibility testing. Many other J2ME emulators are available on the Web for free download, but for the rest of this chapter I'll assume you're using the J2ME Wireless Toolkit 2.0 from Sun.

If you have trouble downloading the toolkit from Sun, keep in mind that you need to register at the Sun site and log in. This shouldn't be a problem—it doesn't cost anything. You have to submit your e-mail address, but Sun has never sent me any spam as a result of my registration, so don't worry about anything.

The J2ME Wireless Toolkit contains a minimal MIDlet development environment (called *KToolbar*), a cell-phone emulator, and a number of helpful demo applications with source code. It also contains a clear and comprehensive manual in Hypertext Markup Language (HTML). I therefore won't take up too much space in this chapter repeating information contained in the manual about using the toolkit. I'll just highlight a few additional points that I noticed about toolkit in the "Compiling and Running from the Command Line" and "Using KToolbar" sections.

## Building an Application for MIDP

I'll stick with tradition and start with the classic "Hello, World" application. This example will illustrate how to get a minimal MIDlet compiled and running.

When you examine the demo applications that are bundled with the toolkit, you'll notice that they consist of a jar file and a jad file. The jar file contains the class files, the resources, and a manifest file (just as you'd expect to find in any jar file). The jad file is a Java properties (text) file that contains information to help the device run the application. The manifest file (MANIFEST.MF) found inside the jar file contains the same information as the jad file minus two properties: MIDlet-Jar-URL and MIDlet-Jar-Size.

Listing 1-1 is an example of the jad file I wrote for my "Hello, World" application. I called this file hello.jar.

*Listing 1-1.* hello.jar

```
MIDlet-1: Hello World, /images/hello.png, net.frog_parrot.hello.Hello
MMIDlet-Description: Hello World for MIDP
MIDlet-Jar-URL: hello.jar
MIDlet-Name: Hello World
MIDlet-Permissions:
MIDlet-Vendor: frog-parrot.net
MIDlet-Version: 2.0
MicroEdition-Configuration: CLDC-1.0
MicroEdition-Profile: MIDP-2.0
MIDlet-Jar-Size: 3201
```

The MIDlet-1 (and MIDlet-2, and so on) property gives the name of the MIDlet, the location of the MIDlet's icon, and the fully qualified name of the MIDlet class to run. The first two items describe how the MIDlet will appear on the menu of MIDlets. The icon should be in the jar file, and its location should be given in the same format as is used by the method Class.getResource(). Thus, in this example, your jar file should contain a top-level folder called images, which contains an icon called hello.png, as shown in Figure 1-1.

*Figure 1-1. This is the icon* hello.png.

The MIDlet-Jar-Size property gives the size of the corresponding jar file in bytes, which you can find by looking at the properties or long listing of the jar file. Be aware that if you rebuild the demos or your own applications using the build script or batch file bundled with the toolkit, you must manually update the size of the jar file in the jad file. If the MIDlet-Jar-Size property in the jad file doesn't match the size of the jar file, the MIDlet won't run.

> **NOTE** *Since the size generally changes with every build, and it's annoying to open your* jad *file in a text editor with every build, I've included some build script modification suggestions in the "Compiling and Running from the Command Line" section.*

The MIDlet-Jar-URL property gives the address of the MIDlet jar relative to the location of the jad file. If the jar file and the jad file are kept in the same directory, this is just the name of the jar file. It's also possible to use a complete Uniform Resource Locator (URL) if the jar file is located somewhere else on the Internet. Chapter 7 discusses the MIDlet-Permissions property, but for simple games, you can omit it or leave it blank. The other properties are self-explanatory.

## Creating the "Hello, World" Application

This section shows the "Hello, World" application. The MIDlet will display the message *Hello World!* on the screen and remove it (or later put it back) when you click the Toggle Msg button. Clicking the Exit button will terminate the MIDlet. The application consists of two classes: the MIDlet subclass called Hello and the Canvas subclass called HelloCanvas. How it works is sufficiently simple that I'll leave the explanations of the various steps in the comments. Chapter 2 includes in-depth discussion of how a MIDlet works. Listing 1-2 shows the code for Hello.java.

*Listing 1-2.* Hello.java

```java
package net.frog_parrot.hello;

import javax.microedition.midlet.*;
import javax.microedition.lcdui.*;

/**
 * This is the main class of the "Hello, World" demo.
 *
 * @author Carol Hamer
 */
public class Hello extends MIDlet implements CommandListener {

  /**
   * The canvas is the region of the screen that has been allotted
   * to the game.
   */
  HelloCanvas myCanvas;
```

```
/**
 * The Command objects appear as buttons in this example.
 */
private Command exitCommand = new Command("Exit", Command.EXIT, 99);


/**
 * The Command objects appear as buttons in this example.
 */
private Command toggleCommand = new Command("Toggle Msg", Command.SCREEN, 1);


/**
 * Initialize the canvas and the commands.
 */
public Hello() {
  myCanvas = new HelloCanvas();
  myCanvas.addCommand(exitCommand);
  myCanvas.addCommand(toggleCommand);
  // you set one command listener to listen to all
  // of the commands on the canvas:
  myCanvas.setCommandListener(this);
}


//-----------------------------------------------------------------
//   implementation of MIDlet

/**
 * Start the application.
 */
public void startApp() throws MIDletStateChangeException {
  // display my canvas on the screen:
  Display.getDisplay(this).setCurrent(myCanvas);
  myCanvas.repaint();
}


/**
 * If the MIDlet was using resources, it should release
 * them in this method.
 */
public void destroyApp(boolean unconditional)
    throws MIDletStateChangeException {
}


/**
 * This method is called to notify the MIDlet to enter a paused
```

```
 * state. The MIDlet should use this opportunity to release
 * shared resources.
 */
public void pauseApp() {
}


//--------------------------------------------------------------------
//   implementation of CommandListener

/*
 * Respond to a command issued on the Canvas.
 * (either reset or exit).
 */
public void commandAction(Command c, Displayable s) {
  if(c == toggleCommand) {
    myCanvas.toggleHello();
  } else if(c == exitCommand) {
    try {
      destroyApp(false);
      notifyDestroyed();
    } catch (MIDletStateChangeException ex) {
    }
  }
}

}
```

Listing 1-3 shows the code for HelloCanvas.java.

*Listing 1-3.* HelloCanvas.java

```
package net.frog_parrot.hello;

import javax.microedition.lcdui.*;

/**
 * This class represents the region of the screen that has been allotted
 * to the game.
 *
 * @author Carol Hamer
 */
public class HelloCanvas extends Canvas {

  //------------------------------------------------------------
  //   fields
```

```
/**
 * whether the screen should currently display the
 * "Hello World" message.
 */
boolean mySayHello = true;


//---------------------------------------------------------
//    initialization and game state changes

/**
 * toggle the hello message.
 */
void toggleHello() {
  mySayHello = !mySayHello;
  repaint();
}


//---------------------------------------------------------
// graphics methods

/**
 * clear the screen and display the "Hello World" message if appropriate.
 */
public void paint(Graphics g) {
  // get the dimensions of the screen:
  int width = getWidth ();
  int height = getHeight();
  // clear the screen (paint it white):
  g.setColor(0xffffff);
  // The first two args give the coordinates of the top
  // left corner of the rectangle.  (0,0) corresponds
  // to the top-left corner of the screen.
  g.fillRect(0, 0, width, height);
  // display the "Hello World" message if appropriate:.
  if(mySayHello) {
    Font font = g.getFont();
    int fontHeight = font.getHeight();
    int fontWidth = font.stringWidth("Hello World!");
    // set the text color to red:
    g.setColor(255, 0, 0);
    g.setFont(font);
```

```
        // write the string in the center of the screen
        g.drawString("Hello World!", (width - fontWidth)/2,
                    (height - fontHeight)/2,
                    g.TOP|g.LEFT);
    }
  }

}
```

The "Hello, World" application is simple enough to run with MIDP 1.0 as well as with MIDP 2.0. Figure 1-2 shows what the "Hello, World" application looks like when running on the Wireless Toolkit 1.0.4's DefaultGrayPhone emulator.

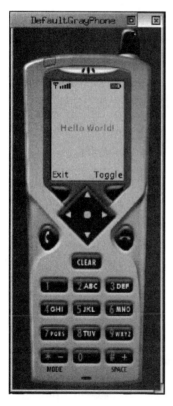

*Figure 1-2. The "Hello, World" application*

## Using KToolbar

The MIDlet development environment KToolbar is easy to use, and it's well documented. Even if you're not planning to use KToolbar, you should definitely browse the documentation a bit so you have a good idea of what sorts of tasks KToolbar can do (you may decide you want to use it after all...).

KToolbar is a "minimal" development environment in the sense that, unlike JBuilder, it doesn't contain a text editor. It'll create and update your jad and manifest files and your project's directory tree for you after you fill in the details in a set of Graphical User Interface (GUI) windows, but you have to create all the source files yourself in your own text editor. Also unlike JBuilder, it doesn't create its own project file describing your project. This is handy because you can open a "project" in KToolbar, even if you created the directory tree for the project yourself, instead of having KToolbar create it for you. All you need to do is make sure your project's root directory is in the right place (in the apps folder inside the WTK2.0 folder), and you can open it as a project in KToolbar.

In addition to setting up your project, KToolbar will preverify and build your project and then run it in the emulator at the click of a GUI button. It also has a whole suite of useful features for debugging and performance monitoring. Plus, it has tools for signing your MIDlet. (Chapter 7 covers more about signing.) Figure 1-3 shows what KToolbar looks like.

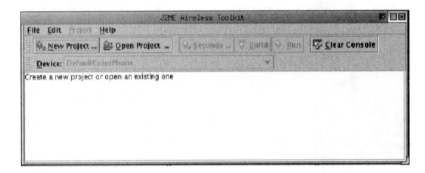

*Figure 1-3. KToolbar*

## Compiling and Running from the Command Line

Running the MIDlet in the emulator from the command line is simple. All I did was go to the bin directory under the toolkit's WTK2.0 directory. From there I typed **./bin/emulator** followed by an option giving the name of the jad descriptor file corresponding to the MIDlet I wanted to run. For example, to run the "Hello, World" application on my system, I typed the following line:

```
./bin/emulator -Xdescriptor:/home/carol/j2me/book/ch02/bin/hello.jad
```

Another useful option when running the emulator from the command line is the option that gives you a choice of different devices. The option is -Xdevice, and the choices are DefaultColorPhone, DefaultGrayPhone, MediaControlSkin, and

QwertyDevice. The previous command including this option looks like this (note that it needs to be typed on a single line):

```
./bin/emulator -Xdevice:Qwerty Device
-Xdescriptor:/home/carol/j2me/book/ch02/bin/hello.jad
```

Figure 1-4 shows the DefaultColorPhone emulator. You'll find other emulator options listed in the toolkit documentation's "Running the Emulator" section.

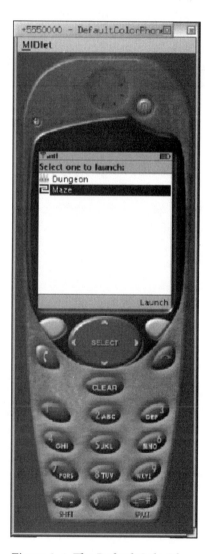

*Figure 1-4. The DefaultColorPhone emulator*

As I mentioned previously, if you rebuild your project from the command line using the scripts bundled with the toolkit, you'll need to update the MIDlet-Jar-Size property in your jad file after rebuilding. This isn't necessary if you're using

KToolbar, but personally I like to build my jar files myself whenever possible so I know what's in them. If you're planning to build your jar files using scripts, you'll probably want to change the build script so you won't have to update the jad file by hand in a text editor after every build. This section assumes that you're using Linux or Unix. (I'd guess that those people who aren't using Linux/Unix are also not building their jar files from the command line, so they probably have already skipped this section.)

The build script in Listing 1-4 requires that the MIDlet-Jar-Size property is the last line of the jad file, as it is in the examples I provided. Note that this script assumes you have a file tree configured as follows: Under your project's main directory, you must have four subdirectories: bin (which contains this script as well as the jad and MANIFEST.MF files), a tmpclasses directory (which may be empty), a classes directory (containing a subdirectory called images that contains all of your image files), and a src directory that contains the directory tree for the source code of the MIDlet you'd like to compile.

*Listing 1-4. Build Script*

```
# This script builds and preverifies the code
# for the example games.

# reset this variable to the path to the correct javac
# command on your system:
JAVA4_HOME=/usr/java/j2sdk1.4.0_01/bin
# reset this variable to the corresct path to the WTK2.0
# directory of the WTK2.0 toolkit that you downloaded:
WTK2_HOME=../../../WTK2.0

echo "clear directories"
# it's better not to leave old class files lying
# around where they may accidentally get picked up
# and create errors...
rm ../tmpclasses/net/frog_parrot/*/*.class
rm ../classes/net/frog_parrot/*/*.class

echo "Compiling source files"

$JAVA4_HOME/javac -bootclasspath $WTK2_HOME/lib/midpapi.zip \
-d ../tmpclasses -classpath ../tmpclasses ../src/net/frog_parrot/*/*.java

echo "Preverifying class files"

$WTK2_HOME/bin/preverify \
-classpath $WTK2_HOME/lib/midpapi.zip:../tmpclasses \
-d ../classes ../tmpclasses
```

```
echo "Jarring preverified class files"
$JAVA4_HOME/jar cmf MANIFEST.MF hello.jar -C ../classes .

echo "Updating JAR size info in JAD file..."

NB=`wc -l hello.jad | awk '{print $1}'`
head --lines=$(($NB-1)) hello.jad > hello.jad1
echo "MIDlet-Jar-Size:" `stat -c '%s' hello.jar`>> hello.jad1
cp hello.jad1 hello.jad
```

## Optimizing Your Game for Different Devices

Ideally it'd be nice to have access to a whole range of devices to test your game on throughout the development phase. But even working for a large corporation you won't necessarily have access to every device on which you may want to run your games. Fortunately, the emulator has a number of performance parameters you can set in order to approximate your target devices as closely as possible. These parameters include the heap size, the virtual machine speed, the refresh speed, and the network speed. You can set these parameters from KToolbar. The toolkit's HTML documentation gives details on how to do it.

The bad news is that according to the emulator's own documentation, "Setting the VM speed parameters does not emulate real device speed, even though a real device skin might be used." Furthermore, the documentation states, "Setting the network throughput speed does not emulate actual network transmission speed." So testing your game with a range of values for these two parameters will give you an idea of how your game will perform on various devices, but it's not perfect. Additionally, it can be difficult to find out precisely what to set these parameters to in order to emulate a given device. The device manufacturer's site usually has some product specs, but not always all the detail you'd like. If the product details aren't in an obvious location, then your best bet is usually to go to Google and search for the device name plus *specs*. A good place to start to get a list of possible devices from various manufacturers to develop for is http://www.microjava.com.

If you have a particular device in mind, the next best thing to testing on the actual target device is to test on an emulator designed by the device's manufacturer. Most major device manufacturers (including Nokia, Motorola, Ericsson, Samsung, and Siemens, to name a few) offer emulators or at least emulator skins you can download. As usual, you can find these by consulting the manufacturer's Web site or Google. (Additionally, I found a comprehensive list of links to emulator downloads at the site http://www.jroller.com/page/shareme/J2MEEmulators.) These often have proprietary class libraries included, so you should probably avoid using a proprietary toolkit as your primary development tool unless you're 100 percent certain you're developing games for only one particular brand of device. On the other hand, if you have plenty of room on your development machine, it wouldn't hurt to install some additional toolkits to fine-tune your games for particular devices.

## Running Your Game on an Actual Cell Phone

The emulator is a helpful development tool, but even though it works well, it's no substitute for testing your game on an actual device. Plus, playing your game on your own cell phone is the fun part! The idea of how to load the file onto the phone is pretty simple, but you need to be aware of a few details.

You have two ways to proceed. The first is to transfer files from your PC using a serial/Universal Serial Bus (USB) cable or an infrared connection. This option doesn't require the data to even leave your house. The second option is more exciting. It consists of placing the required files on a server on the Internet and downloading them using a data connection from the phone—using Global System for Mobile Communications/General Packet Radio Service (GSM/GPRS).

Both methods have advantages. The first method doesn't require you to make a call from the phone and is therefore completely free (except for the cost of the cable if one isn't included with the phone). Also, since the transfer takes place entirely within your own network (generally behind your firewall), there's no danger of your game being downloaded by unauthorized users. But this technique can place additional requirements on your local system. For example, in the case of Nokia, the software that's used to perform the transfer works only on Windows, and the PC that the data is being loaded from must have an infrared port or a separate USB cable.

The second method, placing the games on a Wireless Application Protocol (WAP)–accessible Web page, is clearly preferable if you intend to distribute the games yourself—even if you're distributing it only to your friends. After all, if you set it up so that you can download your game off the Internet, you can tell other people where it is and they can download it as well. For this option you need to be sure that your phone service contract includes WAP access and application downloading. (This is a typical option that's offered with a Java-enabled phone, so the salesperson who sells you the phone will probably suggest it to you before you even have to ask about it.) You'll also need a server on which to place the files. This shouldn't be too difficult to come by since most Internet Service Providers (ISPs) offer some personal Web space with standard Internet access contracts. All additional software needed for this means of data transfer exists in free versions for all platforms.

In this book I'll cover only how to transfer your games to the device through the Internet and not through direct file transfer because transferring the files directly is vendor dependent. If you'd like to transfer the files to your phone directly, then the first step is to go to the Web site of the phone's manufacturer. In the case of Nokia, for example, the necessary software is easy to find on the site and is well documented. The same should be true of most other makers of Connected Limited Device Configuration (CLDC) devices.

## Using WAP

WAP is the protocol that small devices use to access the Internet.

The principle of WAP is that your cell-phone provider makes available a gateway through which your phone can access the Internet. Since small screens make standard browser functions and standard HTML pages unusable, there's another markup language specially designed for cell phones and other small devices called Wireless Markup Language (WML). If your phone contract specifies WAP access and doesn't restrict browsing to some specific portal and sites, you can direct your phone to a WML page listing your MIDlets. From there you can download them. This is similar to a standard HTML Web page embedding a Java applet.

So, to prepare your games for download, you first need to upload them onto a Web server. You need to place the WML file on the server as well as the jar and jad files. In addition, you may have to perform some configuration so that the Web server, when accessed, returns a correct Multipurpose Internet Mail Extensions (MIME) type description for those files. Otherwise, the phone may be unable to recognize them. The following sections explain these steps in detail using the Nokia 6100 as the example phone.

## Preparing the WML File

You can use WML to display interesting content by itself, offering User Interface (UI) elements such as forms, buttons, and so on. But you don't need to do anything fancy to make a page from which your game can be downloaded. In fact, it's better to resist the temptation to make a complex WML page because of the screen limitations of the target device. Try to keep it small and simple. Listing 1-5 shows a minimal example suitable for a download page. The file is called hello.wml.

*Listing 1-5.* hello.wml

```
<?xml version="1.0"?>
<!DOCTYPE wml PUBLIC "-//WAPFORUM//DTD WML 1.1//EN"
  "http://www.WAPforum.org/DTD/wml_1.1.xml">
<wml>
<card id="hello">
<p>
Hello world!
</p>
<p>
<a href="hello.jad">Hello World App</a>
</p>
</card>
</wml>
```

Here's how it works: The first two lines are mandatory to identify the file as WML. The content of the page must be enclosed between the <wml> opening tag and the </wml> closing tag. The <card> tag delimits one screen of data for the device (not much!). As you may guess if you know some HTML or Extensible Markup Language (XML), this page will display one line containing the text *Hello world!* and another line with a link with the text *Hello World App*, as shown in Figure 1-5.

*Figure 1-5. The* hello.wml *WAP page running on the Nokia 6100*

For this link to work, the server directory containing the file hello.wml must contain a jar file called hello.jar and a jad file called hello.jad.

The page can contain multiple game links, and you add them in the obvious way. For example, inside the enclosing <card> tags, you could add a second triple such as the following:

```
<p>
<a href="maze.jad">Amazing Maze!</a>
</p>
```

on the lines immediately following these lines:

```
<p>
<a href="hello.jad">Hello World App</a>
</p>
```

(Obviously, you must also upload the corresponding jar and jad files to the server for this link.) But if you have a large number of downloadable jar files, you'll probably want to arrange them on a series of separate pages. If you have multiple versions of the same game suite that are optimized for different devices, it's a good idea to make a separate WML page for each device rather than making a page for each game suite and having the page contain the versions for multiple devices. Also, it's better to put the lengthy explanations of which version is which on a normal Web page and just put simple descriptive tags on your WML page to save the user the annoyance of excessive scrolling.

One word of warning: The `<p></p>` tags enclosing the links in the previous files aren't optional. In the case of the Nokia 6100, the device failed to recognize the links without the `<p></p>` tags.

## Configuring the Server

Many Web servers aren't configured by default to recognize the file types associated with WAP/WML/J2ME by the file extensions. If you're lucky, just uploading the files (described in the previous section) to a directory in the public area of the server will be sufficient. If you're not, the cell phone will complain that the files are in an unrecognized format (even though the jad file is just text...). If you run into this problem, you'll need to do a little bit of server configuration. I'll explain what to do in the case of the popular Apache server.

If the Apache server is running on your own machine—which is a convenient option if you have cable or Asymmetric Digital Subscriber Line (ADSL)—all you need to do is update the httpd.conf file. (On Red Hat 9, this file is located at /etc/httpd/conf/httpd.conf.) Just add the following lines to the file:

```
#### WAP/WML/JAD
##
AddType text/vnd.wap.wml wml
AddType text/vnd.wap.wmlscript wmls
AddType application/vnd.wap.wmlc wmlc
AddType application/vnd.wap.wmlscriptc wmlsc
AddType image/vnd.wap.wbmp wbmp
AddType text/vnd.sun.j2me.app-descriptor jad
AddType application/java jar
####
```

Then you must restart the server to make this information available. On Red Hat 9 you can restart the server by typing the following command as root:

```
# service httpd restart
```

If the Web server you're using belongs to your ISP, first check if the server is already configured to recognize the required types. (To check, create the page and then try to access it with your cell phone as described in the following section.) If you're using Web space made available by the cell-phone provider, then there's a high probability that the ISP has already taken care of the proper configuration.

If the server hasn't been configured correctly, you may be able to fix it yourself. Here's what to do if your ISP uses an Apache server (other servers may have similar tricks that you can find by consulting the documentation or Google...): You won't be allowed to change the main configuration file, but you can inform Apache of the correct MIME types by placing the same lines as previously in a file called .htaccess somewhere in your Web space area. (Note that you must put such a file in every directory in which you place WAP/WML/J2ME files.) Here's the file .htaccess:

```
#### WAP/WML/JAD
##
AddType text/vnd.wap.wml wml
AddType text/vnd.wap.wmlscript wmls
AddType application/vnd.wap.wmlc wmlc
AddType application/vnd.wap.wmlscriptc wmlsc
AddType image/vnd.wap.wbmp wbmp
AddType text/vnd.sun.j2me.app-descriptor jad
AddType application/java jar
####
```

Of course, you can't ask the ISP to restart its server, but it isn't necessary because Apache will notice the new file automatically. It's possible that the main configuration (which you don't control) forbids this type of user-directed overriding. In that case, you'll have to ask the ISP to change its policy or use another ISP.

## Accessing the WML File and Downloading Applications

Now for the fun part: downloading the games onto the phone! Recall that in this section I'll use the Nokia 6100 as an example. This is a typical CLDC-enabled phone, so you can apply these same ideas to other devices without too much difficulty.

Remember, you need WAP access as mentioned previously. Be sure to check the costs involved in your contract with WAP connections. For friends who simply download your games and keep them in their phones, this is unlikely to be expensive since MIDlets are quite small and the time required for downloading them will rarely exceed a single minute. For the developer, however (that's you!), it's best to get a contract that has a fixed price with unlimited WAP usage since you'll certainly have to perform this operation a number of times (unless you're placing your games on your phone using a direct PC connection during the development phase).

Before you start, you must verify that the WAP access is configured on the phone. This should have been done when you got the phone, or you should have documentation from your phone service and WAP provider giving the details. In my case, I configured the phone by going to a particular Web site and giving the phone number and a PIN code. The server then sent a Short Message Service (SMS) message containing all required information to the phone, which responded by prompting me through the procedure of entering the correct settings. On the Nokia phone you can view or edit the settings by selecting the menu item Menu ➤ Services ➤ Settings ➤ Edit Active Service Settings.

You can then connect to the hello.wml page by selecting the menu item Menu ➤ Services ➤ Go To and typing the URL just as you would for a regular Web page. So, for example, if your domain name is frog-parrot.net, then you'd type **http:// frog-parrot.net/hello.wml** if the hello.wml file is in the top-level directory. (If your hello.wml is in a subdirectory, add the names of the subdirectories to the URL just as you would for any other URL.)

If you're using your own server at home and connecting through cable or ADSL, then you may not have a nice domain name, but you should still have an Internet Protocol (IP) address to which the phone can connect. Depending on how your connection works, your IP address may change from time to time. The operating system will tell you what your current IP address is. In the case of Linux you can find out by looking for the inet addr in the output you get from typing the following command:

```
$ /sbin/ifconfig ppp0
```

If your address is just a set of numbers, it still works perfectly well in the URL. Suppose, for example, that you entered the previous command and you got the following output:

```
ppp0      Link encap:Point-to-Point Protocol
          inet addr:81.49.195.43  P-t-P:193.253.160.3  Mask:255.255.255.255
          UP POINTOPOINT RUNNING NOARP MULTICAST  MTU:1492  Metric:1
          RX packets:1108 errors:0 dropped:0 overruns:0 frame:0
          TX packets:1097 errors:0 dropped:0 overruns:0 carrier:0
          collisions:0 txqueuelen:3
          RX bytes:798514 (779.7 Kb)  TX bytes:98348 (96.0 Kb)
```

In this case, the URL to enter into your phone is **http://81.49.195.43/ hello.wml**.

Merely typing the URL into the phone can be tricky! In the case of the Nokia 6100 you can get a list of symbols by hitting the asterisk+plus key (*+). Navigate through this list using the right and left arrow keys until you find the desired symbol (such as . or / for a URL), and then select Use. Fortunately, the fact that the period (.) is the default symbol may save you a little effort. If you have a fixed IP address or domain name, you can also save yourself some typing by making a bookmark to your page.

Once the URL is entered, click OK, and the phone should open your WML page! From here you can click the link to your game, and your phone will download and install it.

## Making Image Files

If you're wondering where all the image files in this book came from, I drew them myself with a free program called *the gimp*, which you can download from http://www.gimp.org/download.html. If you decide to draw your image files with the gimp and you'd like them to have transparent backgrounds, be sure to select a transparent background when you first create a new image file. (A transparent background is nice for game objects because you don't want the rectangular frame of one game object obscuring another game object.) Then make sure you select Save Background Color when you save the file. Also, you should save it with the .png extension so that the gimp will save it in the right format to be used by a J2ME game.

One thing to keep in mind when making images is that the difference in screen size from one device to another is the factor that's likely to break your game most dramatically when you try to port it from one device to another. With very small screens every pixel counts, so a screen size difference that seems insignificant can translate to a major problem for a game. To make your game more portable, you should of course avoid using hard-coded numerical values when drawing the graphics. Additionally, it helps to make different versions of your images in different sizes. If you have only a few image files, it's probably OK to have the game dynamically choose which images to use based on screen calculations, but if you have quite a number of image files, it's usually preferable to maintain different versions of the game's jar file for different devices. Graphics in the png format tend to be pretty small, but they can add up quickly and therefore significantly impact the size of your jar.

# CHAPTER 2

# Using MIDlets

APPLICATIONS WRITTEN FOR the Mobile Internet Device Profile (MIDP) are called
MIDlets. This chapter shows you how to develop a MIDlet and places a special
emphasis on how to use the Graphical User Interface (GUI) elements. Even if
you've never written a Java GUI before, you don't have to worry about anything.
It's simple. In fact, the javax.microedition.lcdui package is a good place to start
learning GUI programming because the package is so limited. Yet it contains the
core elements of the more complicated Java GUI packages such as the java.awt
packages and the javax.swing packages, so once you've written a few microedition
GUIs, writing a Swing GUI should come pretty naturally.

This chapter's example MIDlet will be a simple maze game that has a size preferences screen that the user can access to modify the maze's size. This example
game will illustrate simple MIDlet concepts such as buttons, menus, changing
screens, forms, and simple graphics, as well as describing the MIDlet life cycle and
highlighting some differences between Java 2 Micro Edition (J2ME) programming
and programming for the other two main Java editions (Standard and Enterprise).

## Using the MIDlet Class

Your starting point when developing a MIDlet will be to extend the MIDlet class.
The MIDlet class is primarily concerned with controlling the application's life
cycle: starting, stopping, and pausing. It also provides the developer with a handle to the device's display so that you can control what appears on the screen.

## Understanding the MIDlet Life Cycle

Just as other Java GUI packages help you understand J2ME GUI writing, your knowl-
edge of Applets will help you grasp MIDlets easily. (Or vice versa—once you've
learned how MIDlets work, you'll discover that you understand Applets, too.) The
parallels are striking. Applets and MIDlets are both run by *application management
software* that acts as a layer of protection between the (possibly untrusted) Applet
or MIDlet and the target Java Virtual Machine (JVM). For Applets, the application
management software is generally a browser. In both cases the application management software performs the same role: It controls the Applet or MIDlet's life
cycle, and it provides a sandbox for the Applet or MIDlet to run in that limits access
to resources. And in both cases, the program's starting point isn't the public static

void main(String[] args) method. An Applet starts with the start() method, and a MIDlet starts with the startApp() method.

After the application management software calls startApp(), it has a few more methods it uses to control the MIDlet's life cycle, namely, pauseApp() and destroyApp(). Both of these are signals that the MIDlet needs to free up shared resources, such as input/output (IO) connections, so other applications can use them. You should think of pauseApp() as the method the application management software will call when the user temporarily switches to using another function on the device but wants to go back to your game later, and destroyApp() is of course the signal that the user is quitting your program. If you disagree with the application management software's decision to start or destroy your MIDlet, you can throw a MIDletStateChangeException to stop it. Bear in mind that if destroyApp() is called with the unconditional argument set to true, your MIDletStateChangeException will be ignored. Since the MIDletStateChangeException is something thrown by the MIDlet developer's code, you can safely ignore any MIDletStateChangeException in a try/catch block (as I've done in the later Listing 2-1) if you're certain that no such Exception will be thrown.

Incidentally, the application management software is allowed to move your application to running in the background at any time. In such a case, your program would still be running but would no longer have control of the screen and also wouldn't receive signals from the buttons. You can find out whether this has happened by calling the isShown() method of your MIDlet's current Displayable or implementing the hideNotify() method if your Displayable is a Canvas (the following section describes the Displayable class). You may expect that you don't need to worry about being sent to the background since a game isn't the sort of program that would be asked to perform its calculations in the background without pausing. But it can certainly happen, especially if your game itself has a set of commands grouped in a menu. When the menu pops up, your program no longer controls the screen, so the game may appear to the user to be paused even though it's still running in the background! If your game is one that performs tasks (such as running a timer) even when the user isn't interacting with it, then you should probably implement the method hideNotify() and have it pause the game. Of course, if the user can pause the game but it can also be paused automatically when hidden, there's a little bit of extra work to do to in the showNotify() to decide whether the game needs to be unpaused. Chapter 4 contains an example of how to deal with this.

Listing 2-1 gives some indication of what may be placed in the destroyApp() method. (I put nothing in the pauseApp() method since the program does nothing if the user isn't actively directing the player dot through the maze.) This example is simple enough that it has no shared resources that it needs to let go of but it's occupying memory (which is valuable on a small device!), so it's a good idea to set your MIDlet's object references to null so that any objects your game was using can be garbage collected. Note that calling `notifyDestroyed()` returns control of the device to the application management software, but it doesn't necessarily cause the JVM to exit (unless the user explicitly stops the Java functions and/or turns the device off). So, particular classes that were loaded by your `MIDlet` will remain in memory even after your game is done. It's especially important to keep this in mind when using `static` fields because they may retain their values from one run to the next, and they occupy space in memory when they're no longer in use.

## Using the Displayable and Display Classes

Every `MIDlet` that displays something on the screen has a currently active instance of the `Displayable` class. It's the object that represents what's currently on the screen. This example game has two `Displayable` objects. The screen that the maze is drawn on is a subclass of `Canvas` (which in turn is a subclass of `Displayable`), and the screen that allows the user to modify the size parameters of the maze is a subclass of `Form` (which is also a subclass of `Displayable` through the intermediate subclass `Screen`). You set the current `Displayable` by calling `setCurrent()` on the `MIDlet`'s unique instance of `Display`.

The `MIDlet`'s instance of `Display` is created for you. It manages the display and input devices (buttons) of the hardware. You can get a handle to it by sending your `MIDlet` instance as an argument to the static method `Display.getDisplay()`. The `setCurrent()` method is probably the most important method in this class, but you can do other fun things with this class such as making the device flash its backlight or vibrate (if the device is capable of doing such things, of course). The `Display` class is also where you find the `isColor()` and `numColors()` methods, which are important if you'd like to write one program that will run on devices with various screen limitations. Yet another useful method is the `setCurrentItem()` method, which sets the input focus to the requested `Item` on a `Form`, first setting the `Item`'s `Form` to the current `Displayable` and scrolling to the `Item` if necessary.

Notice that the example class in Listing 2-1 contains an `Alert`, which is another subclass of `Displayable`. An `Alert` is a temporary screen that's meant to give the user a punctual message, sort of like a `Dialog` except that it takes up the whole screen. In the example program, the `Alert` is there to warn the user that the screen is too small to create a reasonable maze (although in reality the screen would have to be *extremely* small for this program to refuse to draw a maze on it—smaller than the minimum required size for devices that are compliant with Connected Limited Device Configuration (CLDC). Like other `Displayable` subclasses, an `Alert` is displayed by calling `setCurrent()`. It remains for a fixed period of time (or needs to be dismissed by the user depending on how you construct it), and then the previous `Displayable` or another `Displayable` of your choice becomes current.

## Using Buttons and Menus

Although the GUI functionality is contained in the `javax.microedition.lcdui` package, I've organized things by placing some of the main buttons in my `MIDlet` subclass (called `Maze` in this example) because the functions of these buttons relate to my `MIDlet`'s life cycle.

Looking at the `Maze` class in Listing 2-1, you'll notice that buttons and menu items are instances of `javax.microedition.lcdui.Command`. There's no `Button` class and no `MenuItem` class. This is because your target screen and button configurations vary so much from device to device that it doesn't make sense to have the `MIDlet` developer decide which commands should be placed in buttons and which should be placed in menus. You'd have to maintain vastly different versions of your GUI code for each target device or face a situation where your `MIDlet` looks great on one device but looks ridiculous or is difficult to use on another. So you just create a `Command` object and give the device a little bit of information about the `Command`, and the device does the work of arranging your `Commands` for you. This is great news for those of you (like me) who aren't too keen on spending hours or days working out all the intricate ergonomic details of the perfect GUI. The trade-off is of course that you're limited in what you can do, but if one of your target devices is a cell phone, you're already pretty limited in what you can do, so it's nice that the code is correspondingly simple.

The last two arguments of the constructor give the extra information that the `Command` object needs in order to decide where it's to be placed. These arguments are the `commandType` and the `priority`. The `commandType` should be a static field code such as `Command.BACK` or `Command.HELP` that allows standard types of commands to be mapped to their usual buttons on the device. If you add a `Command` that isn't one of the standard types provided, then the `commandType` should be `Command.SCREEN`. The implementation of the priority argument may vary some from device to device, but in general those commands that have higher priority (indicated by a lower priority value) will be more easily accessible to the user. In Listing 2-1, the Exit command has been given a priority of 99, which means that this command is quite unimportant whereas the commands New Maze and Size Preferences are both given priority 1. Yet if you run this program in the emulator, you'll see that the Exit command gets its own button whereas the other two commands are hidden away in a menu. How can this be? It's because there's a particular button that the emulator assigns to the `Command` of type `Command.EXIT`, so the Exit command was mapped to that one. The `Commands` of type `Command.SCREEN` had to fight over what was left.

Then, to respond to the commands, you must implement the interface `javax.microedition.lcdui.CommandListener`. When the user selects a `Command`, the application management software calls the `CommandListener`'s `commandAction()` method. There are two differences between this interface and other GUI listeners such as `java.awt.event.ActionListener`. First, all the `Commands` that have been added to a given instance of `javax.microedition.lcdui.Displayable` have the same

`CommandListener` instead of making every `Button` and other command element have their own list of `ActionListeners`. (You associate the `CommandListener` with a `Displayable` by calling the `Displayable`'s `setCommandListener()` method.) Second, when the `CommandListener` is notified, it receives only a handle to the `Command` and the corresponding `Displayable` instead of having the JVM create a separate `Event` object. As usual, these are memory-saving simplifications that should probably cause you little inconvenience, if any.

You may have noticed in Listing 2-1 below where I create an error `Alert`, I call `setCommandListener()` to set my `MIDlet` as a command listener for the `Alert`, and then I deal with the `Command myAlertDoneCommand` in my implementation of `commandAction()`. When you create an `Alert` in MIDP 2.0 and set its timeout to `Alert.FOREVER`, the `Alert` automatically contains a Done `Command`, which corresponds to the default `Command Alert.DISMISS_COMMAND`. With the default dismiss command, when the user presses the Done button, the previous `Displayable` becomes current (or another `Displayable` of your choice becomes current if you constructed the `Alert` with a `Displayable` as an argument). Therefore, it isn't usually necessary to listen for the `Alert`'s dismiss command. However, in this case, I added my own dismiss command for two reasons: First, I'd like this game to be compatible with MIDP 1.0.4, in which the field `Alert.DISMISS_COMMAND` doesn't exist. Second, if the screen is really the wrong size for the game, I'd like the game to end when the `Alert` is done rather than just going to another `Displayable`. But I can't just end the game right after calling `Display.getDisplay(this).setCurrent(errorAlert)` because that method returns immediately after setting the current display and doesn't wait for the user to be done with the `Alert`. So, if I end the application immediately after setting the `Alert` to being the current `Displayable`, it appears for only a split second and then disappears. Instead I listen for my custom Done `Command` and end the game when the command has been activated.

Listing 2-1 shows the maze game's `MIDlet` subclass called `Maze.java`.

*Listing 2-1.* `Maze.java`

```
package net.frog_parrot.maze;

import javax.microedition.midlet.*;
import javax.microedition.lcdui.*;

/**
 * This is the main class of the maze game.
 *
 * @author Carol Hamer
 */
public class Maze extends MIDlet implements CommandListener {
```

```
//----------------------------------------------------------------
//  game object fields

/**
 * The canvas that the maze is drawn on.
 */
private MazeCanvas myCanvas;

/**
 * The screen that allows the user to alter the size parameters
 * of the maze.
 */
private SelectScreen mySelectScreen;

//----------------------------------------------------------------
//  command fields

/**
 * The button to exit the game.
 */
private Command myExitCommand = new Command("Exit", Command.EXIT, 99);

/**
 * The command to create a new maze.  (This command may appear in a menu.)
 */
private Command myNewCommand = new Command("New Maze", Command.SCREEN, 1);

/**
 * The command to dismiss an alert error message.  In MIDP 2.0
 * an Alert set to Alert.FOREVER automatically has a default
 * dismiss command.  This program does not use it in order to
 * allow backward compatibility
 */
private Command myAlertDoneCommand = new Command("Done", Command.EXIT, 1);

/**
 * The command to go to the screen that allows the user
 * to alter the size parameters.  (This command may appear in a menu)
 */
private Command myPrefsCommand
  = new Command("Size Preferences", Command.SCREEN, 1);

//----------------------------------------------------------------
//  initialization
```

```
/**
 * Initialize the canvas and the commands.
 */
public Maze() {
  try {
    myCanvas = new MazeCanvas(Display.getDisplay(this));
    myCanvas.addCommand(myExitCommand);
    myCanvas.addCommand(myNewCommand);
    myCanvas.addCommand(myPrefsCommand);
    myCanvas.setCommandListener(this);
  } catch(Exception e) {
    // if there's an error during creation, display it as an alert.
    Alert errorAlert = new Alert("error",
                                  e.getMessage(), null, AlertType.ERROR);
    errorAlert.setCommandListener(this);
    errorAlert.setTimeout(Alert.FOREVER);
    errorAlert.addCommand(myAlertDoneCommand);
    Display.getDisplay(this).setCurrent(errorAlert);
  }
}

//-----------------------------------------------------------------
//  implementation of MIDlet

/**
 * Start the application.
 */
public void startApp() throws MIDletStateChangeException {
  if(myCanvas != null) {
    myCanvas.start();
  }
}

/**
 * Clean up.
 */
public void destroyApp(boolean unconditional)
    throws MIDletStateChangeException {
  myCanvas = null;
  System.gc();
}

/**
 * Does nothing since this program occupies no shared resources
 * and little memory.
```

```
   */
  public void pauseApp() {
  }


  //------------------------------------------------------------------
  //   implementation of CommandListener

  /*
   * Respond to a command issued on the Canvas.
   * (reset, exit, or change size prefs).
   */
  public void commandAction(Command c, Displayable s) {
    if(c == myNewCommand) {
      myCanvas.newMaze();
    } else if(c == myAlertDoneCommand) {
      try {
        destroyApp(false);
        notifyDestroyed();
      } catch (MIDletStateChangeException ex) {
      }
    } else if(c == myPrefsCommand) {
      if(mySelectScreen == null) {
        mySelectScreen = new SelectScreen(myCanvas);
      }
      Display.getDisplay(this).setCurrent(mySelectScreen);
    } else if(c == myExitCommand) {
      try {
        destroyApp(false);
        notifyDestroyed();
      } catch (MIDletStateChangeException ex) {
      }
    }
  }

}
```

## Using the Form and Item Classes

The Form class is the subclass of Displayable to use when you want to create a GUI screen. The GUI items you place on it are of class Item. Since some target devices may have small screens, you should probably put only a few Items on any one Form. You can put arbitrarily many Items on a Form, but if you fill it with too many Items, the device may have to make your Form scrollable or fold it into subscreens to fit everything. A multiline TextBox naturally appears alone on the screen because it's a subclass of Screen instead of being an Item that can be placed on a Form.

Since your Form contains only a few Items anyway, you can just append() them to the Form and trust the application management software to lay them out appropriately. But if you have some definite ideas about where you'd like the Items to appear, you can call setLayout() on each Item with one of the static fields of Item such as LAYOUT_CENTER. Be aware that an Item has only one layout int field, so if you'd like to combine two or more layout directives on your Item, you should call setLayout() only once and combine your layout directives in the argument using the "or" operator (for example, setLayout(LAYOUT_RIGHT | LAYOUT_VCENTER)). This same use of the "or" operator appears in the drawString() method of the Graphics class described in the "Using the Graphics and Canvas Classes" section later in this chapter. Also keep in mind that the method setLayout() is new for MIDP 2.0, so if your program doesn't require MIDP 2.0 for anything else, you should probably not bother with this method in order to allow backward compatibility.

In my example game, the Items I've placed on my Form are both of type Gauge. A Gauge is a convenient Item to use when your target device is a cell phone because it allows the user to increase or decrease a numerical value merely by pressing the arrow keys rather than having to enter something. The corresponding value is represented graphically. In this case, I've placed two related Gauges on the same Form (see Figure 2-1). The first one allows the user to modify the width of the maze walls, and the second one (which the user can't control) shows the number of columns that the maze will be divided into, given the width of the walls.

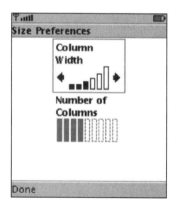

*Figure 2-1. The form containing the two* Gauges

Once you've placed all of your Items on your Form, you'll need to set an ItemCommandListener on any Item that has a Command of type Command.ITEM associated with it or an ItemStateListener on the whole Form if the Form contains Items into which the user can enter data. Item-specific Commands are new to MIDP 2.0. You add them to Items using the method Item.addCommand(), and they appear when the user selects the corresponding Item. If the Item is naturally something that the user can modify (such as a TextField or a Gauge), it's generally not necessary to add Item-specific Commands to it. Setting an ItemStateListener should be sufficient, as it's notified with a call to itemStateChanged() when the user makes a change.

Notice that when you add a Command directly to a Form, it will be mapped to a button or menu, as described in the earlier "Using Buttons and Menus" section. In the example class in Listing 2-2, this is illustrated by the Done Command, which sets the current Displayable to the MazeCanvas (in other words, it exits the size preferences screen and sends the user to the screen with the maze on it).

Listing 2-2 shows the code for the maze game's Form subclass called SelectScreen.java.

*Listing 2-2.* SelectScreen

```
package net.frog_parrot.maze;

import javax.microedition.midlet.*;
import javax.microedition.lcdui.*;

/**
 * This is the screen that allows the user to modify the
 * width of the maze walls.
 *
 * @author Carol Hamer
 */
public class SelectScreen extends Form
  implements ItemStateListener, CommandListener  {

  //-------------------------------------------------------------------
  //  fields

  /**
   * The Done button to exit this screen and return to the maze.
   */
  private Command myExitCommand = new Command("Done", Command.EXIT, 1);

  /**
   * The gauge that modifies the width of the maze walls.
   */
  private Gauge myWidthGauge;
```

```
/**
 * The gauge that displays the number of columns of the maze.
 */
private Gauge myColumnsGauge;

/**
 * A handle to the main game canvas.
 */
private MazeCanvas myCanvas;

//-------------------------------------------------------------------
//  initialization

/**
 * Create the gauges and place them on the screen.
 */
public SelectScreen(MazeCanvas canvas) {
  super("Size Preferences");
  addCommand(myExitCommand);
  setCommandListener(this);
  myCanvas = canvas;
  setItemStateListener(this);
  myWidthGauge = new Gauge("Column Width", true,
                           myCanvas.getMaxColWidth(),
                           myCanvas.getColWidth());
  myColumnsGauge = new Gauge("Number of Columns", false,
                             myCanvas.getMaxNumCols(),
                             myCanvas.getNumCols());
  // Warning: the setLayout method does not exist in
  // MIDP 1.4.  If there is any chance that a target
  // device will be using MIDP 1.4, comment out the
  // following two lines:
  myWidthGauge.setLayout(Item.LAYOUT_CENTER);
  myColumnsGauge.setLayout(Item.LAYOUT_CENTER);
  append(myWidthGauge);
  append(myColumnsGauge);
}

//-------------------------------------------------------------------
//  implementation of ItemStateListener
```

```
/**
 * Respond to the user changing the width.
 */
public void itemStateChanged(Item item) {
  if(item == myWidthGauge) {
    int val = myWidthGauge.getValue();
    if(val < myCanvas.getMinColWidth()) {
      myWidthGauge.setValue(myCanvas.getMinColWidth());
    } else {
      int numCols = myCanvas.setColWidth(val);
      myColumnsGauge.setValue(numCols);
    }
  }
}


//-----------------------------------------------------------------
// implementation of CommandListener

/*
 * Respond to a command issued on this screen.
 * (either reset or exit).
 */
public void commandAction(Command c, Displayable s) {
  if(c == myExitCommand) {
    myCanvas.newMaze();
  }
}

}
```

## Using the Graphics and Canvas Classes

The Canvas class is the subclass of Displayable that you're really interested in as a game developer since not many games lend themselves to being played on a Form. In Chapter 3 I'll talk about the extra things you can do on a GameCanvas. But a GameCanvas is a subclass of Canvas, and a lot of the important functionality is already here. There's enough to draw a simple game at least, as the example code shows.

The main tasks of the Canvas object are to implement the paint() method, which draws the game on the screen, and to implement the keyPressed() method to respond to the user's keystrokes. Implementing keyPressed() is very straightforward. When the user presses a key, the application management software calls keyPressed(), sending a keyCode as a parameter to indicate which key was pressed. In a game, you then need to translate this keyCode into a gameAction (such as Canvas.UP or Canvas.FIRE) using the method getGameAction(). This translation is necessary for portability because the mapping between keyCodes and gameActions may vary from device to device. Once the method keyPressed() returns, the application management software will call keyRepeated() (if the user is still holding down the key, possibly multiple times) and then keyReleased(). You can also implement these two methods as well if your game is interested in such events. Once the underlying game data has changed, you'll probably want to call repaint() and serviceRepaints() to get the application management software to update the screen with a call to paint().

The Graphics object that the Canvas class receives as an argument carries out most of the work in the paint() method. The Graphics class has four built-in shapes that it can draw: arcs, triangles, rectangles, and round rectangles. It can draw filled shapes or just outlines; it can draw in any Red Green Blue (RGB) value or grayscale color and can use a dotted or solid outline. Using just the built-in shapes you can already draw quite a lot of things. You'll notice in Listing 2-3 later in the chapter that I drew the maze itself by filling in a series of white and black rectangles, and I drew the player as a red circle by first calling setColor() with the red argument set to its maximum value and then calling fillRoundRect() with the width, height, arcWidth, and arcHeight arguments all set to the same value as each other. Figure 2-2 shows what the maze looks like on the emulator's screen.

*Figure 2-2. The maze on the emulator's screen*

If the built-in shapes aren't sufficient, you can also draw an Image from a file. But if you're planning to use anything more than the simplest graphics, you'll probably want to use the javax.microedition.lcdui.games package described in Chapter 3 because it contains a lot of additional support for using images.

The X and Y coordinates that are used by the various drawing methods of the Graphics class tell how far (in pixels) a given point is from the top-left corner of the Canvas. The Y value increases as you go *down* and not as you go *up*, which confused me a bit because it's the opposite of what I learned in math class, but I got used to it pretty quickly. To find out how much room you have to paint on, use the getHeight() and getWidth() methods of the Canvas. Using the point (0,0) as your top corner and drawing on a rectangle whose size is given by the getHeight() and getWidth() methods will automatically ensure that your drawing is correctly placed on the screen. If you'd like to do a larger drawing according to your own choice of coordinates and then specify which region is shown, you can do it with the "clip" methods (setClip(), and so on). But, again, I'd use the javax.microedition.lcdui.games package when doing such a complex graphical operation since the class javax.microedition.lcdui.games.LayerManager has additional support for moving the view window on a larger drawing.

The one method in the Graphics class that's a little tricky is the drawString() method. The tricky part is to figure out which anchor point you'd like to use. (Actually it's rather simple, but it's one point where I found the Javadoc explanation a little confusing.) The idea is that when you place a String, you may want to place it by specifying where the top-left corner of the String's bounding rectangle should go. Then again, you may not. For example, if you'd like to place the text near the bottom of the screen, it may be easier to place it by specifying where the bottom of the String's bounding rectangle should go. Or perhaps if you'd like the String to be right justified, you'd prefer to place it in terms of the right side of the String's bounding rectangle. So when you draw a String, its position is based on an anchor point within the String's bounding rectangle. You must choose a horizontal component and a vertical component for your anchor point and then combine them using the "or" operator (for example, BOTTOM|LEFT). The vertical choices are TOP, BASELINE, and BOTTOM, and the horizontal choices are LEFT, HCENTER, and RIGHT. You'll notice in Listing 2-3 that I've centered the String "Maze Completed" by specifying the anchor point as TOP|LEFT and then placing the top-left corner of the String at the point that's at the center of the screen minus the adjustment value of half of the length and height of the String. The adjustment is needed because I'm placing the top-left corner of the String instead of placing the center of the String. You may be wondering why I didn't set the anchor point to the center point of the String. I could have done that for the horizontal placement but not the vertical placement since VCENTER isn't one of the choices for a String's anchor point. (Incidentally, the method drawImage(), which uses anchor points in the same way to place images, allows the choice of VCENTER instead of BASELINE.) But since I had to calculate the location for the top-left corner of the String anyway (so that I could first paint a blank white rectangle to write the text on), I decided it'd be simpler to use TOP|LEFT as my anchor point.

Listing 2-3 shows the code for the maze game's Canvas subclass called MazeCanvas.java.

*Listing 2-3.* `MazeCanvas.java`

```java
package net.frog_parrot.maze;

import javax.microedition.lcdui.*;

/**
 * This class is the display of the game.
 *
 * @author Carol Hamer
 */
public class MazeCanvas extends javax.microedition.lcdui.Canvas {

  //----------------------------------------------------------
  //    static fields

  /**
   * color constant
   */
  public static final int BLACK = 0;

  /**
   * color constant
   */
  public static final int WHITE = 0xffffff;

  //----------------------------------------------------------
  //    instance fields

  /**
   * a handle to the display.
   */
  private Display myDisplay;

  /**
   * The data object that describes the maze configuration.
   */
  private Grid myGrid;

  /**
   * Whether the currently displayed maze has
   * been completed.
   */
  private boolean myGameOver = false;
```

```
/**
 * maze dimension: the width of the maze walls.
 */
private int mySquareSize;

/**
 * maze dimension: the maximum width possible for the maze walls.
 */
private int myMaxSquareSize;

/**
 * maze dimension: the minimum width possible for the maze walls.
 */
private int myMinSquareSize;

/**
 * top corner of the display: X coordinate
 */
private int myStartX = 0;

/**
 * top corner of the display: Y coordinate
 */
private int myStartY = 0;

/**
 * how many rows the display is divided into.
 */
private int myGridHeight;

/**
 * how many columns the display is divided into.
 */
private int myGridWidth;

/**
 * the maximum number columns the display can be divided into.
 */
private int myMaxGridWidth;

/**
 * the minimum number columns the display can be divided into.
 */
private int myMinGridWidth;
```

```
/**
 * previous location of the player in the maze: X coordinate
 * (in terms of the coordinates of the maze grid, NOT in terms
 * of the coordinate system of the Canvas.)
 */
private int myOldX = 1;

/**
 * previous location of the player in the maze: Y coordinate
 * (in terms of the coordinates of the maze grid, NOT in terms
 * of the coordinate system of the Canvas.)
 */
private int myOldY = 1;

/**
 * current location of the player in the maze: X coordinate
 * (in terms of the coordinates of the maze grid, NOT in terms
 * of the coordinate system of the Canvas.)
 */
private int myPlayerX = 1;

/**
 * current location of the player in the maze: Y coordinate
 * (in terms of the coordinates of the maze grid, NOT in terms
 * of the coordinate system of the Canvas.)
 */
private int myPlayerY = 1;

//-------------------------------------------------------
//    gets / sets

/**
 * Changes the width of the maze walls and calculates how
 * this change affects the number of rows and columns
 * the maze can have.
 * @return the number of columns now that the
 *         width of the columns has been updated.
 */
int setColWidth(int colWidth) {
  if(colWidth < 2) {
    mySquareSize = 2;
  } else {
    mySquareSize = colWidth;
```

```
    }
    myGridWidth = getWidth() / mySquareSize;
    if(myGridWidth % 2 == 0) {
      myGridWidth -= 1;
    }
    myGridHeight = getHeight() / mySquareSize;
    if(myGridHeight % 2 == 0) {
      myGridHeight -= 1;
    }
    myGrid = null;
    return(myGridWidth);
  }

  /**
   * @return the minimum width possible for the maze walls.
   */
  int getMinColWidth() {
    return(myMinSquareSize);
  }

  /**
   * @return the maximum width possible for the maze walls.
   */
  int getMaxColWidth() {
    return(myMaxSquareSize);
  }

  /**
   * @return the maximum number of columns the display can be divided into.
   */
  int getMaxNumCols() {
    return(myMaxGridWidth);
  }

  /**
   * @return the width of the maze walls.
   */
  int getColWidth() {
    return(mySquareSize);
  }

  /**
   * @return the number of maze columns the display is divided into.
   */
```

```
int getNumCols() {
  return(myGridWidth);
}


//-------------------------------------------------------
//     initialization and game state changes

/**
 * Constructor performs size calculations.
 * @throws Exception if the display size is too
 *           small to make a maze.
 */
public MazeCanvas(Display d) throws Exception {
  myDisplay = d;
  // a few calculations to make the right maze
  // for the current display.
  int width = getWidth();
  int height = getHeight();
  // tests indicate that 5 is a good default square size,
  // but the user can change it...
  mySquareSize = 5;
  myMinSquareSize = 3;
  myMaxGridWidth = width / myMinSquareSize;
  if(myMaxGridWidth % 2 == 0) {
    myMaxGridWidth -= 1;
  }
  myGridWidth = width / mySquareSize;
  if(myGridWidth % 2 == 0) {
    myGridWidth -= 1;
  }
  myGridHeight = height / mySquareSize;
  if(myGridHeight % 2 == 0) {
    myGridHeight -= 1;
  }
  myMinGridWidth = 15;
  myMaxSquareSize = width / myMinGridWidth;
  if(myMaxSquareSize > height / myMinGridWidth) {
    myMaxSquareSize = height / myMinGridWidth;
  }
  // if the display is too small to make a reasonable maze,
  // then you throw an Exception
  if(myMaxSquareSize < mySquareSize) {
    throw(new Exception("Display too small"));
  }
}
```

```
/**
 * This is called as soon as the application begins.
 */
void start() {
  myDisplay.setCurrent(this);
  repaint();
}


/**
 * discard the current maze and draw a new one.
 */
void newMaze() {
  myGameOver = false;
  // throw away the current maze.
  myGrid = null;
  // set the player back to the beginning of the maze.
  myPlayerX = 1;
  myPlayerY = 1;
  myOldX = 1;
  myOldY = 1;
  myDisplay.setCurrent(this);
  // paint the new maze
  repaint();
}


//-----------------------------------------------------------
//  graphics methods

/**
 * Create and display a maze if necessary. otherwise just
 * move the player.  Since the motion in this game is
 * very simple, it is not necessary to repaint the whole
 * maze each time, just the player + erase the square
 * that the player just left..
 */
protected void paint(Graphics g) {
  // If there is no current maze, create one and draw it.
  if(myGrid == null) {
    int width = getWidth();
    int height = getHeight();
    // create the underlying data of the maze.
    myGrid = new Grid(myGridWidth, myGridHeight);
    // draw the maze:
    // loop through the grid data and color each square the
```

```
    // right color
    for(int i = 0; i < myGridWidth; i++) {
      for(int j = 0; j < myGridHeight; j++) {
        if(myGrid.mySquares[i][j] == 0) {
          g.setColor(BLACK);
        } else {
          g.setColor(WHITE);
        }
        // fill the square with the appropriate color
        g.fillRect(myStartX + (i*mySquareSize),
                   myStartY + (j*mySquareSize),
                   mySquareSize, mySquareSize);
      }
    }
    // fill the extra space outside of the maze
    g.setColor(BLACK);
    g.fillRect(myStartX + ((myGridWidth-1) * mySquareSize),
               myStartY, width, height);
    // erase the exit path:
    g.setColor(WHITE);
    g.fillRect(myStartX + ((myGridWidth-1) * mySquareSize),
               myStartY + ((myGridHeight-2) * mySquareSize), width, height);
    // fill the extra space outside of the maze
    g.setColor(BLACK);
    g.fillRect(myStartX,
               myStartY + ((myGridHeight-1) * mySquareSize), width, height);
}
// draw the player (red):
g.setColor(255, 0, 0);
g.fillRoundRect(myStartX + (mySquareSize)*myPlayerX,
                myStartY + (mySquareSize)*myPlayerY,
                mySquareSize, mySquareSize,
                mySquareSize, mySquareSize);
// erase the previous location
if((myOldX != myPlayerX) || (myOldY != myPlayerY)) {
  g.setColor(WHITE);
  g.fillRect(myStartX + (mySquareSize)*myOldX,
             myStartY + (mySquareSize)*myOldY,
             mySquareSize, mySquareSize);
}
// if the player has reached the end of the maze,
// you display the end message.
if(myGameOver) {
  // perform some calculations to place the text correctly:
  int width = getWidth();
```

```
              int height = getHeight();
              Font font = g.getFont();
              int fontHeight = font.getHeight();
              int fontWidth = font.stringWidth("Maze Completed");
              g.setColor(WHITE);
              g.fillRect((width - fontWidth)/2, (height - fontHeight)/2,
                              fontWidth + 2, fontHeight);
              // write in red
              g.setColor(255, 0, 0);
              g.setFont(font);
              g.drawString("Maze Completed", (width - fontWidth)/2,
                          (height - fontHeight)/2,
                              g.TOP|g.LEFT);
          }
      }


      /**
       * Move the player.
       */
      public void keyPressed(int keyCode) {
        if(! myGameOver) {
          int action = getGameAction(keyCode);
          switch (action) {
          case LEFT:
            if((myGrid.mySquares[myPlayerX-1][myPlayerY] == 1) &&
               (myPlayerX != 1)) {
              myOldX = myPlayerX;
              myOldY = myPlayerY;
              myPlayerX -= 2;
              repaint();
            }
            break;
          case RIGHT:
            if(myGrid.mySquares[myPlayerX+1][myPlayerY] == 1) {
              myOldX = myPlayerX;
              myOldY = myPlayerY;
              myPlayerX += 2;
              repaint();
            } else if((myPlayerX == myGrid.mySquares.length - 2) &&
                      (myPlayerY == myGrid.mySquares[0].length - 2)) {
              myOldX = myPlayerX;
              myOldY = myPlayerY;
              myPlayerX += 2;
```

```
            myGameOver = true;
            repaint();
          }
          break;
        case UP:
          if(myGrid.mySquares[myPlayerX][myPlayerY-1] == 1) {
            myOldX = myPlayerX;
            myOldY = myPlayerY;
            myPlayerY -= 2;
            repaint();
          }
          break;
        case DOWN:
          if(myGrid.mySquares[myPlayerX][myPlayerY+1] == 1) {
            myOldX = myPlayerX;
            myOldY = myPlayerY;
            myPlayerY += 2;
            repaint();
          }
          break;
      }
    }
  }

}
```

## Using the java.util Package

If you're not careful, you may not notice that the java.util package that comes with MIDP is any different from the java.util package you already know and love. I found some of my favorite classes there (Vector and Random), and all the methods I wanted to use were in the usual places. You can see how I used some java.util classes in the code in Listing 2-4. But beware! Many of the standard java.util classes are simply not there, and the ones that are there are missing some of their functionality.

Fortunately, most of the core classes are there, so even if you don't have a LinkedHashMap, you can probably make due with a Hashtable, and you can probably get around using a StringTokenizer with a little extra programming. One thing I miss is using Locale and ResourceBundle for internationalization. That was such an elegant application of the "write once, run anywhere" philosophy! But while my enterprise clients didn't mind my cluttering up their hard drives with GUI labels for every language from Icelandic to Swahili, it's not really an appropriate use of the limited memory of a cell phone. (Other localization features are also missing such as formatting for dates, currencies, and times. The only help you get is the system property microedition.locale, which tells you the locale to which the device is set.) So what do you do about internationalization? It looks like it's difficult to avoid maintaining separate versions of your code for different countries. You could automate the changes from one country to the next using scripts. Since memory conservation is so important in J2ME, it would have been a good idea to include a standard (optional) precompilation phase like in C. This would not only simplify internationalization but would also allow other memory-saving tricks such as inline functions and constants that are numbers in the compiled code instead of being public static final variables. But they probably figured that Java programmers don't want to deal with the headaches of reading other people's macros.

The example class for this section is the class that contains the maze generation algorithm. I'm leaving the description of how it works for the comments since it's just pure math, and there's nothing J2ME specific about it. Notice that the java.util classes Vector and Random are used in the usual way.

Listing 2-4 shows the code for Grid.java.

*Listing 2-4.* Grid.java

```
package net.frog_parrot.maze;

import java.util.Random;
import java.util.Vector;

/**
 * This class contains the data necessary to draw the maze.
 *
 * @author Carol Hamer
 */
public class Grid {

  /**
   * Random number generator to create a random maze.
   */
  private Random myRandom = new Random();

  /**
   * data for which squares are filled and which are blank.
   * 0 = black
   * 1 = white
   * values higher than 1 are used during the maze creation
   * algorithm.
   * 2 = the square could possibly be appended to the maze this round.
```

```
 * 3 = the square's color is not yet decided, and the square is
 * not close enough to be appended to the maze this round.
 */
int[][] mySquares;


//----------------------------------------------------------
//  maze generation methods

/**
 * Create a new maze.
 */
public Grid(int width, int height) {
  mySquares = new int[width][height];
  // initialize all the squares to white except a lattice
  // framework of black squares.
  for(int i = 1; i < width - 1; i++) {
    for(int j = 1; j < height - 1; j++) {
      if((i % 2 == 1) || (j % 2 == 1)) {
        mySquares[i][j] = 1;
      }
    }
  }
  // the entrance to the maze is at (0,1).
  mySquares[0][1] = 1;
  createMaze();
}


/**
 * This method randomly generates the maze.
 */
private void createMaze() {
  // create an initial framework of black squares.
  for(int i = 1; i < mySquares.length - 1; i++) {
    for(int j = 1; j < mySquares[i].length - 1; j++) {
      if((i + j) % 2 == 1) {
        mySquares[i][j] = 0;
      }
    }
  }
  // initialize the squares that can be either black or white
  // depending on the maze.
  // first you set the value to 3, which means undecided.
  for(int i = 1; i < mySquares.length - 1; i+=2) {
    for(int j = 1; j < mySquares[i].length - 1; j+=2) {
```

```
            mySquares[i][j] = 3;
      }
   }
   // Then those squares that can be selected to be open
   // (white) paths are given the value of 2.
   // You randomly select the square where the tree of maze
   // paths will begin.  The maze is generated starting from
   // this initial square and branches out from here in all
   // directions to fill the maze grid.
   Vector possibleSquares = new Vector(mySquares.length
                                       * mySquares[0].length);
   int[] startSquare = new int[2];
   startSquare[0] = getRandomInt(mySquares.length / 2)*2 + 1;
   startSquare[1] = getRandomInt(mySquares[0].length / 2)*2 + 1;
   mySquares[startSquare[0]][startSquare[1]] = 2;
   possibleSquares.addElement(startSquare);
   // Here you loop to select squares one by one to append to
   // the maze pathway tree.
   while(possibleSquares.size() > 0) {
      // the next square to be joined on is selected randomly.
      int chosenIndex = getRandomInt(possibleSquares.size());
      int[] chosenSquare = (int[])possibleSquares.elementAt(chosenIndex);
      // you set the chosen square to white and then
      // remove it from the list of possibleSquares (i.e. squares
      // that can possibly be added to the maze), and you link
      // the new square to the maze.
      mySquares[chosenSquare[0]][chosenSquare[1]] = 1;
      possibleSquares.removeElementAt(chosenIndex);
      link(chosenSquare, possibleSquares);
   }
   // now that the maze has been completely generated, you
   // throw away the objects that were created during the
   // maze creation algorithm and reclaim the memory.
   possibleSquares = null;
   System.gc();
}

/**
 * internal to createMaze.  Checks the four squares surrounding
 * the chosen square.  Of those that are already connected to
 * the maze, one is randomly selected to be joined to the
 * current square (to attach the current square to the
 * growing maze).  Those squares that were not previously in
 * a position to be joined to the maze are added to the list
```

```
 * of "possible" squares (that can be chosen to be attached
 * to the maze in the next round).
 */
private void link(int[] chosenSquare, Vector possibleSquares) {
  int linkCount = 0;
  int i = chosenSquare[0];
  int j = chosenSquare[1];
  int[] links = new int[8];
  if(i >= 3) {
    if(mySquares[i - 2][j] == 1) {
      links[2*linkCount] = i - 1;
      links[2*linkCount + 1] = j;
      linkCount++;
    } else if(mySquares[i - 2][j] == 3) {
      mySquares[i - 2][j] = 2;
      int[] newSquare = new int[2];
      newSquare[0] = i - 2;
      newSquare[1] = j;
      possibleSquares.addElement(newSquare);
    }
  }
  if(j + 3 <= mySquares[i].length) {
    if(mySquares[i][j + 2] == 3) {
      mySquares[i][j + 2] = 2;
      int[] newSquare = new int[2];
      newSquare[0] = i;
      newSquare[1] = j + 2;
      possibleSquares.addElement(newSquare);
    } else if(mySquares[i][j + 2] == 1) {
      links[2*linkCount] = i;
      links[2*linkCount + 1] = j + 1;
      linkCount++;
    }
  }
  if(j >= 3) {
    if(mySquares[i][j - 2] == 3) {
      mySquares[i][j - 2] = 2;
      int[] newSquare = new int[2];
      newSquare[0] = i;
      newSquare[1] = j - 2;
      possibleSquares.addElement(newSquare);
    } else if(mySquares[i][j - 2] == 1) {
      links[2*linkCount] = i;
      links[2*linkCount + 1] = j - 1;
```

```
              linkCount++;
            }
          }
      if(i + 3 <= mySquares.length) {
        if(mySquares[i + 2][j] == 3) {
          mySquares[i + 2][j] = 2;
          int[] newSquare = new int[2];
          newSquare[0] = i + 2;
          newSquare[1] = j;
          possibleSquares.addElement(newSquare);
        } else if(mySquares[i + 2][j] == 1) {
          links[2*linkCount] = i + 1;
          links[2*linkCount + 1] = j;
          linkCount++;
        }
      }
      if(linkCount > 0) {
        int linkChoice = getRandomInt(linkCount);
        int linkX = links[2*linkChoice];
        int linkY = links[2*linkChoice + 1];
        mySquares[linkX][linkY] = 1;
        int[] removeSquare = new int[2];
        removeSquare[0] = linkX;
        removeSquare[1] = linkY;
        possibleSquares.removeElement(removeSquare);
      }
    }


  /**
   * a randomization utility.
   * @param upper the upper bound for the random int.
   * @return a random non-negative int less than the bound upper.
   */
  public int getRandomInt(int upper) {
    int retVal = myRandom.nextInt() % upper;
    if(retVal < 0) {
      retVal += upper;
    }
    return(retVal);
  }


}
```

As you can see from this example, if your game is simple enough, you can write it using entirely MIDP 1.0 classes and methods. However, for a fast-paced game with more complicated graphics, you'll undoubtedly want to use the additional functionality provided by the `javax.microedition.lcdui.game` package, described in the next chapter.

# CHAPTER 3

# Using the MIDP 2.0 Games API

NOW IT'S TIME TO LOOK at the most important package you'll be dealing with when writing games with Mobile Internet Device Profile (MIDP) 2.0: the package `javax.microedition.lcdui.game.*`. In this chapter, I show you the main parts of a MIDP 2.0 game by explaining the code of an example game called Tumbleweed. The game involves a cowboy walking through a prairie jumping over tumbleweeds. It's kind of a silly game, but it illustrates most of the basics you'll need when writing more reasonable games.

As in the earlier chapters, I've included all of the code necessary to build the example, and you can download the code from the Downloads section of the Apress Web site (`http://www.apress.com`) with all its resources.

## Starting with the MIDlet Class

As usual, the application starts with the `MIDlet` class. In this case, my `MIDlet` subclass is called `Jump`. This class is essentially the same as the `MIDlet` subclass from the previous chapter, so if you'd like a detailed explanation of what's going on in it, please see the "Using the MIDlet Class" section in Chapter 2. The only differences here are the use of a separate `GameThread` class and the fact that when the user presses a command button, I have the `MIDlet` change the command that's available on the screen. The command change is because the user can pause the game only when it's unpaused, can unpause the game only when it's paused, and can start over only when the game has ended.

Listing 3-1 shows the game's `MIDlet` subclass called `Jump.java`.

*Listing 3-1.* `Jump.java`

```
package net.frog_parrot.jump;

import javax.microedition.midlet.*;
import javax.microedition.lcdui.*;

/**
 * This is the main class of the Tumbleweed game.
```

```
 *
 * @author Carol Hamer
 */
public class Jump extends MIDlet implements CommandListener {

  //----------------------------------------------------------
  //    commands

  /**
   * the command to end the game.
   */
  private Command myExitCommand = new Command("Exit", Command.EXIT, 99);

  /**
   * the command to start moving when the game is paused.
   */
  private Command myGoCommand = new Command("Go", Command.SCREEN, 1);

  /**
   * the command to pause the game.
   */
  private Command myPauseCommand = new Command("Pause", Command.SCREEN, 1);

  /**
   * the command to start a new game.
   */
  private Command myNewCommand = new Command("Play Again", Command.SCREEN, 1);

  //----------------------------------------------------------
  //    game object fields

  /**
   * the canvas that all of the game will be drawn on.
   */
  private JumpCanvas myCanvas;

  /**
   * the thread that advances the cowboy.
   */
  private GameThread myGameThread;

  //----------------------------------------------------------
  //     initialization and game state changes
```

```java
/**
 * Initialize the canvas and the commands.
 */
public Jump() {
  try {
    myCanvas = new JumpCanvas(this);
    myCanvas.addCommand(myExitCommand);
    myCanvas.addCommand(myPauseCommand);
    myCanvas.setCommandListener(this);
  } catch(Exception e) {
    errorMsg(e);
  }
}

/**
 * Switch the command to the play again command.
 */
void setNewCommand () {
  myCanvas.removeCommand(myPauseCommand);
  myCanvas.removeCommand(myGoCommand);
  myCanvas.addCommand(myNewCommand);
}

/**
 * Switch the command to the go command.
 */
private void setGoCommand() {
  myCanvas.removeCommand(myPauseCommand);
  myCanvas.removeCommand(myNewCommand);
  myCanvas.addCommand(myGoCommand);
}

/**
 * Switch the command to the pause command.
 */
private void setPauseCommand () {
  myCanvas.removeCommand(myNewCommand);
  myCanvas.removeCommand(myGoCommand);
  myCanvas.addCommand(myPauseCommand);
}

//-----------------------------------------------------------------
// implementation of MIDlet
// these methods may be called by the application management
```

```
// software at any time, so you always check fields for null
// before calling methods on them.

/**
 * Start the application.
 */
public void startApp() throws MIDletStateChangeException {
  if(myCanvas != null) {
    if(myGameThread == null) {
      myGameThread = new GameThread(myCanvas);
      myCanvas.start();
      myGameThread.start();
    } else {
      myCanvas.removeCommand(myGoCommand);
      myCanvas.addCommand(myPauseCommand);
      myCanvas.flushKeys();
      myGameThread.resumeGame();
    }
  }
}

/**
 * stop and throw out the garbage.
 */
public void destroyApp(boolean unconditional)
    throws MIDletStateChangeException {
  if(myGameThread != null) {
    myGameThread.requestStop();
  }
  myGameThread = null;
  myCanvas = null;
  System.gc();
}

/**
 * request the thread to pause.
 */
public void pauseApp() {
  if(myCanvas != null) {
    setGoCommand();
  }
  if(myGameThread != null) {
    myGameThread.pauseGame();
  }
```

```
    }


    //-------------------------------------------------------------------
    //   implementation of CommandListener

    /*
     * Respond to a command issued on the Canvas.
     * (either reset or exit).
     */
    public void commandAction(Command c, Displayable s) {
      if(c == myGoCommand) {
        myCanvas.removeCommand(myGoCommand);
        myCanvas.addCommand(myPauseCommand);
        myCanvas.flushKeys();
        myGameThread.resumeGame();
      } else if(c == myPauseCommand) {
        myCanvas.removeCommand(myPauseCommand);
        myCanvas.addCommand(myGoCommand);
        myGameThread.pauseGame();
      } else if(c == myNewCommand) {
        myCanvas.removeCommand(myNewCommand);
        myCanvas.addCommand(myPauseCommand);
        myCanvas.reset();
        myGameThread.resumeGame();
      } else if((c == myExitCommand) || (c == Alert.DISMISS_COMMAND)) {
        try {
          destroyApp(false);
          notifyDestroyed();
        } catch (MIDletStateChangeException ex) {
        }
      }
    }


    //---------------------------------------------------------
    //   error methods

    /**
     * Converts an exception to a message and displays
     * the message..
     */
    void errorMsg(Exception e) {
      if(e.getMessage() == null) {
        errorMsg(e.getClass().getName());
      } else {
```

```
          errorMsg(e.getClass().getName() + ":" + e.getMessage());
      }
  }

  /**
   * Displays an error message alert if something goes wrong.
   */
  void errorMsg(String msg) {
    Alert errorAlert = new Alert("error",
                                  msg, null, AlertType.ERROR);
    errorAlert.setCommandListener(this);
    errorAlert.setTimeout(Alert.FOREVER);
    Display.getDisplay(this).setCurrent(errorAlert);
  }

}
```

## Using the Thread Class

This game requires only the simplest use of the Thread class. Chapter 4 covers how to use threads. But even in this simple case, I'd like to mention a few points.

In this case, it really is necessary to spawn a new thread. The animation in this game is always moving, even when the user doesn't press a button, so I need to have a game loop that repeats constantly until the end of the game. I can't use the main thread for the game loop because the application management software may need to use the main thread while my game is running. While testing the game in the emulator, I found that if I use the main thread for my game's animation loop, the emulator is unable to respond to keystrokes. Of course, in general, it's good practice to spawn a new thread when you plan to go into a loop that's to be repeated throughout the duration of your program's active life cycle.

Here's how my Thread subclass (called GameThread) works: Once the thread starts, it goes into the main loop (inside the while(true) block). The first step is to check if the Jump class has called requestStop() since the last cycle. If so, you break out of the loop, and the run() method returns. Otherwise, if the user hasn't paused the game, you prompt the GameCanvas to respond to the user's keystrokes and advance the game animation. Then you do a short pause of one millisecond. This is partially to be sure that the freshly painted graphics stay on the screen for an instant before the next paint, but it's also useful to help the keystroke query work correctly. As mentioned, the information about the user's keystrokes is updated on another thread, so it's necessary to put a short wait inside your game loop to make sure that the other thread gets a turn and has the opportunity to update the key state's value in a timely fashion. This allows your game to respond immediately when the user presses a key. Even a millisecond will do the trick. (I earlier wrote a racecar game in which I neglected to put a wait in the main game loop, and I found that the car would go halfway around the track between the time I pressed the lane change key and the time the car actually changed lanes...).

Listing 3-2 shows the code for GameThread.java.

*Listing 3-2.* GameThread.java

```java
package net.frog_parrot.jump;

/**
 * This class contains the loop that keeps the game running.
 *
 * @author Carol Hamer
 */
public class GameThread extends Thread {

  //-----------------------------------------------------------
  //   fields

  /**
   * Whether the main thread would like this thread
   * to pause.
   */
  private boolean myShouldPause;

  /**
   * Whether the main thread would like this thread
   * to stop.
   */
  private boolean myShouldStop;

  /**
   * A handle back to the graphical components.
   */
  private JumpCanvas myJumpCanvas;

  //-----------------------------------------------------------
  //   initialization

  /**
   * standard constructor.
   */
  GameThread(JumpCanvas canvas) {
    myJumpCanvas = canvas;
  }
```

```
//------------------------------------------------------------
//   actions

/**
 * pause the game.
 */
void pauseGame() {
  myShouldPause = true;
}

/**
 * restart the game after a pause.
 */
synchronized void resumeGame() {
  myShouldPause = false;
  notify();
}

/**
 * stops the game.
 */
synchronized void requestStop() {
  myShouldStop = true;
  notify();
}

/**
 * start the game..
 */
public void run() {
  // flush any keystrokes that occurred before the
  // game started:
  myJumpCanvas.flushKeys();
  myShouldStop = false;
  myShouldPause = false;
  while(true) {
    if(myShouldStop) {
      break;
    }
    synchronized(this) {
      while(myShouldPause) {
        try {
          wait();
        } catch(Exception e) {}
```

```
      }
    }
    myJumpCanvas.checkKeys();
    myJumpCanvas.advance();
    // you do a short pause to allow the other thread
    // to update the information about which keys are pressed:
    synchronized(this) {
      try {
        wait(1);
      } catch(Exception e) {}
    }
  }
}

}
```

## Using the GameCanvas Class

Now you'll look at the class that allows you to paint customized game graphics to the screen.

### How GameCanvas Differs from Canvas

The GameCanvas class represents the area of the screen that the device has allotted to your game. The javax.microedition.lcdui.game.GameCanvas class differs from its superclass javax.microedition.lcdui.Canvas in two important ways: graphics buffering and the ability to query key states. Both of these changes give the game developer enhanced control over precisely when the program deals with events such as keystrokes and screen repainting.

The graphics buffering allows all the graphical objects to be created behind the scenes and then flushed to the screen all at once when they're ready. This makes animation smoother. I've illustrated how to use it in the method advance() in Listing 3-3. (Recall that the method advance() is called from the main loop of my GameThread object.) Notice that to update and repaint the screen, all you need to do is call paint(getGraphics()) and then call flushGraphics(). To make your program more efficient, there's even a version of the flushGraphics() method that allows you to repaint just a subset of the screen if you know that only part has changed. As an experiment I tried replacing the calls to paint(getGraphics()) and flushGraphics() with calls to repaint() and then serviceRepaints() as you might if your class extended Canvas instead of GameCanvas. In my simple examples it didn't make much difference, but if your game has a lot of complicated graphics, the GameCanvas version will undoubtedly make a big difference.

The ability to query key states is helpful for the game's organization. When you extend the Canvas class directly, you must implement the keyPressed(int keyCode) if your game is interested in keystrokes. The application management software then calls this method when the user presses a button. But if your program is running on its own thread, this might happen at any point in your game's algorithm. If you're not careful about using synchronized blocks, this could potentially cause errors if one thread is updating data about the game's current state and the other is using that data to perform calculations. The program is simpler and easier to follow if you get the keystroke information when you want it by calling the GameCanvas method getKeyStates().

An additional advantage of the getKeyStates() method is that it can tell you if multiple keys are being pressed simultaneously. The keyCode that's passed to the keyPressed(int keyCode) method can tell you only about a single key and therefore will be called multiple times even if the user presses two keys at the same time. In a game, the precise timing of each keystroke is often important, so the Canvas method keyPressed() loses valuable information. Looking at the method checkKeys() in Listing 3-3, you can see that the value returned by getKeyStates() contains all the keystroke information. All you need to do is perform a bit-wise "and" (&) between the getKeyStates() return value and a static field such as GameCanvas.LEFT_PRESSED to tell if a given key is currently being pressed.

This is a large classfile, but you can see the main idea of how it works by recalling that the main loop of the GameThread class first tells my GameCanvas subclass (called JumpCanvas) to query the key states (see the method JumpCanvas.checkKeys() in Listing 3-3 for details). Then once the key events have been dealt with, the main loop of the GameThread class calls JumpCanvas.advance(), which tells the LayerManager to make appropriate updates in the graphics (more on that in the next sections) and then paints the screen.

Listing 3-3 shows the code for JumpCanvas.java.

*Listing 3-3.* JumpCanvas.java

```
package net.frog_parrot.jump;

import javax.microedition.lcdui.*;
import javax.microedition.lcdui.game.*;

/**
 * This class is the display of the game.
 *
 * @author Carol Hamer
 */
public class JumpCanvas extends javax.microedition.lcdui.game.GameCanvas {
```

```
//----------------------------------------------------------
//    dimension fields
//    (constant after initialization)

/**
 * the height of the green region below the ground.
 */
static final int GROUND_HEIGHT = 32;

/**
 * a screen dimension.
 */
static final int CORNER_X = 0;

/**
 * a screen dimension.
 */
static final int CORNER_Y = 0;

/**
 * a screen dimension.
 */
static int DISP_WIDTH;

/**
 * a screen dimension.
 */
static int DISP_HEIGHT;

/**
 * a font dimension.
 */
static int FONT_HEIGHT;

/**
 * the default font.
 */
static Font FONT;

/**
 * a font dimension.
 */
static int SCORE_WIDTH;
```

```
/**
 * The width of the string that displays the time,
 * saved for placement of time display.
 */
static int TIME_WIDTH;

/**
 * color constant
 */
public static final int BLACK = 0;

/**
 * color constant
 */
public static final int WHITE = 0xffffff;

//-----------------------------------------------------------
//   game object fields

/**
 * a handle to the display.
 */
private Display myDisplay;

/**
 * a handle to the MIDlet object (to keep track of buttons).
 */
private Jump myJump;

/**
 * the LayerManager that handles the game graphics.
 */
private JumpManager myManager;

/**
 * whether the game has ended.
 */
private boolean myGameOver;

/**
 * the player's score.
 */
private int myScore = 0;
```

```
/**
 * How many ticks you start with.
 */
private int myInitialGameTicks = 950;

/**
 * this is saved to determine if the time string needs
 * to be recomputed.
 */
private int myOldGameTicks = myInitialGameTicks;

/**
 * the number of game ticks that have passed.
 */
private int myGameTicks = myOldGameTicks;

/**
 * you save the time string to avoid recreating it
 * unnecessarily.
 */
private static String myInitialString = "1:00";

/**
 * you save the time string to avoid recreating it
 * unnecessarily.
 */
private String myTimeString = myInitialString;

//-------------------------------------------------------
//     gets/sets

/**
 * This is called when the game ends.
 */
void setGameOver() {
  myGameOver = true;
  myJump.pauseApp();
}

//-------------------------------------------------------
//     initialization and game state changes

/**
 * Constructor sets the data, performs dimension calculations,
```

```
     * and creates the graphical objects.
     */
   public JumpCanvas(Jump midlet) throws Exception {
     super(false);
     myDisplay = Display.getDisplay(midlet);
     myJump = midlet;
     // calculate the dimensions
     DISP_WIDTH = getWidth();
     DISP_HEIGHT = getHeight();
     Display disp = Display.getDisplay(myJump);
     if(disp.numColors() < 256) {
       throw(new Exception("game requires 256 shades"));
     }
     if((DISP_WIDTH < 150) || (DISP_HEIGHT < 170)) {
       throw(new Exception("Screen too small"));
     }
     if((DISP_WIDTH > 250) || (DISP_HEIGHT > 250)) {
       throw(new Exception("Screen too large"));
     }
     FONT = getGraphics().getFont();
     FONT_HEIGHT = FONT.getHeight();
     SCORE_WIDTH = FONT.stringWidth("Score: 000");
     TIME_WIDTH = FONT.stringWidth("Time: " + myInitialString);
     if(myManager == null) {
       myManager = new JumpManager(CORNER_X, CORNER_Y + FONT_HEIGHT*2,
             DISP_WIDTH, DISP_HEIGHT - FONT_HEIGHT*2 - GROUND_HEIGHT);
     }
   }


   /**
    * This is called as soon as the application begins.
    */
   void start() {
     myGameOver = false;
     myDisplay.setCurrent(this);
     repaint();
   }


   /**
    * sets all variables back to their initial positions.
    */
   void reset() {
     myManager.reset();
     myScore = 0;
```

```
    myGameOver = false;
    myGameTicks = myInitialGameTicks;
    myOldGameTicks = myInitialGameTicks;
    repaint();
  }

  /**
   * clears the key states.
   */
  void flushKeys() {
    getKeyStates();
  }

  /**
   * This version of the game does not deal with what happens
   * when the game is hidden, so I hope it won't be hidden...
   * see the version in the next chapter for how to implement
   * hideNotify and showNotify.
   */
  protected void hideNotify() {
  }

  /**
   * This version of the game does not deal with what happens
   * when the game is hidden, so I hope it won't be hidden...
   * see the version in the next chapter for how to implement
   * hideNotify and showNotify.
   */
  protected void showNotify() {
  }

  //----------------------------------------------------------
  //  graphics methods

  /**
   * paint the game graphic on the screen.
   */
  public void paint(Graphics g) {
    // clear the screen:
    g.setColor(WHITE);
    g.fillRect(CORNER_X, CORNER_Y, DISP_WIDTH, DISP_HEIGHT);
    // color the grass green
    g.setColor(0, 255, 0);
```

```
            g.fillRect(CORNER_X, CORNER_Y + DISP_HEIGHT - GROUND_HEIGHT,
                        DISP_WIDTH, DISP_HEIGHT);
            // paint the layer manager:
            try {
                myManager.paint(g);
            } catch(Exception e) {
                myJump.errorMsg(e);
            }
            // draw the time and score
            g.setColor(BLACK);
            g.setFont(FONT);
            g.drawString("Score: " + myScore,
                            (DISP_WIDTH - SCORE_WIDTH)/2,
                            DISP_HEIGHT + 5 - GROUND_HEIGHT, g.TOP|g.LEFT);
            g.drawString("Time: " + formatTime(),
                            (DISP_WIDTH - TIME_WIDTH)/2,
                            CORNER_Y + FONT_HEIGHT, g.TOP|g.LEFT);
            // write game over if the game is over
            if(myGameOver) {
                myJump.setNewCommand();
                // clear the top region:
                g.setColor(WHITE);
                g.fillRect(CORNER_X, CORNER_Y, DISP_WIDTH, FONT_HEIGHT*2 + 1);
                int goWidth = FONT.stringWidth("Game Over");
                g.setColor(BLACK);
                g.setFont(FONT);
                g.drawString("Game Over", (DISP_WIDTH - goWidth)/2,
                                CORNER_Y + FONT_HEIGHT, g.TOP|g.LEFT);
            }
        }


    /**
     * a simple utility to make the number of ticks look like a time...
     */
    public String formatTime() {
        if((myGameTicks / 16) + 1 != myOldGameTicks) {
            myTimeString = "";
            myOldGameTicks = (myGameTicks / 16) + 1;
            int smallPart = myOldGameTicks % 60;
            int bigPart = myOldGameTicks / 60;
            myTimeString += bigPart + ":";
            if(smallPart / 10 < 1) {
                myTimeString += "0";
            }
            myTimeString += smallPart;
```

```java
    }
    return(myTimeString);
  }


  //-------------------------------------------------------
  //   game movements

  /**
   * Tell the layer manager to advance the layers and then
   * update the display.
   */
  void advance() {
    myGameTicks--;
    myScore += myManager.advance(myGameTicks);
    if(myGameTicks == 0) {
      setGameOver();
    }
    // paint the display
    try {
      paint(getGraphics());
      flushGraphics();
    } catch(Exception e) {
      myJump.errorMsg(e);
    }
  }

  /**
   * Respond to keystrokes.
   */
  public void checkKeys() {
    if(! myGameOver) {
      int keyState = getKeyStates();
      if((keyState & LEFT_PRESSED) != 0) {
        myManager.setLeft(true);
      }
      if((keyState & RIGHT_PRESSED) != 0) {
        myManager.setLeft(false);
      }
      if((keyState & UP_PRESSED) != 0) {
        myManager.jump();
      }
    }
  }

}
```

## Using the Graphics Class with a GameCanvas

Chapter 2 covered using the Graphics class. In this section, I just go over the main points of how the Graphics class is used in the example game.

In the Tumbleweed game I need to draw a cowboy walking through a prairie jumping over tumbleweeds. Figure 3-1 shows the game.

*Figure 3-1. The Tumbleweed game*

As you can see, I've put the score on the bottom and the time remaining on the top. (To simplify the game, I just have it end when the player runs out of time.) As the cowboy is walking along, I'd like his background to scroll to the right or to the left (otherwise he won't have very far to go on such a small screen...), but I'd like the time and the score to stay in place. To accomplish this, I have my JumpCanvas class take care of painting the stable strip on the top and the bottom of the screen, and I delegate the interesting graphics to the LayerManager (more details on that in the next section).

When the JumpCanvas is first created, you start by analyzing the screen with which you have to work. Some of the information about the screen's capacities comes from the Graphics object, some from the display object, and some directly from methods of the GameCanvas. This information calculates where the objects should be placed, including calculating the dimensions of the region that will be painted by the LayerManager subclass (JumpManager). If you're interested in maintaining Java's "write once, run anywhere" philosophy, it's obviously better to base the screen layout on the (dynamically determined) dimensions of the current screen rather than basing the dimensions on fixed constants. Of course, if massive changes to the game are needed when going from one target device to another, it may be better to save device memory by maintaining multiple versions of the game rather than putting all of the code together in a single version and using the display information to determine which version to run. In my example game, if the screen is too different from the screen I wrote the game for (the emulator that came with the toolkit in this case), I throw an Exception that the Jump class will catch and show it to the user as an Alert. When using this technique professionally, you'd of course make sure the Alert clearly states that the user needs to download a different version of the game for the current device.

At the risk of belaboring the obvious, I'll point out that once I know the appropriate sizes for the top and bottom regions, the paint(Graphics g) method paints the top one white and the bottom one green with g.fillRect(), and then the method g.drawString() adds the time and the score. Chapter 2 discussed the drawString() method. (Don't ask me why my prairie has both green grass and tumbleweeds; my only excuse is that I know more about Java than I know about the Wild West...).

## Using the LayerManager Class

The interesting graphical objects in an MIDP game are usually represented by subclasses of the javax.microedition.lcdui.game.Layer class. The background layers could be instances of javax.microedition.lcdui.game.TiledLayer, and the player (and his enemies) would likely be instances of javax.microedition.lcdui.game.Sprite, both of which are subclasses of Layer. The LayerManager class helps you to organize all these graphical layers. The order in which you append your Layers to your LayerManager determines the order in which they'll be painted. (The first one appended is the last one painted.) The top layers will cover the lower layers, but you can allow parts of the lower layers to show through by creating image files that have transparent regions.

Probably the most useful aspect of the LayerManager class is that you can create a graphical painting that's much larger than the screen and then choose which section of it will appear on the screen. Imagine drawing a huge, elaborate drawing and then covering it with a piece of paper that has a small rectangular hole you can move. The whole drawing represents what you can stock into the LayerManager, and the hole is the window showing the part that appears on the screen at any given time. Allowing the possibility of a virtual screen that's much larger than the actual screen is extremely helpful for games on devices with small screens. It'll save you huge amounts of time and effort if, for example, your game involves a player exploring an elaborate dungeon (see Chapter 5 for just such an example). The confusing part is that this means you have to deal with two separate coordinate systems. The Graphics object of the GameCanvas has one coordinate system, but the various Layers need to be placed in the LayerManager according to the LayerManager's coordinate system. So, keep in mind that the method LayerManager.paint(Graphics g, int x, int y) paints the layer on the screen according to the coordinates of the GameCanvas, and the method LayerManager.setViewWindow(int x, int y, int width, int height) sets the visible rectangle of the LayerManager in terms of the LayerManager's coordinate system.

In my example I have a simple background (it's just a repeating series of patches of grass), but I'd like the cowboy to stay in the middle of the screen as he walks to the right and left, so I need to continuously change which part of the `LayerManager`'s graphical area is visible. I do this by calling the method `setViewWindow(int x, int y, int width, int height)` from the `paint(Graphics g)` method of my subclass of `LayerManager` (called `JumpManager`). More precisely, what happens is the following: The main loop in the `GameThread` calls `JumpCanvas.checkKeys()`, which queries the key states and tells the `JumpManager` class whether the cowboy should be walking to the right or to the left and whether he should be jumping. `JumpCanvas` passes this information along to `JumpManager` by calling the methods `setLeft(boolean left)`or `jump()`. If the message is to jump, the `JumpManager` calls `jump()` on the cowboy `Sprite`. If the message is that the cowboy is going to the left (or similarly to the right), then when the `GameThread` calls the `JumpCanvas` to tell the `JumpManager` to advance (in the next step of the loop), the `JumpManager` tells the cowboy `Sprite` to move one pixel to the left and compensates by moving the view window one pixel to the right to keep the cowboy in the center of the screen. You can accomplish these two actions by incrementing the field `myCurrentLeftX` (which is the X coordinate that's sent to the method `setViewWindow(int x, int y, int width, int height)`) and then calling `myCowboy .advance(gameTicks, myLeft)`. Of course, I could keep the cowboy centered by not moving him and not appending him to the `LayerManager` but, rather, painting him separately afterward, but it's easier to keep track of everything by putting all of the moving graphics on one set of layers and then keeping the view window focused on the cowboy `Sprite`. While telling the cowboy to advance his position, I also have the tumbleweed `Sprites` advance their positions, and I have the grass `TiledLayer` advance its animation. Then I check if the cowboy has collided with any tumbleweeds (I'll go into more detail about those steps in the following sections). After moving the game pieces around, the `JumpManager` calls the method `wrap()` to see if the view window has reached the edge of the background and, if so, move all of the game objects so that the background appears to continue indefinitely in both directions. Then the `JumpCanvas` repaints everything, and the game loop begins again.

I'll just add a few words here about the method `wrap()`. The class `LayerManager` unfortunately doesn't have a built-in wrapping capability for the case in which you have a simple background you'd like to have repeat indefinitely. The `LayerManager`'s graphical area will appear to wrap when the coordinates sent to `setViewWindow` `(int x, int y, int width, int height)` exceed the value `Integer.MAX_VALUE`, but that's unlikely to help you. Thus, you have to write your own functions to prevent the player `Sprite` from leaving the region that contains background graphics. In my example, the background grass repeats after the number of pixels given by `Grass.TILE_WIDTH*Grass.CYCLE`. So, whenever the X coordinate of the view window (`myCurrentLeftX`) is an integer multiple of the length of the background, I move the view window back to the center and also move all of the `Sprites` in the same direction, which seamlessly prevents the player from reaching the edge.

Listing 3-4 shows the code for `JumpManager.java`.

*Listing 3-4.* JumpManager.java

```java
package net.frog_parrot.jump;

import javax.microedition.lcdui.*;
import javax.microedition.lcdui.game.*;

/**
 * This handles the graphics objects.
 *
 * @author Carol Hamer
 */
public class JumpManager extends javax.microedition.lcdui.game.LayerManager {

  //----------------------------------------------------------
  //    dimension fields
  //    (constant after initialization)

  /**
   * The X coordinate of the place on the game canvas where
   * the LayerManager window should appear, in terms of the
   * coordinates of the game canvas.
   */
  static int CANVAS_X;

  /**
   * The Y coordinate of the place on the game canvas where
   * the LayerManager window should appear, in terms of the
   * coordinates of the game canvas.
   */
  static int CANVAS_Y;

  /**
   * The width of the display window.
   */
  static int DISP_WIDTH;

  /**
   * The height of this object's graphical region. This is
   * the same as the height of the visible part because
   * in this game the layer manager's visible part scrolls
   * only left and right but not up and down.
   */
  static int DISP_HEIGHT;
```

```
//----------------------------------------------------------
//    game object fields

/**
 * the player's object.
 */
private Cowboy myCowboy;

/**
 * the tumbleweeds that enter from the left.
 */
private Tumbleweed[] myLeftTumbleweeds;

/**
 * the tumbleweeds that enter from the right.
 */
private Tumbleweed[] myRightTumbleweeds;

/**
 * the object representing the grass in the background..
 */
private Grass myGrass;

/**
 * Whether the player is currently going left.
 */
private boolean myLeft;

/**
 * The leftmost X coordinate that should be visible on the
 * screen in terms of this objects internal coordinates.
 */
private int myCurrentLeftX;

//--------------------------------------------------------
//    gets/sets

/**
 * This tells the player to turn left or right.
 * @param left whether the turn is toward the left.
 */
void setLeft(boolean left) {
  myLeft = left;
}
```

```
//------------------------------------------------------
//    initialization and game state changes

/**
 * Constructor sets the data and constructs the graphical objects.
 * @param x The X coordinate of the place on the game canvas where
 * the LayerManager window should appear, in terms of the
 * coordinates of the game canvas.
 * @param y The Y coordinate of the place on the game canvas where
 * the LayerManager window should appear, in terms of the
 * coordinates of the game canvas.
 * @param width the width of the region that is to be
 * occupied by the LayoutManager.
 * @param height the height of the region that is to be
 * occupied by the LayoutManager.
 */
public JumpManager(int x, int y, int width, int height)
    throws Exception {
  CANVAS_X = x;
  CANVAS_Y = y;
  DISP_WIDTH = width;
  DISP_HEIGHT = height;
  myCurrentLeftX = Grass.CYCLE*Grass.TILE_WIDTH;
  setViewWindow(0, 0, DISP_WIDTH, DISP_HEIGHT);
  // create the player:
  if(myCowboy == null) {
    myCowboy = new Cowboy(myCurrentLeftX + DISP_WIDTH/2,
                          DISP_HEIGHT - Cowboy.HEIGHT - 2);
    append(myCowboy);
  }
  // create the tumbleweeds to jump over:
  if(myLeftTumbleweeds == null) {
    myLeftTumbleweeds = new Tumbleweed[2];
    for(int i = 0; i < myLeftTumbleweeds.length; i++) {
      myLeftTumbleweeds[i] = new Tumbleweed(true);
      append(myLeftTumbleweeds[i]);
    }
  }
  if(myRightTumbleweeds == null) {
    myRightTumbleweeds = new Tumbleweed[2];
    for(int i = 0; i < myRightTumbleweeds.length; i++) {
      myRightTumbleweeds[i] = new Tumbleweed(false);
      append(myRightTumbleweeds[i]);
    }
```

71

```
    }
    // create the background object:
    if(myGrass == null) {
      myGrass = new Grass();
      append(myGrass);
    }
  }


  /**
   * sets all variables back to their initial positions.
   */
  void reset() {
    if(myGrass != null) {
      myGrass.reset();
    }
    if(myCowboy != null) {
      myCowboy.reset();
    }
    if(myLeftTumbleweeds != null) {
      for(int i = 0; i < myLeftTumbleweeds.length; i++) {
        myLeftTumbleweeds[i].reset();
      }
    }
    if(myRightTumbleweeds != null) {
      for(int i = 0; i < myRightTumbleweeds.length; i++) {
        myRightTumbleweeds[i].reset();
      }
    }
    myLeft = false;
    myCurrentLeftX = Grass.CYCLE*Grass.TILE_WIDTH;
  }


  //--------------------------------------------------------
  //  graphics methods

  /**
   * paint the game graphic on the screen.
   */
  public void paint(Graphics g) {
    setViewWindow(myCurrentLeftX, 0, DISP_WIDTH, DISP_HEIGHT);
    paint(g, CANVAS_X, CANVAS_Y);
  }
```

```java
/**
 * If the cowboy gets to the end of the graphical region,
 * move all of the pieces so that the screen appears to wrap.
 */
private void wrap() {
  if(myCurrentLeftX % (Grass.TILE_WIDTH*Grass.CYCLE) == 0) {
    if(myLeft) {
      myCowboy.move(Grass.TILE_WIDTH*Grass.CYCLE, 0);
      myCurrentLeftX += (Grass.TILE_WIDTH*Grass.CYCLE);
      for(int i = 0; i < myLeftTumbleweeds.length; i++) {
        myLeftTumbleweeds[i].move(Grass.TILE_WIDTH*Grass.CYCLE, 0);
      }
      for(int i = 0; i < myRightTumbleweeds.length; i++) {
        myRightTumbleweeds[i].move(Grass.TILE_WIDTH*Grass.CYCLE, 0);
      }
    } else {
      myCowboy.move(-(Grass.TILE_WIDTH*Grass.CYCLE), 0);
      myCurrentLeftX -= (Grass.TILE_WIDTH*Grass.CYCLE);
      for(int i = 0; i < myLeftTumbleweeds.length; i++) {
        myLeftTumbleweeds[i].move(-Grass.TILE_WIDTH*Grass.CYCLE, 0);
      }
      for(int i = 0; i < myRightTumbleweeds.length; i++) {
        myRightTumbleweeds[i].move(-Grass.TILE_WIDTH*Grass.CYCLE, 0);
      }
    }
  }
}


//--------------------------------------------------------
//  game movements

/**
 * Tell all of the moving components to advance.
 * @param gameTicks the remaining number of times that
 *        the main loop of the game will be executed
 *        before the game ends.
 * @return the change in the score after the pieces
 *         have advanced.
 */
int advance(int gameTicks) {
  int retVal = 0;
  // first you move the view window
  // (so you are showing a slightly different view of
```

```
    // the manager's graphical area.)
    if(myLeft) {
      myCurrentLeftX--;
    } else {
      myCurrentLeftX++;
    }
    // now you tell the game objects to move accordingly.
    myGrass.advance(gameTicks);
    myCowboy.advance(gameTicks, myLeft);
    for(int i = 0; i < myLeftTumbleweeds.length; i++) {
      retVal += myLeftTumbleweeds[i].advance(myCowboy, gameTicks,
                     myLeft, myCurrentLeftX, myCurrentLeftX + DISP_WIDTH);
      retVal -= myCowboy.checkCollision(myLeftTumbleweeds[i]);
    }
    for(int i = 0; i < myLeftTumbleweeds.length; i++) {
      retVal += myRightTumbleweeds[i].advance(myCowboy, gameTicks,
            myLeft, myCurrentLeftX, myCurrentLeftX + DISP_WIDTH);
      retVal -= myCowboy.checkCollision(myRightTumbleweeds[i]);
    }
    // now you check if you have reached an edge of the viewable
    // area, and if so, you move the view area and all of the
    // game objects so that the game appears to wrap.
    wrap();
    return(retVal);
  }

  /**
   * Tell the cowboy to jump..
   */
  void jump() {
    myCowboy.jump();
  }

}
```

## Using the Sprite Class

A Sprite is a graphical object represented by one image (at a time). The fact
that a Sprite is composed of only one image is the principal difference between
a Sprite and a TiledLayer, which is a region that's covered with images that can
be manipulated. (The Sprite class has a few extra features, but the fact that it uses

one image rather than filling an area with images is the most obvious difference.) So, a Sprite is generally used for small, active game objects (such as your spaceship and the asteroids that are coming to crash into it), and a TiledLayer would be more likely to be used for an animated background. One cool feature of Sprite is that even though a Sprite is represented by only one image at a time, it can be easily represented by different images under different circumstances, including by a series of images that make up an animation. In my example game, the cowboy has three different images in which he's walking and one in which he's jumping. All of the images used for a given Sprite need to be stored together in a single image file. (To indicate where to find the image file to use, send the address of the image within the jar in the same format that's used to find resources in the method Class.getResource(); see Chapter 1 for more details.) Multiple frames are stored in a single Image object, which is a convenience that means you don't have to manipulate multiple Image objects to determine which face your Sprite is wearing at any given time. Figure 3-2 shows the image file for the cowboy Sprite.

*Figure 3-2. The image file to use for the cowboy* Sprite

The tumbleweed image file consists of three frames that give a rolling animation when shown in sequence (see Figure 3-3).

*Figure 3-3. The tumbleweed image*

The way to select which frame is shown at any given time is intuitive. First, if your image file comprises multiple images (as these two do), you should construct the Sprite with the constructor that specifies the width and height (in pixels) that you'd like your Sprite to be. The width and height of the Image should be integer multiples of the width and height you send to the constructor. In other words, the computer should be able to divide your image file evenly into rectangles of the size you specify. As you can see from the previous examples, you can arrange the subimages arranged horizontally or vertically. You can even arrange them in a grid with multiple rows and columns. Then, to identify the individual frames, they're numbered starting with zero at the top-left corner, continuing to the right and then continuing to the lower rows, in the same order in which you're reading the letters on this page. To select the frame that's currently displayed, use the method setFrame(int sequenceIndex), sending the frame number as an argument.

The Sprite class has some added support for animation that allows you to define a frame sequence with the method setFrameSequence(int[] sequence). As you can see in Listing 3-5, I've set a frame sequence of { 1, 2, 3, 2 } for my cowboy and { 0, 1, 2 } for my tumbleweed. (Note that for the tumbleweed, the frame sequence I'd like to use is just the default frame sequence, so I don't have to set the Tumbleweed's frame sequence in the code.) To advance your Sprite's animation from one frame to the next, you use the method nextFrame() (or, if you prefer, prevFrame()). This is convenient in cases such as my tumbleweed where all the available frames are used in the animation. It's slightly less convenient in cases such as my cowboy that have an image or images that fall outside of the frame sequence of the animation. This is because once a frame sequence has been set, the argument to the method setFrame(int sequenceIndex) gives the index of an entry in the frame sequence instead of giving the index of the frame itself. What that means is that once I've set my cowboy's frame sequence to { 3, 2, 1, 2 }, if I call setFrame(0), it'll show frame number 1, setFrame(1) will show frame number 2, setFrame(2) will show frame number 3, and setFrame(3) will show frame number 2. But when the cowboy is jumping, I'd like it to show frame number 0, which is no longer accessible. So, when my cowboy jumps, I have to set my frame sequence to null before calling setFrame(0), and then I have to set my frame sequence back to the animation sequence { 1, 2, 3, 2 } afterward. Listing 3-5 shows this in the methods jump() and advance(int tickCount, boolean left).

In addition to changing your Sprite's appearance by changing frames, you can change it by applying simple transforms such as rotations or mirror images. Both my cowboy and my tumbleweed in Listings 3-5 and 3-6 can be going either left or right, so of course I need to use the mirror image transform to change from one direction to the other. Once you start applying transforms, you need to keep track of the Sprite's reference pixel. This is because when you transform your Sprite, the reference pixel is the pixel that doesn't move. You might expect that if your Sprite's image is square, then after a transformation the Sprite's image will continue to occupy the same square of area on the screen. This isn't the case. The best way to illustrate what happens is to imagine an example Sprite of a standing person facing left whose reference pixel has been defined to be the tip of his toe. Then after applying a 90-degree rotation, your person will be in the spot he'd be in if he had tripped and fallen forward. Clearly, this has its applications if your Sprite has a special pixel (such as the tip of an arrow) that should stay put after a transformation. But if you want your Sprite to continue to occupy the same space on the screen after a transformation, then you should first call defineReferencePixel(int x, int y) and set your Sprite's reference pixel to the center of the Sprite, as I did in the Cowboy constructor in Listing 3-5. (Another trick to keep the Sprite from moving after a transformation is to use getX() and getY() to get the absolute coordinates of the Sprite's upper-left corner before the transformation and then after the transformation, use setPosition() to set the upper-left corner back to the earlier location.) Be aware that the coordinates in defineReferencePixel(int x, int y) are relative to the top corner of the Sprite whereas the coordinates sent to setRefPixelPosition(int x, int y) tell where to place the Sprite's reference pixel on the screen in terms of the screen's coordinates. To be more precise, the coordinates sent to setRefPixelPosition(int x, int y) refer to the coordinate system of the Canvas if the Sprite is painted directly onto the Canvas, but if the Sprite is painted by a LayerManager, these coordinates should be given in terms of the LayerManager's coordinate system. (I explained how these coordinate systems fit together in the earlier "Using the LayerManager Class" section.) The coordinates in the various methods to set and get the position of the reference pixel or to set and get the position of the pixel in the top-left corner refer to the coordinates of the appropriate Canvas or LayerManager. Also note that if you perform multiple transformations, the later transformations are applied to the original image and not to its current state. In other words, if I apply setTransform(TRANS_MIRROR) twice in a row, the second transform won't mirror my image back to its original position; it'll just repeat the action of setting the Image to being a mirror image of the original Image. If you want to set a transformed Sprite back to normal, use setTransform(TRANS_NONE). This is illustrated in the top of the Cowboy.advance(int tickCount, boolean left) method.

Another great feature of the Layer class (including both Sprites and TiledLayers) is the support it gives you for placing your objects in relative terms instead of in absolute terms. If your Sprite needs to move over three pixels regardless of where it currently is, you can just call move(int x, int y), sending it the x and y distances it should move from its current position, as opposed to calling setRefPixelPosition(int x, int y) with the absolute coordinates of the Sprite's new location. Even more useful is the set of collidesWith() methods. This allows you to check if a Sprite is occupying the same space as another Sprite or TiledLayer or even an Image. It's easy to see that this saves you quite a number of comparisons, especially since when you send the pixelLevel argument as true, it will consider the two Layers as having collided only if their opaque pixels overlap.

In the Tumbleweed game, after advancing all of the Sprites, I check if the cowboy has collided with any tumbleweeds. (This happens in the

Cowboy.checkCollision(Tumbleweed tumbleweed) method that's called from
JumpManager.advance(int gameTicks).) I check the collisions between the cowboy
and all of the tumbleweeds each time because it automatically returns false for
any tumbleweeds that aren't currently visible anyway, so I'm not really being
wasteful by checking the cowboy against tumbleweeds that aren't currently in
use. In many cases, however, you can save some effort by checking only for collisions that you know are possible rather than checking all of the Sprites against
each other. Note that in my example I don't bother to check if the tumbleweeds
collide with each other or if anything collides with the background grass because
that's irrelevant. If you're checking for pixel-level collisions, you'll want to be sure
your images have a transparent background. (This is also helpful in general so
that your Sprite doesn't paint an ugly rectangle of background color over another
Sprite or Image.) You can find some discussion of creating the image files correctly
in the sidebar "Making Image Files" in Chapter 1.

Listing 3-5 shows the code for Cowboy.java.

*Listing 3-5.* Cowboy.java

```
package net.frog_parrot.jump;

import javax.microedition.lcdui.*;
import javax.microedition.lcdui.game.*;

/**
 * This class represents the player.
 *
 * @author Carol Hamer
 */
public class Cowboy extends Sprite {

  //-----------------------------------------------------------
  //    dimension fields

  /**
   * The width of the cowboy's bounding rectangle.
   */
  static final int WIDTH = 32;

  /**
   * The height of the cowboy's bounding rectangle.
   */
  static final int HEIGHT = 48;
```

```
/**
 * This is the order that the frames should be displayed
 * for the animation.
 */
static final int[] FRAME_SEQUENCE = { 3, 2, 1, 2 };


//-----------------------------------------------------------
//     instance fields

/**
 * the X coordinate of the cowboy where the cowboy starts
 * the game.
 */
private int myInitialX;

/**
 * the Y coordinate of the cowboy when not jumping.
 */
private int myInitialY;

/**
 * The jump index that indicates that no jump is
 * currently in progress..
 */
private int myNoJumpInt = -6;

/**
 * Where the cowboy is in the jump sequence.
 */
private int myIsJumping = myNoJumpInt;

/**
 * If the cowboy is currently jumping, this keeps track
 * of how many points have been scored so far during
 * the jump.  This helps the calculation of bonus points since
 * the points being scored depend on how many tumbleweeds
 * are jumped in a single jump.
 */
private int myScoreThisJump = 0;


//-----------------------------------------------------------
//     initialization
```

```
/**
 * constructor initializes the image and animation.
 */
public Cowboy(int initialX, int initialY) throws Exception {
  super(Image.createImage("/images/cowboy.png"),
        WIDTH, HEIGHT);
  myInitialX = initialX;
  myInitialY = initialY;
  // you define the reference pixel to be in the middle
  // of the cowboy image so that when the cowboy turns
  // from right to left (and vice versa) he does not
  // appear to move to a different location.
  defineReferencePixel(WIDTH/2, 0);
  setRefPixelPosition(myInitialX, myInitialY);
  setFrameSequence(FRAME_SEQUENCE);
}

//----------------------------------------------------------
//   game methods

/**
 * If the cowboy has landed on a tumbleweed, you decrease
 * the score.
 */
int checkCollision(Tumbleweed tumbleweed) {
  int retVal = 0;
  if(collidesWith(tumbleweed, true)) {
    retVal = 1;
    // once the cowboy has collided with the tumbleweed,
    // that tumbleweed is done for now, so you call reset
    // which makes it invisible and ready to be reused.
    tumbleweed.reset();
  }
  return(retVal);
}

/**
 * set the cowboy back to its initial position.
 */
void reset() {
  myIsJumping = myNoJumpInt;
  setRefPixelPosition(myInitialX, myInitialY);
  setFrameSequence(FRAME_SEQUENCE);
```

```
    myScoreThisJump = 0;
    // at first the cowboy faces right:
    setTransform(TRANS_NONE);
}


//-----------------------------------------------------------
//   graphics

/**
 * alter the cowboy image appropriately for this frame..
 */
void advance(int tickCount, boolean left) {
    if(left) {
        // use the mirror image of the cowboy graphic when
        // the cowboy is going toward the left.
        setTransform(TRANS_MIRROR);
        move(-1, 0);
    } else {
        // use the (normal, untransformed) image of the cowboy
        // graphic when the cowboy is going toward the right.
        setTransform(TRANS_NONE);
        move(1, 0);
    }
    // this section advances the animation:
    // every third time through the loop, the cowboy
    // image is changed to the next image in the walking
    // animation sequence:
    if(tickCount % 3 == 0) { // slow the animation down a little
        if(myIsJumping == myNoJumpInt) {
            // if he's not jumping, set the image to the next
            // frame in the walking animation:
            nextFrame();
        } else {
            // if he's jumping, advance the jump:
            // the jump continues for several passes through
            // the main game loop, and myIsJumping keeps track
            // of where you are in the jump:
            myIsJumping++;
            if(myIsJumping < 0) {
                // myIsJumping starts negative, and while it's
                // still negative, the cowboy is going up.
                // here you use a shift to make the cowboy go up a
                // lot in the beginning of the jump and ascend
```

```
                    // more and more slowly as he reaches his highest
                    // position:
                    setRefPixelPosition(getRefPixelX(),
                                   getRefPixelY() - (2<<(-myIsJumping)));
           } else {
                    // once myIsJumping is negative, the cowboy starts
                    // going back down until he reaches the end of the
                    // jump sequence:
                    if(myIsJumping != -myNoJumpInt - 1) {
                        setRefPixelPosition(getRefPixelX(),
                                      getRefPixelY() + (2<<myIsJumping));
                    } else {
                        // once the jump is done, you reset the cowboy to
                        // his nonjumping position:
                        myIsJumping = myNoJumpInt;
                        setRefPixelPosition(getRefPixelX(), myInitialY);
                        // you set the image back to being the walking
                        // animation sequence rather than the jumping image:
                        setFrameSequence(FRAME_SEQUENCE);
                        // myScoreThisJump keeps track of how many points
                        // were scored during the current jump (to keep
                        // track of the bonus points earned for jumping
                        // multiple tumbleweeds).  Once the current jump is done,
                        // you set it back to zero.
                        myScoreThisJump = 0;
                    }
               }
           }
       }
}

/**
 * makes the cowboy jump.
 */
void jump() {
    if(myIsJumping == myNoJumpInt) {
        myIsJumping++;
        // switch the cowboy to use the jumping image
        // rather than the walking animation images:
        setFrameSequence(null);
        setFrame(0);
    }
}
```

```
/**
 * This is called whenever the cowboy clears a tumbleweed
 * so that more points are scored when more tumbleweeds
 * are cleared in a single jump.
 */
int increaseScoreThisJump() {
  if(myScoreThisJump == 0) {
    myScoreThisJump++;
  } else {
    myScoreThisJump *= 2;
  }
  return(myScoreThisJump);
}

}
```

Listing 3-6 shows the code for Tumbleweed.java.

*Listing 3-6.* Tumbleweed.java

```
package net.frog_parrot.jump;

import java.util.Random;

import javax.microedition.lcdui.*;
import javax.microedition.lcdui.game.*;

/**
 * This class represents the tumbleweeds that the player
 * must jump over.
 *
 * @author Carol Hamer
 */
public class Tumbleweed extends Sprite {

  //----------------------------------------------------------
  //    dimension fields

  /**
   * The width of the tumbleweed's bounding square.
   */
  static final int WIDTH = 16;
```

```
//------------------------------------------------------------
//    instance fields

/**
 * Random number generator to randomly decide when to appear.
 */
private Random myRandom = new Random();

/**
 * whether this tumbleweed has been jumped over.
 * This is used to calculate the score.
 */
private boolean myJumpedOver;

/**
 * whether this tumbleweed enters from the left.
 */
private boolean myLeft;

/**
 * the Y coordinate of the tumbleweed.
 */
private int myY;

//------------------------------------------------------------
//    initialization

/**
 * constructor initializes the image and animation.
 * @param left whether this tumbleweed enters from the left.
 */
public Tumbleweed(boolean left) throws Exception {
  super(Image.createImage("/images/tumbleweed.png"),
        WIDTH, WIDTH);
  myY = JumpManager.DISP_HEIGHT - WIDTH - 2;
  myLeft = left;
  if(!myLeft) {
    setTransform(TRANS_MIRROR);
  }
  myJumpedOver = false;
  setVisible(false);
}
```

```
//------------------------------------------------------------
//    graphics

/**
 * move the tumbleweed back to its initial (inactive) state.
 */
void reset() {
  setVisible(false);
  myJumpedOver = false;
}


/**
 * alter the tumbleweed image appropriately for this frame..
 * @param left whether the player is moving left
 * @return how much the score should change by after this
 *         advance.
 */
int advance(Cowboy cowboy, int tickCount, boolean left,
              int currentLeftBound, int currentRightBound) {
  int retVal = 0;
  // if the tumbleweed goes outside of the display
  // region, set it to invisible since it is
  // no longer in use.
  if((getRefPixelX() + WIDTH <= currentLeftBound) ||
     (getRefPixelX() - WIDTH >= currentRightBound)) {
    setVisible(false);
  }
  // If the tumbleweed is no longer in use (i.e. invisible)
  // it is given a 1 in 100 chance (per game loop)
  // of coming back into play:
  if(!isVisible()) {
    int rand = getRandomInt(100);
    if(rand == 3) {
      // when the tumbleweed comes back into play,
      // you reset the values to what they should
      // be in the active state:
      myJumpedOver = false;
      setVisible(true);
      // set the tumbleweed's position to the point
      // where it just barely appears on the screen
      // to that it can start approaching the cowboy:
      if(myLeft) {
        setRefPixelPosition(currentRightBound, myY);
        move(-1, 0);
```

```
        } else {
          setRefPixelPosition(currentLeftBound, myY);
          move(1, 0);
        }
      }
  } else {
    // when the tumbleweed is active, you advance the
    // rolling animation to the next frame and then
    // move the tumbleweed in the right direction across
    // the screen.
    if(tickCount % 2 == 0) { // slow the animation down a little
      nextFrame();
    }
    if(myLeft) {
      move(-3, 0);
      // if the cowboy just passed the tumbleweed
      // (without colliding with it) you increase the
      // cowboy's score and set myJumpedOver to true
      // so that no further points will be awarded
      // for this tumbleweed until it goes off the screen
      // and then is later reactivated:
      if((! myJumpedOver) &&
         (getRefPixelX() < cowboy.getRefPixelX())) {
        myJumpedOver = true;
        retVal = cowboy.increaseScoreThisJump();
      }
    } else {
      move(3, 0);
      if((! myJumpedOver) &&
         (getRefPixelX() > cowboy.getRefPixelX() + Cowboy.WIDTH)) {
        myJumpedOver = true;
        retVal = cowboy.increaseScoreThisJump();
      }
    }
  }
  return(retVal);
}

/**
 * Gets a random int between
 * zero and the param upper.
 */
public int getRandomInt(int upper) {
  int retVal = myRandom.nextInt() % upper;
```

```
    if(retVal < 0) {
      retVal += upper;
    }
    return(retVal);
  }

}
```

## Using the TiledLayer Class

As mentioned, the TiledLayer class is similar to the Sprite class except that a TiledLayer can comprise multiple cells, each of which is painted with an individually set image frame. The other differences between TiledLayer and Sprite are mostly related to functionality missing from TiledLayer; TiledLayer has no transforms, reference pixel, or frame sequence.

Of course, the mere fact that you're simultaneously managing multiple images complicates things a bit. I'll explain it by going over my subclass of TiledLayer, which I've called Grass. This class represents a row of grass in the background that waves back and forth as the game is being played (see Figure 3-4). To make it more interesting, some of the cells in my TiledLayer have animated grasses, and others have no tall grasses and hence just consist of a green line representing the ground at the bottom of the cell.

*Figure 3-4. The image file that's used by the* Grass TiledLayer

> **CAUTION** *The tile index for* Sprite *starts with* 0, *but the tile index for* TiledLayer *starts with* 1! *This is a little confusing (it caused me to get an* IndexOutOfBoundsException *the first time I made a* Sprite *because I assumed that the* Sprite *images were numbered like the* TiledLayer *images). Yet the system is completely logical. In a* TiledLayer, *the tile index* 0 *indicates a blank tile (in other words, paint nothing in the cell if the cell's tile index is set to* 0). *A* Sprite, *however, comprises only one cell, so if you want that cell to be blank, then you can just call* setVisible(false), *meaning that* Sprite *doesn't need to reserve a special index to indicate a blank tile. This little confusion in the indices shouldn't pose a big problem, but it's something to keep in mind if you can't figure out why your animation appears to be displaying the wrong images. Aside from this point, the image file is divided into individual frames or tiles in* TiledLayer *just as in* Sprite, *explained previously.*

The first step in creating your TiledLayer is to decide how many rows and columns of cells you'll need. If you don't want your layer to be rectangular, it isn't a problem because any unused cells are by default set to being blank, which prevents them from getting in the way of other images. In my example, shown in Listing 3-7, I have only one row, and I calculate the number of columns based on the width of the screen.

Once you've set how many rows and columns you'll be using, you can fill each cell with a tile using the method setCell(int col, int row, int tileIndex). The "Using the Sprite Class" section explained the tileIndex argument. If you'd like some of the cells to be filled with animated images, you need to create an animated tile by calling createAnimatedTile(int staticTileIndex), which returns the tile index that has been allotted to your new animated tile. You can make as many animated tiles as you want, but remember that each animated tile can be used in multiple cells if you want the cells to display the same animation simultaneously. In my case, I create only one animated tile and reuse it because I want all of my animated grass to be waving in sync. The cells are set in the constructor of Grass in Listing 3-7. To advance the animation you don't get built-in frame-sequence functionality as in Sprite, so you have to set the frames with the method setAnimatedTile(int animatedTileIndex, int staticTileIndex). This sets the current frame of the given animated tile. Thus, all the cells that have been set to contain the animated tile corresponding to animatedTileIndex will change to the image given by the argument staticTileIndex. To simplify the animation updates, it's easy to add your own frame-sequence functionality; see the method Grass.advance(int tickCount) for an idea of how to do it.

Listing 3-7 shows the code for the last class, Grass.java.

*Listing 3-7.* Grass.java

```java
package net.frog_parrot.jump;

import javax.microedition.lcdui.*;
import javax.microedition.lcdui.game.*;

/**
 * This class draws the background grass.
 *
 * @author Carol Hamer
 */
public class Grass extends TiledLayer {

  //-----------------------------------------------------------
  //     dimension fields
  //   (constant after initialization)

  /**
   * The width of the square tiles that make up this layer..
   */
  static final int TILE_WIDTH = 20;

  /**
   * This is the order that the frames should be displayed
   * for the animation.
   */
  static final int[] FRAME_SEQUENCE = { 2, 3, 2, 4 };

  /**
   * This gives the number of squares of grass to put along
   * the bottom of the screen.
   */
  static int COLUMNS;

  /**
   * After how many tiles does the background repeat.
   */
  static final int CYCLE = 5;

  /**
   * the fixed Y coordinate of the strip of grass.
   */
  static int TOP_Y;
```

```
//-----------------------------------------------------------
//     instance fields

/**
 * Which tile you are currently on in the frame sequence.
 */
private int mySequenceIndex = 0;

/**
 * The index to use in the static tiles array to get the
 * animated tile..
 */
private int myAnimatedTileIndex;

//-----------------------------------------------------------
//   gets / sets

/**
 * Takes the width of the screen and sets my columns
 * to the correct corresponding number
 */
static int setColumns(int screenWidth) {
  COLUMNS = ((screenWidth / 20) + 1)*3;
  return(COLUMNS);
}

//-----------------------------------------------------------
//   initialization

/**
 * constructor initializes the image and animation.
 */
public Grass() throws Exception {
  super(setColumns(JumpCanvas.DISP_WIDTH), 1,
        Image.createImage("/images/grass.png"),
        TILE_WIDTH, TILE_WIDTH);
  TOP_Y = JumpManager.DISP_HEIGHT - TILE_WIDTH;
  setPosition(0, TOP_Y);
  myAnimatedTileIndex = createAnimatedTile(2);
  for(int i = 0; i < COLUMNS; i++) {
    if((i % CYCLE == 0) || (i % CYCLE == 2)) {
      setCell(i, 0, myAnimatedTileIndex);
```

```
      } else {
        setCell(i, 0, 1);
      }
    }
  }

  //---------------------------------------------------------
  //   graphics

  /**
   * sets the grass back to its initial position.
   */
  void reset() {
    setPosition(-(TILE_WIDTH*CYCLE), TOP_Y);
    mySequenceIndex = 0;
    setAnimatedTile(myAnimatedTileIndex, FRAME_SEQUENCE[mySequenceIndex]);
  }

  /**
   * alter the background image appropriately for this frame..
   * @param left whether the player is moving left
   */
  void advance(int tickCount) {
    if(tickCount % 2 == 0) { // slow the animation down a little
      mySequenceIndex++;
      mySequenceIndex %= 4;
      setAnimatedTile(myAnimatedTileIndex, FRAME_SEQUENCE[mySequenceIndex]);
    }
  }

}
```

So, now you've seen a basic game that illustrates how to use all of the classes of the javax.microedition.lcdui.game package, and the Tumbleweed game example especially shows how to take advantage of the graphics and animation features. In the next chapter, you'll take the same game and improve it by adding some more threads to play music and to optimize performance.

# CHAPTER 4

# Using Threads and Tones

**IN THIS CHAPTER,** you'll improve the Tumbleweed game from the previous chapter by adding some new threads. One of the new threads will make the algorithm that releases the tumbleweeds more efficient, and the other new thread will play background music. You won't need to change some of the classes for this version, and therefore the code for certain classes won't be repeated in this chapter. Please see Chapter 3 if you'd like to review the source code for GameThread.java, Cowboy.java, and Grass.java (which the current example also uses). The following listings include the code for the modified classes.

## Using Threads

Working with threads is a standard skill that most Java developers learn pretty quickly. But since threading is so important in games, and because there are a few extra things to keep in mind when using threads with the Connected Limited Device Configuration (CLDC), I'll devote almost the whole chapter to threading strategies and threading issues. If you're already comfortable with threads and you just want to see an example of how to add music to your game, you can skip to the "Adding Music" section.

### Differences Between CLDC Threads and Threads in Standard Java

Two main thread-related items have been eliminated in the CLDC: the class ThreadGroup and the possibility of marking your threads as daemon threads. You won't miss them. This is another case of the CLDC specification authors eliminating something that you didn't need anyway.

Daemon threads can be useful in many programs. Marking a thread as a daemon is a way of telling the program not to wait around for the thread to finish—if the rest of the program is done, just exit. For example, in a game you may use a daemon thread to move around background items. Throughout the game you want the background items to keep moving, but once the player's character is dead, of course you don't want the program to keep going just for the sake of the background animation. But in a Mobile Internet Device Profile (MIDP) program, daemon threads wouldn't work as you may like them to work. Since a MIDlet is run by application management software, the end of the MIDlet's life cycle doesn't correspond to the Java Virtual Machine (JVM) exiting. Regardless of how many threads the MIDlet has started, and regardless of whether they're active, the MIDlet's active life ends when it's destroyed. It's therefore not even clear what it'd mean for a thread to be a daemon in this case.

The ThreadGroup class, on the other hand, is essentially useless even for versions of Java that allow its use. Its original purpose was to group the threads of a program to simplify pausing, restarting, and stopping them all at once. But as you probably know, the methods Thread.suspend(), Thread.resume(), and Thread.stop() were all deprecated because they're inherently unsafe. ThreadGroup's uncaughtException() method can be useful, but without the thread lifecycle methods, putting your threads in a ThreadGroup isn't significantly more useful than grouping them in a Vector.

You may wonder then what you're supposed to do to pause or stop your game if it has multiple threads running. If you've done much programming with threads, you probably already know the answer. Your thread classes should have fields that serve as flags, telling the thread to pause or stop. Other classes can set these fields, and then your Thread subclass can query the fields and pause or stop when it becomes convenient to do so. In fact, this is exactly what I did in the GameThread class of the previous version of Tumbleweed. Since that class will not be changed for this version of Tumbleweed, I won't reprint it here. See the "Using the Thread Class" section in Chapter 3 to review how it works. The pause flags are set by my MIDlet subclass (called Jump). I've included the code for Jump in Listing 4-1 because there are some changes in this version. Basically, since I've added some more threads, I've separated the code to start and stop the threads and grouped it. Also, since one of my new threads plays music and since I want to allow the user to turn the music on and off while the game is running, I've added code to just pause and unpause the music alone.

Listing 4-1 shows the code for the new version of Jump.java.

*Listing 4-1.* Jump.java

```
package net.frog_parrot.jump;

import javax.microedition.midlet.*;
import javax.microedition.lcdui.*;

/**
 * This is the main class of the Tumbleweed game.
 *
 * @author Carol Hamer
 */
public class Jump extends MIDlet implements CommandListener {
```

```
//------------------------------------------------------------
//    commands

/**
 * the command to end the game.
 */
private Command myExitCommand = new Command("Exit", Command.EXIT, 99);

/**
 * the command to start moving when the game is paused.
 */
private Command myGoCommand = new Command("Go", Command.SCREEN, 1);

/**
 * the command to pause the game.
 */
private Command myPauseCommand = new Command("Pause", Command.SCREEN, 1);

/**
 * the command to start a new game.
 */
private Command myNewCommand = new Command("Play Again", Command.SCREEN, 1);

/**
 * The command to start/pause the music.  (This command may appear in a menu.)
 */
private Command myMusicCommand = new Command("Music", Command.SCREEN, 2);

//------------------------------------------------------------
//    game object fields

/**
 * the canvas that all the game will be drawn on.
 */
private JumpCanvas myCanvas;

//------------------------------------------------------------
//    thread fields

/**
 * the thread that advances the cowboy.
 */
private GameThread myGameThread;
```

```java
/**
 * The class that plays music if the user wants.
 */
private MusicMaker myMusicMaker;
//private ToneControlMusicMaker myMusicMaker;

/**
 * The thread that sets tumbleweeds in motion at random
 * intervals.
 */
private TumbleweedThread myTumbleweedThread;

/**
 * if the user has paused the game.
 */
private boolean myGamePause;

/**
 * if the game is paused because it is hidden.
 */
private boolean myHiddenPause;

//-------------------------------------------------------
//     initialization and game state changes

/**
 * Initialize the canvas and the commands.
 */
public Jump() {
  try {
    myCanvas = new JumpCanvas(this);
    myCanvas.addCommand(myExitCommand);
    myCanvas.addCommand(myMusicCommand);
    myCanvas.addCommand(myPauseCommand);
    myCanvas.setCommandListener(this);
  } catch(Exception e) {
    errorMsg(e);
  }
}

/**
 * Switch the command to the play again command.
 */
void setNewCommand() {
```

```
    myCanvas.removeCommand(myPauseCommand);
    myCanvas.removeCommand(myGoCommand);
    myCanvas.addCommand(myNewCommand);
}


/**
 * Switch the command to the go command.
 */
private void setGoCommand() {
    myCanvas.removeCommand(myPauseCommand);
    myCanvas.removeCommand(myNewCommand);
    myCanvas.addCommand(myGoCommand);
}


/**
 * Switch the command to the pause command.
 */
private void setPauseCommand() {
    myCanvas.removeCommand(myNewCommand);
    myCanvas.removeCommand(myGoCommand);
    myCanvas.addCommand(myPauseCommand);
}


//------------------------------------------------------------------
//   implementation of MIDlet
// these methods may be called by the application management
// software at any time, so you always check fields for null
// before calling methods on them.

/**
 * Start the application.
 */
public void startApp() throws MIDletStateChangeException {
    try {
        if(myCanvas != null) {
            myCanvas.start();
            myCanvas.flushKeys();
            systemStartThreads();
        }
    } catch(Exception e) {
        errorMsg(e);
    }
}
```

```
/**
 * stop and throw out the garbage.
 */
public void destroyApp(boolean unconditional)
    throws MIDletStateChangeException {
  try {
    stopThreads();
    myCanvas = null;
    System.gc();
  } catch(Exception e) {
    errorMsg(e);
  }
}


/**
 * request the game to pause. This method is called
 * by the application management software, not in
 * response to a user pausing the game.
 */
public void pauseApp() {
  try {
    if(myCanvas != null) {
      setGoCommand();
      systemPauseThreads();
    }
  } catch(Exception e) {
    errorMsg(e);
  }
}


//-----------------------------------------------------------------
//   implementation of CommandListener

/*
 * Respond to a command issued on the Canvas.
 * (either reset or exit).
 */
public void commandAction(Command c, Displayable s) {
  try {
    if(c == myGoCommand) {
      myCanvas.removeCommand(myGoCommand);
      myCanvas.addCommand(myPauseCommand);
      myCanvas.flushKeys();
      userStartThreads();
```

```
      } else if(c == myPauseCommand) {
        myCanvas.removeCommand(myPauseCommand);
        myCanvas.addCommand(myGoCommand);
        userPauseThreads();
      } else if(c == myNewCommand) {
        myCanvas.removeCommand(myNewCommand);
        myCanvas.addCommand(myPauseCommand);
        System.gc();
        myCanvas.reset();
        myCanvas.flushKeys();
        myHiddenPause = false;
        myGamePause = false;
        startThreads();
      } else if(c == myMusicCommand) {
        if(myMusicMaker != null) {
          myMusicMaker.toggle();
          myCanvas.repaint();
          myCanvas.serviceRepaints();
        }
      } else if((c == myExitCommand) || (c == Alert.DISMISS_COMMAND)) {
        try {
          destroyApp(false);
          notifyDestroyed();
        } catch (MIDletStateChangeException ex) {
        }
      }
    } catch(Exception e) {
      errorMsg(e);
    }
  }


  //-------------------------------------------------------
  //  thread methods

  /**
   * start up all the game's threads.
   * Creates them if necessary.
   * to be called when the user hits the go command.
   */
  private synchronized void userStartThreads() throws Exception {
    myGamePause = false;
    if(! myHiddenPause) {
      startThreads();
    }
  }
```

```
/**
 * start up all the game's threads.
 * Creates them if necessary.
 * used by showNotify
 */
synchronized void systemStartThreads() throws Exception {
  myHiddenPause = false;
  if(! myGamePause) {
    startThreads();
  }
}

/**
 * start up all the game's threads.
 * Creates them if necessary.
 * internal version.
 * note: if this were synchronized, would it cause deadlock?
 */
private void startThreads() throws Exception {
  if(myGameThread == null) {
    myGameThread = new GameThread(myCanvas);
    myGameThread.start();
  } else {
    myGameThread.resumeGame();
  }
  if(myTumbleweedThread == null) {
    myTumbleweedThread = new TumbleweedThread(myCanvas);
    myTumbleweedThread.start();
  } else {
    myTumbleweedThread.resumeGame();
  }
  if(myMusicMaker == null) {
    //myMusicMaker = new ToneControlMusicMaker();
    myMusicMaker = new MusicMaker();
    myMusicMaker.start();
  } else {
    myMusicMaker.resumeGame();
  }
}

/**
 * Pause all the threads started by this game.
 * to be called when the user hits the pause command.
 */
```

```
synchronized void userPauseThreads() {
  myGamePause = true;
  pauseThreads();
}

/**
 * Pause all the threads started by this game.
 * used by hideNotify
 */
void systemPauseThreads() {
  myHiddenPause = true;
  pauseThreads();
}

/**
 * pause all the game's threads.
 * Creates them if necessary.
 * internal version.
 * note: if this were synchronized, would it cause deadlock?
 */
private void pauseThreads() {
  if(myGameThread != null) {
    myGameThread.pauseGame();
  }
  if(myTumbleweedThread != null) {
    myTumbleweedThread.pauseGame();
  }
  if(myMusicMaker != null) {
    myMusicMaker.pauseGame();
  }
}

/**
 * Stop all the threads started by this game and
 * delete them as they are no longer usable.
 */
private synchronized void stopThreads() {
  if(myGameThread != null) {
    myGameThread.requestStop();
  }
  if(myTumbleweedThread != null) {
    myTumbleweedThread.requestStop();
  }
  if(myMusicMaker != null) {
```

```
        myMusicMaker.requestStop();
    }
    myGameThread = null;
    myTumbleweedThread = null;
    myMusicMaker = null;
}

//-----------------------------------------------------------
//  error methods

/**
 * Converts an exception to a message and displays
 * the message.
 */
void errorMsg(Exception e) {
    if(e.getMessage() == null) {
        errorMsg(e.getClass().getName());
    } else {
        errorMsg(e.getClass().getName() + ":" + e.getMessage());
    }
}

/**
 * Displays an error message alert if something goes wrong.
 */
void errorMsg(String msg) {
    Alert errorAlert = new Alert("error",
                                 msg, null, AlertType.ERROR);
    errorAlert.setCommandListener(this);
    errorAlert.setTimeout(Alert.FOREVER);
    Display.getDisplay(this).setCurrent(errorAlert);
}

}
```

The other big change you'll encounter when working with CLDC threads is a practical one, namely, the computing power of the device. The types of devices that use the CLDC almost certainly don't have the capacity to do parallel processing. So if you're accustomed to dividing your calculations between two threads to get them done faster, don't waste your energy on it here: your threads will merely take turns, and performance won't be enhanced.

## *Strategies for Deciding When to Use a New Thread*

At the risk of stating something totally obvious, a good rule of thumb is that you should have a new thread for each event that happens repeatedly but doesn't occur at the same rhythm as events on existing threads. It's also a good idea to spawn a new thread for long calculations that can be performed in the background while the user is interacting with the program in the foreground. In the tumbleweed example, you spawn three threads, which means there are really at least four threads running, counting the main thread. The main thread is controlled by the application management software, which uses it to query the hardware for keystrokes. Then you have the GameThread object, which contains the main game loop that updates the timer and moves all the graphical objects and then repaints them. Then you have a thread that plays the music. If you use a Player to play your game's music, then you won't need to spawn a new thread because Player will do that for you (see the "Playing Tones with a Player" section). But if you want the music to be synchronized with screen events, it's a good idea to devote a thread to playing the music (see the "Playing Simple Tones" section) and then keep the music and the screen events aligned by keeping the two threads in contact with each other. The final thread that's spawned by the Tumbleweed game is a loop to decide when to start each new tumbleweed rolling.

In the earlier version of the Tumbleweed game, the technique I used to determine when a tumbleweed should start crossing the screen again once it was done with its previous pass wasn't very efficient. Basically, if the tumbleweed wasn't currently on the screen, then for every game tick (every pass through the main game animation loop), the tumbleweed generated a random number. If the number was the right one, the tumbleweed would start rolling across the screen again. But this means I'm wasting quite a lot of computing power to generate several random numbers for each game tick when I could just generate one random number to select a random length of time to wait before sending another tumbleweed across the screen. So, since the tumbleweeds starting off on their journeys across the screen is a repeated event that doesn't coincide with the repeated events on the other threads, I've created a new thread (called TumbleweedThread) to control this event.

The TumbleweedThread has a simple, standard design with a main loop where the action takes place and methods that allow the MIDlet to pause or stop it.

Listing 4-2 shows the code for TumbleweedThread.java.

*Listing 4-2.* TumbleweedThread.java

```java
package net.frog_parrot.jump;

import java.util.Random;

/**
 * This class contains the loop that sets the tumbleweeds in motion.
 *
 * @author Carol Hamer
 */
public class TumbleweedThread extends Thread {

  //------------------------------------------------------------
  //   fields

  /**
   * Whether the main thread would like this thread
   * to pause.
   */
  private boolean myShouldPause;

  /**
   * Whether the main thread would like this thread
   * to stop.
   */
  private boolean myShouldStop;

  /**
   * A handle back to the graphical components.
   */
  private Tumbleweed[] myTumbleweeds;

  /**
   * Random number generator to randomly decide when to appear.
   */
  private Random myRandom = new Random();

  //------------------------------------------------------------
  //   initialization

  /**
   * standard constructor, sets data.
   */
```

```
TumbleweedThread(JumpCanvas canvas) throws Exception {
  myTumbleweeds = canvas.getTumbleweeds();
}


//----------------------------------------------------------
//   actions

/**
 * pause the thread.
 */
void pauseGame() {
  myShouldPause = true;
}


/**
 * restart the thread after a pause.
 */
synchronized void resumeGame() {
  myShouldPause = false;
  notify();
}


/**
 * stops the thread.
 */
synchronized void requestStop() {
  myShouldStop = true;
  notify();
}


/**
 * start the thread.
 */
public void run() {
  myShouldStop = false;
  myShouldPause = false;
  while(true) {
    if(myShouldStop) {
      break;
    }
    synchronized(this) {
      while(myShouldPause) {
        try {
          wait();
```

```
          } catch(Exception e) {}
        }
      }
      // wait a random length of time:
      int waitTime = (1 + getRandomInt(10)) * 100;
      synchronized(this) {
        try {
          wait(waitTime);
        } catch(Exception e) {}
      }
      if(!myShouldPause) {
        // randomly select which one to set in motion and
        // tell it to go.  If the chosen tumbleweed is
        // currently visible, it will not be affected
        int whichWeed = getRandomInt(myTumbleweeds.length);
        myTumbleweeds[whichWeed].go();
      }
    }
  }
}


//-----------------------------------------------------------
//   randomization utilities

/**
 * Gets a random int between
 * zero and the param upper (exclusive).
 */
public int getRandomInt(int upper) {
  int retVal = myRandom.nextInt() % upper;
  if(retVal < 0) {
    retVal += upper;
  }
  return(retVal);
}

}
```

Listing 4-3 shows the modified version of `Tumbleweed.java`.

*Listing 4-3. The Modified* `Tumbleweed.java`

```
package net.frog_parrot.jump;

import javax.microedition.lcdui.*;
import javax.microedition.lcdui.game.*;
```

```
/**
 * This class represents the tumbleweeds that the player
 * must jump over.
 *
 * @author Carol Hamer
 */
public class Tumbleweed extends Sprite {

  //-----------------------------------------------------------
  //    dimension fields

  /**
   * The width of the tumbleweed's bounding square.
   */
  static final int WIDTH = 16;

  //-----------------------------------------------------------
  //    instance fields

  /**
   * whether this tumbleweed has been jumped over.
   * This calculates the score.
   */
  private boolean myJumpedOver;

  /**
   * whether this tumbleweed enters from the left.
   */
  private boolean myLeft;

  /**
   * the Y coordinate of the tumbleweed.
   */
  private int myY;

  /**
   * the leftmost visible pixel.
   */
  private int myCurrentLeftBound;

  /**
   * the rightmost visible pixel.
   */
  private int myCurrentRightBound;
```

```
//-----------------------------------------------------------
//   initialization

/**
 * constructor initializes the image and animation.
 * @param left whether this tumbleweed enters from the left.
 */
public Tumbleweed(boolean left) throws Exception {
  super(Image.createImage("/images/tumbleweed.png"),
        WIDTH, WIDTH);
  myY = JumpManager.DISP_HEIGHT - WIDTH - 2;
  myLeft = left;
  if(!myLeft) {
    setTransform(TRANS_MIRROR);
  }
  myJumpedOver = false;
  setVisible(false);
}

//-----------------------------------------------------------
//   game actions

/**
 * Set the tumbleweed in motion if it is not currently visible.
 */
synchronized boolean go() {
  boolean retVal = false;
  if(!isVisible()) {
    retVal = true;
    //System.out.println("Tumbleweed.go-->not visible");
    myJumpedOver = false;
    setVisible(true);
    // set the tumbleweed's position to the point
    // where it just barely appears on the screen
    // to that it can start approaching the cowboy:
    if(myLeft) {
      setRefPixelPosition(myCurrentRightBound, myY);
      move(-1, 0);
    } else {
      setRefPixelPosition(myCurrentLeftBound, myY);
      move(1, 0);
    }
  } else {
    //System.out.println("Tumbleweed.go-->visible");
```

```
    }
    return(retVal);
  }


  //-----------------------------------------------------------
  //    graphics

  /**
   * move the tumbleweed back to its initial (inactive) state.
   */
  void reset() {
    setVisible(false);
    myJumpedOver = false;
  }


  /**
   * alter the tumbleweed image appropriately for this frame.
   * @param left whether the player is moving left
   * @return how much the score should change by after this
   *           advance.
   */
  synchronized int advance(Cowboy cowboy, int tickCount, boolean left,
                int currentLeftBound, int currentRightBound) {
    int retVal = 0;
    myCurrentLeftBound = currentLeftBound;
    myCurrentRightBound = currentRightBound;
    // if the tumbleweed goes outside of the display
    // region, set it to invisible since it is
    // no longer in use.
    if((getRefPixelX() - WIDTH >= currentRightBound) && (!myLeft)) {
      setVisible(false);
    }
    if((getRefPixelX() + WIDTH <= currentLeftBound) && myLeft) {
      setVisible(false);
    }
    if(isVisible()) {
      // when the tumbleweed is active, you advance the
      // rolling animation to the next frame and then
      // move the tumbleweed in the right direction across
      // the screen.
      if(tickCount % 2 == 0) { // slow the animation down a little
        nextFrame();
      }
      if(myLeft) {
```

```
            move(-3, 0);
            // if the cowboy just passed the tumbleweed
            // (without colliding with it), you increase the
            // cowboy's score and set myJumpedOver to true
            // so that no further points will be awarded
            // for this tumbleweed until it goes off the screen
            // and then is later reactivated:
            if((! myJumpedOver) &&
               (getRefPixelX() < cowboy.getRefPixelX())) {
              myJumpedOver = true;
              retVal = cowboy.increaseScoreThisJump();
            }
          } else {
            move(3, 0);
            if((! myJumpedOver) &&
               (getRefPixelX() > cowboy.getRefPixelX() + Cowboy.WIDTH)) {
              myJumpedOver = true;
              retVal = cowboy.increaseScoreThisJump();
            }
          }
        }
      }
      return(retVal);
   }

}
```

Note that the changes to Tumbleweed.java require adding the method shown in Listing 4-4 to JumpManager.java.

*Listing 4-4. Additions to* JumpManager.java

```
/**
   * @return a handle to the tumbleweed objects.
   */
  Tumbleweed[] getTumbleweeds() {
    Tumbleweed[] retArray = new Tumbleweed[myLeftTumbleweeds.length
                                      + myRightTumbleweeds.length];
    for(int i = 0; i < myLeftTumbleweeds.length; i++) {
      retArray[i] = myLeftTumbleweeds[i];
    }
    for(int i = 0; i < myRightTumbleweeds.length; i++) {
      retArray[i + myLeftTumbleweeds.length] = myRightTumbleweeds[i];
    }
    return(retArray);
  }
```

You must also add a corresponding method to JumpCanvas.java as well as slightly modify the setGameOver() method. Additionally, I've added implementations to showNotify() and hideNotify(). The changes to showNotify() and hideNotify() are necessary because the added command to toggle the music forced the emulator to put some commands in a menu. When the menu pops up, the game is hidden. But it wouldn't be fair for the tumbleweeds to keep rolling by and crashing into the cowboy while the user is busy with the menu. (In fact, while the menu is open, the game doesn't receive keystroke information and the display isn't updated, so the user may think the game is paused even if it's not.) So, I'd like for the game to pause when it's hidden and start again when it's displayed. My first solution was to put a call to pauseGame() in hideNotify() and a call to resumeGame() in showNotify(). The problem with this is that if the user selects the pause command from the menu, showNotify() will be called as soon as the menu goes away, starting the game again against the user's wishes! That's why I've created two distinct functions in the Jump code in Listing 4-1: userPauseThreads() and systemPauseThreads(). That way, the game proceeds only if the user wants it to proceed *and* the application management software verifies that the game isn't hidden.

Listing 4-5 shows the added and modified parts of JumpCanvas.java.

*Listing 4-5. Additions and Changes to* JumpCanvas.java

```
//-------------------------------------------------------
  //    gets/sets

  /**
   * This is called when the game ends.
   */
  void setGameOver() {
    myGameOver = true;
    myJump.userPauseThreads();
  }

  /**
   * @return a handle to the tumbleweed objects.
   */
  Tumbleweed[] getTumbleweeds() {
    return(myManager.getTumbleweeds());
  }

  //-------------------------------------------------------
  //    initialization and game state changes
```

```
/**
 * pause the game when it's hidden.
 */
protected void hideNotify() {
  try {
    myJump.systemPauseThreads();
  } catch(Exception oe) {
    myJump.errorMsg(oe);
  }
}

/**
 * When it comes back into view, unpause it.
 */
protected void showNotify() {
  try {
    myJump.systemStartThreads();
  } catch(Exception oe) {
    myJump.errorMsg(oe);
  }
}
```

## Avoiding Race Conditions and Deadlock

Synchronization issues are some of the hardest problems to locate and debug. This is because the errors they create are often rare and almost impossible to reproduce. You therefore have to do all your thread synchronization debugging by pure thought. To give you an idea of how to do it, I'll go over using the synchronized keyword in this example program and suggest how to keep your program thread safe. This section will contain nothing new for experienced Java programmers, but because keeping your program thread safe is at once tricky and important, I'll include this material for those readers who are new to it.

Recall the basics of how synchronization works: Each instance of an object has a lock, and each class has a lock for its static methods. Suppose the instance is called myObject. If a thread enters a method for that instance marked with the synchronized keyword or if the thread enters a block of code contained in a block delineated by synchronized(myObject), then the thread picks up the instance's lock. If one thread is holding the lock for a particular instance, then no other thread can enter any method or synchronized block for that particular instance until the thread currently holding the lock exits the synchronized method or block. This is a means of preventing *race conditions* in which two or more threads are at risk of modifying and/or acting on the values of data simultaneously. Clearly there's going to be problems if one thread completes the phrase if(x == y) and then another thread changes the value of x before the first thread executes all the statements in the if block.

Obviously, the problem arises when two or more threads are using the same data at the same time and at least one of those threads might modify that data. A naive solution is to use the synchronized keyword on every method that reads or modifies data. That would force all the threads to take turns using data-related methods. But that strategy would almost certainly lead to frequent *deadlock*, which is when two threads get stuck because each one is waiting for the other to give up a lock.

The best strategy is to analyze each class method by method to see where synchronization is needed and where it isn't. That's not as terrible as it sounds since it becomes second nature once you're used to doing it. Here are a few little tips:

- Use local method variables instead of class fields when you can because this avoids the necessity of making the method synchronized (local method variables can't be altered by other threads).

- Make each synchronized segment as small and simple as possible.

- Try to avoid grabbing a second lock from within a synchronized section.

You'll now see how these ideas apply to GameThread. Using synchronization in the other two thread classes is nearly identical to how you use it in GameThread. The run() method has two synchronized blocks and two other synchronized methods. Listing 4-6 shows what they look like.

*Listing 4-6. Synchronized Blocks and Methods*

```
/**
* restart the game after a pause.
*/
synchronized void resumeGame() {
  myShouldPause = false;
  notify();
}

/**
 * stops the game.
 */
synchronized void requestStop() {
  myShouldStop = true;
  notify();
}
```

```
/**
 * start the game.
 */
public void run() {
  // flush any keystrokes that occurred before the
  // game started:
  myJumpCanvas.flushKeys();
  myShouldStop = false;
  myShouldPause = false;
  while(true) {
    if(myShouldStop) {
      break;
    }
    synchronized(this) {
      while(myShouldPause) {
        try {
          wait();
        } catch(Exception e) {}
      }
    }
    myJumpCanvas.checkKeys();
    myJumpCanvas.advance();
    // you do a very short pause to allow the other thread
    // to update the information about which keys are pressed:
    synchronized(this) {
      try {
        wait(1);
      } catch(Exception e) {}
    }
  }
}
```

The first thing to verify is that none of these synchronized segments can cause deadlock. Clearly they can't. The two methods merely set a data field and then call notify(), so they certainly return without doing anything that would cause the thread to need to grab another lock before it could continue. Similarly, the two blocks in the run() method are safe because all they do is check data and then wait. Waiting with a lock may seem dangerous, but in fact the thread lets go of its lock as soon as it starts waiting (and then grabs it again once it's notified), so in these blocks the thread lets go of the lock almost immediately after grabbing it.

The second thing to analyze is why these particular blocks are synchronized. To begin with, the methods wait() and notify() must always be called from within a synchronized block or method. You must synchronize on the same object that you call the method wait() or notify() on, so, for example, calling myObject.wait() must be done from within a block marked by synchronized(myObject). In most cases, the least confusing thing to do is to synchronize on this as I've done in this example. Of course, you may notice in Listing 4-6 that I included the phrase while(myShouldPause) inside the synchronized block. I did this to avoid a race condition. Imagine what might happen if the synchronized block contained only the call to the method wait(). Suppose that the thread just finished the line while(myShouldPause) and determined that myShouldPause is true. Then, before this thread gets to the next line, another thread calls resumeGame(), which sets myShould Pause to false and then calls notify(). At this point notify() has no effect because the thread isn't waiting. Then the original thread starts up again and executes the next line, which is a call to wait(). The result of all this is that the program has just asked the game to start up again, and the game thread is stuck waiting, which is not what's supposed to happen. Since the call to wait() depends on the data checked on the previous line and that data could potentially be changed on another thread, you group the two within the same synchronized block.

The final question is, why is there so little synchronization in the rest of the code? Many of the classes have places where the action on one line depends strongly on data checked on the previous line. But the difference is that only a single thread can modify the data in the graphical game objects. You can see in Listing 4-6 that GameThread first prompts the GameCanvas to query for keystrokes (which prompts all the keystroke-related data updates) and then prompts the GameCanvas to advance the animation accordingly. No other thread can modify the data objects concurrently to mess up things.

I have one last comment to add about thread scheduling: As I mentioned previously, a cell phone or other small device generally does doesn't parallel processors and hence must run the threads one at a time. In fact, it turns out that in most CLDC implementations the processor switches from one thread to another only when the currently active thread waits or finishes. This means that if one of your threads has an infinite loop, it needs to occasionally wait, as described in the "Using the Thread Class" section in Chapter 3. It also means that none of the race condition or deadlock situations discussed should ever create problems in practice even if you're sloppy with the synchronized keyword. But it's good practice to synchronize correctly anyway.

## Adding Music

The MIDP 2.0 Application Programming Interface (API) provides two possible strategies for adding music to your game: Either you can play music from a music file, or you can create your own music by playing tones. You'll build the music for the example game with tones. Custom tonal music is much more adapted to MIDP game applications than playing complex music from music files, but music files can have their applications (see the "Using Audio Files" section for more about playing music files). The audio functionality in MIDP is part of a larger Mobile Media API, which is used by various Java 2 Micro Edition (J2ME) profiles.

In the following sections, I'll give two different example classes you could use to add music to the Tumbleweed game. They both play the same tune, and they both create the tune by playing tones. The difference is that the first one illustrates how to write a program that will play the tones itself, one by one, and in the second version, you use the simpler technique of passing the music data to a `Player` and having the `Player` play the tones. The advantage of the first approach is that you have more control. You can more easily synchronize the game animation with the music since you know exactly when each note is being played. This is the way to go if you're programming a game where the music plays a part in the game, such as the popular Dance-Dance Revolution. The advantage of the second version is that it's easier on the programmer. The MIDP classes will do some of the work for you, such as spawning a new `Thread` on which the `Player` can run. The second approach is probably the one you want to use if the music in your game does nothing but provide background atmosphere.

## Playing Simple Tones

Playing tonal music with MIDP is the easiest thing you can possibly imagine. As usual, the situation is that the target devices have limited abilities. The disadvantage is that your possibilities are limited, and the advantage is that what you can do is really simple. All you need to do is call the static method `javax.microedition.media.Manager.playTone()` with the note, volume, and time duration you'd like.

The trickiest part is figuring out which integer value corresponds to which note. For fun, I'll quote to you the Javadoc on the subject:

*[SEMITONE_CONST = 17.31234049066755 = 1/(ln(2^(1/12)))*

*note = ln(freq/8.176)\*SEMITONE_CONST*

*The musical note A = MIDI note 69 (0x45) = 440 Hz.]*

I imagine this formula would be useful for the people writing JVM implementations, and I assume that's who the audience is for this part of the Javadoc. But allow me to explain how it works in English, assuming that (like me) you haven't done any advanced studies in music theory. As the previous quote states, the number 69 is the note A. To find the number corresponding to another note, count how many piano keys it is away from the note A, including the black keys (the sharps and flats). For example, the following are two scales in the key of A: { 57, 59, 61, 62, 64, 66, 68, 69 } and { 69, 71, 73, 74, 76, 78, 80 81 }.

Keep in mind that the method playTone() is *nonblocking*, which means the thread returns as soon as the note *starts* playing, not when the note finishes playing. The easiest strategy is therefore to have one thread devoted to playing music and, as soon as it plays a note, have it wait for the same length of time that the note is played for before starting the next note. That's what I've done in the example code in Listing 4-7.

But what do you do if you need the musical notes to be synchronized with game/animation events? Unfortunately, no version of playTone() allows you to say to the machine, "Play this note until I tell you to stop." So if you want the music and the game events to line up, you have to match the game events to the music, not vice versa. It's probably better that way anyway since you don't really want the rhythm of the music to depend on how the calculations in your game loop are going. What I recommend in that case is to still use a separate music thread and game/animation thread. Then, when the animation thread gets to the point where it shouldn't do anything more until the beginning of the next note, have that thread wait until the music thread notifies it that the next note is about to start. The one thing to be careful of is that the game/animation calculations may occasionally take longer than expected, and that thread may not be waiting yet when the music thread calls notify(). But that's easy to deal with by creating and setting appropriate flags.

Listing 4-7 shows the code for MusicMaker.java.

*Listing 4-7.* MusicMaker.java

```
package net.frog_parrot.jump;

import javax.microedition.media.*;

/**
 * This is the class that plays a little tune while you
 * play the game.
 *
 * @author Carol Hamer
 */
public class MusicMaker extends Thread {

  //-------------------------------------------------------------
  //   fields

  /**
   * Whether the main thread would like this thread
   * to stop.
   */
  public static final int NOTE_LENGTH = 250;
```

```
/**
 * Whether the main thread would like this thread
 * to pause.
 */
private boolean myShouldPause;

/**
 * If the whole game is paused, you pause the music, too.
 */
private boolean myGamePause;

/**
 * Whether the main thread would like this thread
 * to stop.
 */
private static boolean myShouldStop;

/**
 * The tune played by the game, stored as an array
 * of notes and durations.
 *
 * NOTE: 69 is A. To get other notes, just add or subtract
 * their difference from A on the keyboard including the
 * black keys in the calculation.  See the following scales
 * for an idea.
 *
 */
private byte[][] myTune = { { 69, 1 }, { 69, 1 }, { 69, 1 }, { 71, 1 },
                    { 73, 2 }, { 71, 2 }, { 69, 1 }, { 73, 1 },
                    { 71, 1 }, { 71, 1 }, { 69, 4 },
                    { 69, 1 }, { 69, 1 }, { 69, 1 }, { 71, 1 },
                    { 73, 2 }, { 71, 2 }, { 69, 1 }, { 73, 1 },
                    { 71, 1 }, { 71, 1 }, { 69, 4 },
                    { 71, 1 }, { 71, 1 }, { 71, 1 }, { 71, 1 },
                    { 66, 2 }, { 66, 2 }, { 71, 1 }, { 69, 1 },
                    { 68, 1 }, { 66, 1 }, { 64, 4 },
                    { 69, 1 }, { 69, 1 }, { 69, 1 }, { 71, 1 },
                    { 73, 2 }, { 71, 2 }, { 69, 1 }, { 73, 1 },
                    { 71, 1 }, { 71, 1 }, { 69, 4 }
};

/**
 * An example "tune" that is just a scale.
 * not used.
 */
```

```
private byte[][] myScale = { { 69, 1 }, { 71, 1 }, { 73, 1 }, { 74, 1 },
                { 76, 1 }, { 78, 1 }, { 80, 1 }, { 81, 1 } };


/**
 * An example "tune" that is just a scale.
 * not used.
 */
private byte[][] myScale2 = { { 57, 1 }, { 59, 1 }, { 61, 1 }, { 62, 1 },
                { 64, 1 }, { 66, 1 }, { 68, 1 }, { 69, 1 } };


//-----------------------------------------------------------
//    actions

/**
 * call this when the game pauses.
 */
void pauseGame() {
  myGamePause = true;
}


/**
 * call this when the game resumes.
 */
synchronized void resumeGame() {
  myGamePause = false;
  this.notify();
}


/**
 * toggle the music.
 * (pause it if it's going, start it again if it's paused).
 */
synchronized void toggle() {
  myShouldPause = !myShouldPause;
  this.notify();
}


/**
 * stops the music.
 */
synchronized void requestStop() {
  myShouldStop = true;
  this.notify();
}
```

```
/**
 * start the music.
 */
public void run() {
  myShouldStop = false;
  myShouldPause = true;
  myGamePause = false;
  int counter = 0;
  while(true) {
    if(myShouldStop) {
      break;
    }
    synchronized(this) {
      while((myShouldPause) || (myGamePause)) {
        try {
          wait();
        } catch(Exception e) {}
      }
    }
    try {
      Manager.playTone(myTune[counter][0],
                       myTune[counter][1]*NOTE_LENGTH, 50);
    } catch(Exception e) {
      // the music isn't necessary, so you ignore exceptions.
    }
    synchronized(this) {
      try {
        wait(myTune[counter][1]*NOTE_LENGTH);
      } catch(Exception e) {}
    }
    counter++;
    if(counter >= myTune.length) {
      counter = 0;
    }
  }
}
```

## Playing Tones with a Player

Now you'll see how to create a `Player` to take over some of the work of playing the music.

Just as with the previous version, the most important part of creating the music is writing an array of data to describe the tune. In this case, to pass the data to the Player, you call setSequence() on the ToneControl object associated with the Player.

The tune data used by a Player needs to be stored in a particular format, called *augmented BNF notation*. This notation is pretty simple. It's essentially a sequence of pairs of bytes that give the note and the length of time the note should be played. The correspondence between numbers and notes works in the same way for a Player as it did in the previous section when playing the notes with the Manager (in other words, 69 is A, and you can find the numbers of the other notes by counting how many piano keys there are from A and adding or subtracting that number from 69). In addition to the notes and their lengths, you have a few extra components to add to the data array, such as codes for the version and the tempo, as you can see in Listing 4-8 (in the field myTune). Also, you can define the tune in terms of blocks, which is convenient for the tune I used because the tune has one line that's repeated three times. But it isn't necessary to define the music data in terms of blocks of notes, and if you do use blocks of notes, you can alternate them with sequences of notes that aren't defined as blocks. If you don't want to do anything too fancy, you can more or less work from the example in Listing 4-8. For more details, the precise syntax of the augmented BNF notation is given in the Javadoc of the javax.microedition. media.control.ToneControl class.

In addition to using the ToneControl interface in the example class, I also used the VolumeControl to set the volume. All I did was set the volume to its maximum (100), but you could easily write code that would allow the user to access a Form screen containing a Gauge that uses a VolumeControl to control the volume. See the "Using the Form and Item Classes" in Chapter 2 for a review of using MIDP Graphical User Interface (GUI) components.

One main structural difference to notice between this version of the MusicMaker code and the version from the previous section is that by using a Player I avoid having to create a separate thread for the music. When you call start() on the Player, the method returns immediately, and the music runs on its own thread. So I have one less thread to keep track of myself. If I want the music to repeat, the simplest way to do it is to call setLoopCount(). In a professional game I would have made the music repeat indefinitely by setting the loop count to -1. But instead I decided to illustrate the use of the PlayerListener interface to make the music repeat. With the PlayerListener interface, you can listen for state changes in the Player such as starting, stopping, changing volume, and so on. In Listing 4-8, I have it listen for END_OF_MEDIA, and when the end of the tune is reached, I tell it to play it again.

One more point in the fields of this class may require some explanation. Just as in the other version, I maintain two different fields to keep track of whether the music has been paused by the system or by the user. This is necessary because I don't want to start the music after a pause unless both the system and the user want the music to be unpaused. An example of what can go wrong without this double-checking is that the user might decide to turn off the music, but then later when the game is hidden by a menu and then unhidden, the method showNotify() (called by the application management software) may trigger the music to start up again if you're not keeping track of the user's desire to have the music stay turned off.

Note that to have the game use this version of the MusicMaker class instead of the one from the previous section, you must make a small change in the Jump class. You must change the field myMusicMaker from being declared as a MusicMaker to being declared as a ToneControlMusicMaker. This change involves modifying only two lines, and I've provided the alternate lines (commented out) in the Jump code in the "Differences Between CLDC Threads and Threads in Standard Java" section.

Listing 4-8 shows the code for ToneControlMusicMaker.java.

*Listing 4-8.* ToneControlMusicMaker.java

```
package net.frog_parrot.jump;

import javax.microedition.media.*;
import javax.microedition.media.control.*;

/**
 * This is the class that plays a little tune while you
 * play the game. This version uses the Player and
 * Control interfaces.
 *
 * @author Carol Hamer
 */
public class ToneControlMusicMaker implements PlayerListener {

  //-----------------------------------------------------------
  //   fields

  /**
   * The player object that plays the tune.
   */
  private Player myPlayer;

  /**
   * Whether the player wants to pause the music.
   */
  private boolean myShouldPause;
```

```
/**
 * Whether the system wants to pause the music.
 */
private boolean myGamePause;

/**
 * The tune played by the game, stored as an array
 * of bytes in BNF notation.
 */
private byte[] myTune = {
        // first set the version
        ToneControl.VERSION, 1,
        // set the tempo
        ToneControl.TEMPO, 30,
        // define the first line of the song
        ToneControl.BLOCK_START, 0,
        69,8, 69,8, 69,8, 71,8,
        73,16, 71,16, 69,8, 73,8,
        71,8, 71,8, 69,32,
        ToneControl.BLOCK_END, 0,
        // define the other line of the song
        ToneControl.BLOCK_START, 1,
        71,8, 71,8, 71,8, 71,8,
        66,16, 66,16, 71,8, 69,8,
        68,8, 66,8, 64,32,
        ToneControl.BLOCK_END, 1,
        // play the song
        ToneControl.PLAY_BLOCK, 0,
        ToneControl.PLAY_BLOCK, 0,
        ToneControl.PLAY_BLOCK, 1,
        ToneControl.PLAY_BLOCK, 0,
};


//----------------------------------------------------------
//   actions

/**
 * call this when the game pauses.
 * This method does not affect the field
 * myShouldPause because this method is called only
 * when the system pauses the music, not when the
 * player pauses the music.
 */
```

```
void pauseGame() {
  try {
    myGamePause = true;
    myPlayer.stop();
    // when the application pauses the game, resources
    // are supposed to be released, so you close the
    // player and throw it away.
    myPlayer.close();
    myPlayer = null;
  } catch(Exception e) {
    // the music isn't necessary, so you ignore exceptions.
  }
}

/**
 * call this when the game resumes.
 * This method does not affect the field
 * myShouldPause because this method is called only
 * when the system resumes the music, not when the
 * player pauses the music.
 */
synchronized void resumeGame() {
  try {
    myGamePause = false;
    if(! myShouldPause) {
      // if the player is null, you create a new one.
      if(myPlayer == null) {
        start();
      }
      // start the music.
      myPlayer.start();
    }
  } catch(Exception e) {
    // the music isn't necessary, so you ignore exceptions.
  }
}

/**
 * toggle the music.
 * (pause it if it's going, start it again if it's paused).
 */
```

```
synchronized void toggle() {
  try {
    myShouldPause = !myShouldPause;
    if(myShouldPause) {
      if(myPlayer != null) {
        myPlayer.stop();
      }
    } else if(! myGamePause) {
      // if the player is null, you create a new one.
      if(myPlayer == null) {
        start();
      }
      // start the music.
      myPlayer.start();
    }
  } catch(Exception e) {
    // the music isn't necessary, so you ignore exceptions.
  }
}


/**
 * stops the music.
 */
synchronized void requestStop() {
  try {
    myPlayer.stop();
    // this is called when the game is over to you close
    // up the player to release the resources.
    myPlayer.close();
  } catch(Exception e) {
    // the music isn't necessary, so you ignore exceptions.
  }
}


//------------------------------------------------------------
//   initialization

/**
 * start the music.
 * Here the method is "start" instead of "run" because
 * it is not necessary to create a thread for the Player.
```

```
 * the Player runs on its own thread.
 */
public void start() {
  ToneControl control = null;
  try {
    myPlayer = Manager.createPlayer(Manager.TONE_DEVICE_LOCATOR);
    // do the preliminary setup:
    myPlayer.realize();
    // set a listener to listen for the end of the tune:
    myPlayer.addPlayerListener(this);
    // get the ToneControl object in order to set the tune data:
    control = (ToneControl)myPlayer.getControl("ToneControl");
    control.setSequence(myTune);
    // set the volume to the highest possible volume:
    VolumeControl vc = (VolumeControl)myPlayer.getControl("VolumeControl");
    vc.setLevel(100);
  } catch(Exception e) {
    // the music isn't necessary, so you ignore exceptions.
  }
}


//------------------------------------------------------------
//    implementation of PlayerListener

/**
 * If you reach the end of the song, play it again...
 */
public void playerUpdate(Player player, String event, Object eventData) {
  if(event.equals(PlayerListener.END_OF_MEDIA)) {
    if((! myShouldPause) && (! myGamePause)) {
      try {
        myPlayer.start();
      } catch(Exception e) {
        // the music isn't necessary, so you ignore exceptions.
      }
    }
  }
}

}
```

## Finding Public Domain Music

If you're planning to distribute your game, don't forget that the background music can potentially give you some legal headaches if you're not careful about the copyright. A tune that you reproduce from memory in tones could easily be owned by someone who may not want you reselling it along with your game. This goes double for reproducing tunes from copyrighted sheet music or for using music files of uncertain origin. Unless using a particular tune is really important for your game and your company is big enough to have a legal department, you probably should avoid using copyrighted music.

Ideally, you're a brilliant composer in addition to being a brilliant game developer, in which case you can just compose a tune yourself, and your problem is solved. If you're not, the easiest solution is to use music that's in the public domain. If you play the Tumbleweed game with music, you may recognize that it plays an old French folk tune called *Au Clair de la Lune* instead of some modern (copyrighted) piece.

Fortunately, plenty of resources exist on the Web that will help you find public domain music. The site at http://www.pdinfo.com/ is full of helpful legal information about how the public domain works, plus it has a list of titles of more than 3,500 public domain songs, many with sheet music you can order. The site at http://www.pdmusic.org/ also has a long list of song titles, many of which have associated .midi music files, but it doesn't give much information on how to get the associated sheet music. The site at http://www.cpdl.org/ has a huge list of songs to choose from, and it allows you to download the sheet music for free in .pdf format. The site at http://www.sheetmusic1.com/new.great.music.html also has sheet music you can download for free, but the selection appears to be slightly more limited. The site at http://members.aol.com/katzmarek/pdmusic.htm claims to be the largest supplier of public domain books and music in the United States. The sheet music isn't free, but you can order it online at the site.

The previous list is certainly not exhaustive. You can find plenty of similar sites by typing **public domain music** into Google.

## Using Audio Files

By playing music files instead of creating music through tones, you can give your game a much richer musical background. Unfortunately, playing music files has several drawbacks that make them inappropriate for many applications, especially on small devices such as cell phones. First, devices that run MIDP 2.0 aren't required to support playback of audio files, so there's a good chance your target devices won't even give you this option. Second, the audio files can be quite large, especially compared to the total amount of storage space on the device. Third, playing an audio file requires a lot of effort on the part of the processor and will likely slow down your game's animation and response time. A fourth drawback is that it's hard to synchronize the music with the game. (You can use the getMediaTime() method of the Player interface to find out where you are in the music file, but it's not guaranteed to work.)

Dealing with memory and processor consumption is a really serious issue. Your target device must be a high-end MIDP device to even consider it. Verify that even with the audio file in the jar your program doesn't take up too much of the device's memory. Having the game download the audio file at run time is generally not a good solution for keeping the jar size down since having the device download data during the game and/or read the whole audio file into a buffer will dramatically diminish the computing resources available for your game.

The one place where playing audio from an audio file is typically appropriate for a game on a small device is to play it along with a few seconds of introductory animation before your game starts. That way, you can start by impressing your customer with a cool startup sequence without having the music eat up your computing power during the game itself. But even for this use it's important to verify that your target device can handle it.

Once you've decided you want to use an audio file in your game, it's easy to implement. Listing 4-9 shows an example code block to demonstrate.

*Listing 4-9. Playing an Audio File*

```
/**
 * Read the audio file from the jar and play it.
 */
void playMusic() {
  try {
    // create an input stream that can be used to read the
    // music data from a file called music.wav in a directory
    // called resources in this program's jar file.
    InputStream is = getClass().getResourceAsStream("resources/music.wav");
    // create a media player to play the music file, and
    // inform the player that the format is "audio/X-wav"
    Player player = Manager.createPlayer(is, "audio/X-wav");
    // start the music
    player.start();
  } catch (IOException ioe) {
    // deal with the exception
  } catch (MediaException me) {
    // deal with the exception
  }
}
```

Before creating the `Player`, you can verify that the implementation supports playback of files in your chosen format by calling `Manager.getSupportedContentTypes()`. Some common types include .wav audio files (MIME type: `audio/x-wav`), .au audio files (MIME type: `audio/basic`), .mp3 audio files (MIME type: `audio/mpeg`), and .midi files (MIME type: `audio/midi`). Once you have an instance of `Player`, you have a number of methods at your disposition for controlling the `Player`'s life cycle. Using `realize()`, you can tell the player to do any preliminary construction steps without acquiring device resources, and the methods `prefetch()` and `deallocate()` allow you to instruct the `Player` to acquire (and release) the resources that the player needs in order to play. Then you can start and stop the music using the aptly named `start()` and `stop()` methods and close the player down with the method `close()`.

# CHAPTER 5

# Storing and Retrieving Data

I**T TURNS OUT THAT** storing bytes of data locally on a device that's equipped for the Mobile Internet Device Profile (MIDP) is easy. Therefore, this chapter starts with an extremely simple example: You'll take the maze game example from Chapter 3 and store the user's preferred size information. Then, each time the user restarts the game, the game will automatically create the maze with walls of the user's chosen width rather than starting at the default width.

The hard part of data storage and retrieval is when you have more complicated data to store. MIDP allows you to store arrays of bytes only. But what if the data you want to store isn't in the form of bytes? The simplest thing to do is to use the classes `java.io.DataInputStream` and `java.io.DataOutputStream` to convert other types of data to bytes. But since memory can be scarce on a small device, it's a good idea to understand how you convert integers to bytes, and vice versa, so you can compact your data to store it more efficiently. Therefore, in this chapter, you'll see a utility class that converts ints to bytes and back again, compacting the data appropriately if it falls within a certain size range. Then you'll see a complete game example (using the utility class) in which the user can save a game that's currently in play and start it again later from that point. This example illustrates how to store complex data in a real game situation.

## Saving Simple Data

The MIDP Record Management System (RMS) is simple. Its package `javax.microedition.rms` has only one class: `RecordStore`. A `RecordStore` is a collection of records, which are in fact just byte arrays. A `RecordStore` is identified by the property `MIDlet-Vendor` and the property `MIDlet-Name` in the `jad` file, as well as by the name given to the `RecordStore` by the `MIDlet` that created it. This means that within a `MIDlet` *suite* (a group of `MIDlet`s in the same `jar` file), the `MIDlet`s share the `RecordStore`s they've created, but `MIDlet` suites don't share `RecordStore`s with other `MIDlet` suites (unless they're explicitly given permission to do so; you'll learn more about that in the sidebar "Using Secure Connections While Selling Your Game" in Chapter 7). A `RecordStore` is identified by the `MIDlet-Vendor` and the `MIDlet-Name` properties in addition to the store's name, so you don't have to start your RecordStore's name with your own package name to keep it in a separate namespace from the RecordStores of other unrelated MIDlets. It's a good thing, too, because the name of the RecordStore can be only 32 (case-sensitive) characters long, so you don't want to waste too many of them.

To create a RecordStore, all you have to do is call the static method RecordStore.openRecordStore() with the name of the RecordStore you want to create and the value true as arguments. The second argument true answers the question of whether to create the RecordStore if it doesn't already exist. Once you have a handle to a RecordStore (either by creating it or by opening an existing RecordStore), you can get or set the records. Note that a *record* isn't a separate class; it's merely a byte array. The RMS assigns each record an integer record ID that you use to get or replace the data array using getRecord() or setRecord(). The first record is assigned the ID of one, and the record IDs go up incrementally from there. If you don't like hard-coding numerical constants into your code (a reasonable inhibition), you can call enumerateRecords to get a RecordEnumerator to help you. The RecordEnumerator won't necessarily give you the records in the same order they'd appear in if you had gotten them by number using getRecord(). If you'd like to traverse the records in a particular order, you can create a RecordFilter and/or a RecordComparator, which allows you to define, respectively, which subset of the records will be returned and in what order to return them. Both RecordFilter and RecordComparator are interfaces you must implement yourself if you'd like to use them. These interfaces were obviously designed with address book–type applications in mind rather than games, but you may find a use for them.

In this first example, you'll create the simplest possible RecordStore. It'll contain only one record, and that record will contain only 1 byte. The example works as follows: You start with the maze game from Chapter 3. After the user selects the preferred width for the maze walls and presses Done, the game calls the new class (PrefsStorage) with the preferred size information, and the PrefsStorage class then saves that information in a RecordStore. The game also consults the PrefsStorage class when the user first opens the game to check for a stored size preference to use when building the maze. If no preferred size has been stored, the PrefsStorage returns the default value.

In addition to adding the PrefsStorage class listed next, you need to modify a few other classes a bit. In the class MazeCanvas, you need to replace the following line:

```
mySquareSize = 5;
```

with the following line:

```
mySquareSize = PrefsStorage.getSquareSize();
```

Next, in the class SelectScreen, you need to add the following line:

```
PrefsStorage.setSquareSize(myWidthGauge.getValue());
```

to the method commandAction, as follows:

```
public void commandAction(Command c, Displayable s) {
  if(c == myExitCommand) {
    PrefsStorage.setSquareSize(myWidthGauge.getValue());
    myCanvas.newMaze();
  }
}
```

Aside from those changes, the code for this example is identical to the code of the maze example from Chapter 3.

Listing 5-1 shows the code for PrefsStorage.java.

*Listing 5-1.* PrefsStorage.java

```
package net.frog_parrot.maze;

import javax.microedition.rms.*;

/**
 * This class helps to store and retrieve the data about
 * the maze size preferences.
 *
 * This is a utility class that does not contain instance data,
 * so to simplify access, all the methods are static.
 *
 * @author Carol Hamer
 */
public class PrefsStorage {

  //-----------------------------------------------------------
  //    static fields

  /**
   * The name of the datastore.
   */
  public static final String STORE = "SizePrefs";

  //-----------------------------------------------------------
  //    business methods
```

```
/**
 * This gets the preferred square size from the stored data.
 */
static int getSquareSize() {
  // if data retrieval fails, the default value is 5
  int retVal = 5;
  RecordStore store = null;
  try {
    // if the record store does not yet exist, the second
    // arg "true" tells it to create.
    store = RecordStore.openRecordStore(STORE, true);
    int numRecords = store.getNumRecords();
    if(numRecords > 0) {
      // the first record has id number 1
      // (In fact this program stores only one record)
      byte[] rec = store.getRecord(1);
      retVal = rec[0];
    }
  } catch(Exception e) {
    // data storage is not critical for this game and you're
    // not creating a log, so if data retrieval fails, you
    // just skip it and move on.
  } finally {
    try {
      store.closeRecordStore();
    } catch(Exception e) {
      // if the record store is open, this shouldn't throw.
    }
  }
  return(retVal);
}

/**
 * This saves the preferred square size.
 */
static void setSquareSize(int size) {
  RecordStore store = null;
  try {
    // since you're storing the int as a single byte,
    // it's important that its value be less than
    // 128.  In fact, in real life the value would never
    // get anywhere near this high, but I'm adding this
    // little size check as a last line of defense against
    // errors:
```

```
      if(size > 127) {
        size = 127;
      }
      // if the record store doesn't yet exist, the second
      // arg "true" tells it to create.
      store = RecordStore.openRecordStore(STORE, true);
      byte[] record = new byte[1];
      record[0] = (new Integer(size)).byteValue();
      int numRecords = store.getNumRecords();
      if(numRecords > 0) {
        store.setRecord(1, record, 0, 1);
      } else {
        store.addRecord(record, 0, 1);
      }
    } catch(Exception e) {
      // data storage isn't critical for this game and you're
      // not creating a log, so if data storage fails, you
      // just skip it and move on.
    } finally {
      try {
        store.closeRecordStore();
      } catch(Exception e) {
        // if the record store is open, this shouldn't throw.
      }
    }
  }

}
```

I need to mention one last point before you're done with this little example—namely, the technique for converting back and forth between int values and byte values. The value I'm saving is an int, yet I save it in the form of a byte with little regard for the fact that an int and a byte in Java aren't the same thing at all. (In particular, an int occupies 4 bytes of memory!) Yet you'll notice that in the method setSquareSize() I get a byte value for the argument size merely by calling byteValue(), and in the other direction (in the method getSquareSize()) I convert the byte rec[0] to an int without any sort of conversion operation at all. What's going on here? The answer is, I know the argument size is between -128 and 127 in value, so I know it can be stored as a single byte without losing any data. This simple conversion between ints and bytes is useful, but only if you're 100 percent certain your int isn't going to fall outside the appropriate range. If you'd like to store your int value with more precision, you can use alternate conversion techniques, discussed in the next section.

## Serializing More Complex Data Using Streams

Java doesn't make it easy for the programmer to take one kind of data and directly reinterpret it as another type of data. This can be frustrating if you've done any programming in C and are used to looking at data in terms of bytes. But maintaining strongly typed data is integral to Java's internal security, so if you want to program in Java, you might as well get used to it.

You can easily convert all of Java's simple data types into byte arrays and back again using the classes java.io.ByteArrayInputStream, java.io.ByteArrayOutputStream, java.io.DataInputStream, and java.io.DataOutputStream. The pair of methods shown in Listing 5-2 demonstrates how you can use these classes to convert between byte arrays and ints.

*Listing 5-2. Converting Between Arrays and Ints*

```
/**
 * Uses an input stream to convert an array of bytes to an int.
 */
public static int parseInt(byte[] data) throws IOException {
  DataInputStream stream
    = new DataInputStream(new ByteArrayInputStream(data));
  int retVal = stream.readInt();
  stream.close();
  return(retVal);
}


/**
 * Uses an output stream to convert an int to four bytes.
 */
public static byte[] intToFourBytes(int i) throws IOException {
  ByteArrayOutputStream baos = new ByteArrayOutputStream(4);
  DataOutputStream dos = new DataOutputStream(baos);
  dos.writeInt(i);
  baos.close ();
  dos.close();
  byte[] retArray = baos.toByteArray();
  return(retArray);
}
```

This same technique works for all of Java's simple data types. For Strings, you can use the methods readUTF() and writeUTF(). One design note in Listing 5-2 is that in most applications you wouldn't want to make multiple calls to utility functions like these because each call creates two stream objects that clutter memory and will later need to be garbage collected. Usually, if you plan to save a record that comprises multiple chunks of data, you'd create the appropriate OutputStream as you did previously and then write the entire record to it before closing it. My example game uses the previous methods because, as you'll see next, each record contains only one int that needs to be saved using a stream.

## Using Data Types and Byte Arithmetic

Using InputStream and OutputStream to encode and decode your data for storage purposes would be sufficient if your target device had an infinite amount of memory, which is far from the case for many small devices. And the DataOutputStream uses a full byte to record a single Boolean when of course you could squeeze eight Booleans into the same space, and as mentioned previously, DataOutputStream uses 4 bytes to store an int when you often know in advance that the value will be small enough to fit into 1 or 2 bytes. Of course, you have a little bit of design strategy to consider when deciding whether to store your data in the standard way or whether to compact it. Compacting your data not only complicates your program, but it makes your data less portable. If you're using custom compression algorithms, it's easier to render your data completely unsalvageable with a small error than it is when your data is serialized in a standard format. Therefore, if you're storing only a little data, then it's generally better to serialize it using the standard methods. In the case of this chapter's example program, however, data compression makes a nontrivial difference. In the game, a player is exploring a maze-like dungeon that's created by a 16×16 square grid. I'd like to allow for the possibility of having a large series of different boards for this game, and each board is stored as a chunk of data that tells which squares of the grid should be empty and which should be filled. Therefore, you create the background of this game with a 16×16 two-dimensional array of ones and zeros—or, in other words, with 256 Booleans. If I plan to store multiple boards, I'd prefer not to store this as an array of 256 bytes (or worse, as 256 ints that would equal 1024 bytes!) when I could store it compactly as 32 bytes.

It's not hard to compact data if you know a little bit about byte arithmetic. And Java 2 Micro Edition (J2ME) programmers naturally need to use byte arithmetic more than the average Java programmer. Recall that you use the bitwise "or" operator for placing strings and images (see the "Using the Graphics and Canvas Classes" section in Chapter 2) and for layout directives (see the "Using the Form and Item classes" section in Chapter 2), and you use a bitwise "and" operator to get all the information about the current key states (see the "Using the GameCanvas Class" section in Chapter 3). To stock eight Booleans into a byte, all you need to do is add the ones and zeros to the byte one by one and use the shift operator to shift the result up one bit between each new addition. To get the data out again, you just perform a bitwise "and" between the byte and a series of appropriate flag bytes. For example, 128 corresponds to the top bit of a byte, so to find out if the top bit of a given byte is set, all you have to do is perform a bitwise "and" with your chosen byte and a flag byte whose value is equal to 128. The value returned by the operation will be nonzero if and only if the top bit of your byte was set. You can get all the other flag bytes easily from the initial flag by shifting down the flag byte.

The class in Listing 5-3 is the complete version of my integer compression utility class (called DataConverter). It contains methods to pack eight Booleans into a byte as described previously, as well as methods to convert integers in various size ranges to bytes. I've even included methods that will convert an int to an array of 4 bytes giving exactly the same values as you'd get using DataInputStream and DataInputStream. I include these only so you can see the precise Java's algorithm for internally representing integers, not because you should choose to use these utilities over DataInputStream and DataOutputStream.

The only tricky part in any of the algorithms in Listing 5-3 is dealing with when a byte is considered to be signed and when it's considered to be unsigned. Signed bytes range in value from -128 to 127, and unsigned bytes range in value from 0 to 255. Any byte can be regarded as signed or unsigned; it's just a question of whether you consider the top bit to indicate a negative sign or 128. If you convert a single byte to an int, Java will consider the byte to be signed when returning the value. If you wanted its value as an unsigned byte, then you can fix it by adding 256 if the value is negative (that is, add 128 to get the value into the positive range and then add another 128 for the value of the top bit that was set). An integer obviously needs only one sign, so when Java represents an integer internally as 4 bytes, only the high byte (which is the first of the 4 bytes) is regarded as signed. Dealing with the interplay between signed and unsigned bytes is a little bit confusing, but I hope that the code example in Listing 5-3 will help clarify how it works.

Listing 5-3 shows the code for DataConverter.java.

*Listing 5-3.* DataConverter.java

```
package net.frog_parrot.util;

import java.io.*;

/**
 * This class is a set of simple utility functions that
 * can be used to convert standard data types to bytes
 * and back again. It is used especially for data storage,
 * but also for sending and receiving data.
 *
 * @author Carol Hamer
 */
public class DataConverter {
```

```
//-----------------------------------------------------------
//  utilities to encode small, compactly stored small ints.

/**
 * Encodes a coordinate pair into a byte.
 * @param coordPair a pair of integers to be compacted into
 * a single byte for storage.
 * WARNING: each of the two values MUST BE
 * between 0 and 15 (inclusive).  This method does not
 * verify the length of the array (which must be 2!)
 * and it doesn't verify that the ints are of the right size.
 */
public static byte encodeCoords(int[] coordPair) {
  // get the byte value of the first coordinate:
  byte retVal = (new Integer(coordPair[0])).byteValue();
  // move the first coordinate's value up to the top
  // half of the storage byte:
  retVal = (new Integer(retVal << 4)).byteValue();
  // store the second coordinate in the lower half
  // of the byte:
  retVal += (new Integer(coordPair[1])).byteValue();
  return(retVal);
}

/**
 * Encodes eight ints into a byte.
 * This could be easily modified to encode eight Booleans.
 * @param eight an array of at least eight ints.
 * WARNING: all values must be 0 or 1!  This method does
 * not verify that the values are in the correct range
 * and it doesn't verify that the array is long enough.
 * @param offset the index in the array eight to start
 * reading data from.  (should usually be 0)
 */
public static byte encode8(int[] eight, int offset) {
  // get the byte value of the first int:
  byte retVal = (new Integer(eight[offset])).byteValue();
  // progressively move the data up one bit in the
  // storage byte and then record the next int in
  // the lowest spot in the storage byte:
  for(int i = offset + 1; i < 8 + offset; i++) {
    retVal = (new Integer(retVal << 1)).byteValue();
    retVal += (new Integer(eight[i])).byteValue();
```

```
    }
    return(retVal);
}


//----------------------------------------------------------
// utilities to decode small, compactly stored small ints.

/**
 * Turns a byte into a pair of coordinates.
 */
public static int[] decodeCoords(byte coordByte) {
    int[] retArray = new int[2];
    // you perform a bitwise and with the value 15
    // in order to just get the bits of the lower
    // half of the byte:
    retArray[1] = coordByte & 15;
    // To get the bits of the upper half of the
    // byte, you perform a shift to move them down:
    retArray[0] = coordByte >> 4;
    // bytes in Java are generally assumed to be
    // signed, but in this coding algorithm you
    // would like to treat them as unsigned:
    if(retArray[0] < 0) {
        retArray[0] += 16;
    }
    return(retArray);
}


/**
 * Turns a byte into eight ints.
 */
public static int[] decode8(byte data) {
    int[] retArray = new int[8];
    // The flag allows us to look at each bit individually
    // to determine if it is 1 or 0.  The number 128
    // corresponds to the highest bit of a byte, so you
    // start with that one.
    int flag = 128;
    // You use a loop that checks
    // the data bit by bit by performing a bitwise
    // and (&) between the data byte and a flag:
    for(int i = 0; i < 8; i++) {
        if((flag & data) != 0) {
            retArray[i] = 1;
        } else {
```

```
      retArray[i] = 0;
    }
    // move the flag down one bit so you can
    // check the next bit of data on the next pass
    // through the loop:
    flag = flag >> 1;
  }
  return(retArray);
}



//-----------------------------------------------------------
//  standard integer interpretation

/**
 * Uses an input stream to convert an array of bytes to an int.
 */
public static int parseInt(byte[] data) throws IOException {
  DataInputStream stream
    = new DataInputStream(new ByteArrayInputStream(data));
  int retVal = stream.readInt();
  stream.close();
  return(retVal);
}

/**
 * Uses an output stream to convert an int to four bytes.
 */
public static byte[] intToFourBytes(int i) throws IOException {
  ByteArrayOutputStream baos = new ByteArrayOutputStream(4);
  DataOutputStream dos = new DataOutputStream(baos);
  dos.writeInt(i);
  baos.close();
  dos.close();
  byte[] retArray = baos.toByteArray();
  return(retArray);
}

//-----------------------------------------------------------
//  integer interpretation illustrated

/**
 * Java appears to treat a byte as being signed when
 * returning it as an int--this function converts from
 * the signed value to the corresponding unsigned value.
```

```
 * This method is used by nostreamParseInt.
 */
public static int unsign(int signed) {
  int retVal = signed;
  if(retVal < 0) {
    retVal += 256;
  }
  return(retVal);
}

/**
 * Takes an array of bytes and returns an int.
 * This version will return the same value as the
 * method parseInt previously.  This version is included
 * in order to illustrate how Java encodes int values
 * in terms of bytes.
 * @param data an array of 1, 2, or 4 bytes.
 */
public static int nostreamParseInt(byte[] data) {
  // byte 0 is the high byte, which is assumed
  // to be signed.  As you add the lower bytes
  // one by one, you unsign them because because
  // a single byte alone is interpreted as signed,
  // but in an int only the top byte should be signed.
  // (note that the high byte is the first one in the array)
  int retVal = data[0];
  for(int i = 1; i < data.length; i++) {
    retVal = retVal << 8;
    retVal += unsign(data[i]);
  }
  return(retVal);
}

/**
 * Takes an arbitrary int and returns
 * an array of 4 bytes.
 * This version will return the same byte array
 * as the method intToFourBytes previous. This version
 * is included in order to illustrate how Java encodes
 * int values in terms of bytes.
 */
public static byte[] nostreamIntToFourBytes(int i) {
  byte[] fourBytes = new byte[4];
  // when you take the byte value of an int, it
  // only gives you the lowest byte. So you
```

```
      // get all 4 bytes by taking the lowest
      // byte four times and moving the whole int
      // down by one byte between each one.
      // (note that the high byte is the first one in the array)
      fourBytes[3] = (new Integer(i)).byteValue();
      i = i >> 8;
      fourBytes[2] = (new Integer(i)).byteValue();
      i = i >> 8;
      fourBytes[1] = (new Integer(i)).byteValue();
      i = i >> 8;
      fourBytes[0] = (new Integer(i)).byteValue();
      return(fourBytes);
    }


    /**
     * Takes an int between -32768 and 32767 and returns
     * an array of 2 bytes. This does not verify that
     * the argument is of the right size. If the absolute
     * value of i is too high, it will not be encoded
     * correctly.
     */
    public static byte[] nostreamIntToTwoBytes(int i) {
      byte[] twoBytes = new byte[2];
      // when you take the byte value of an int, it
      // only gives you the lowest byte. So you
      // get the lower two bytes by taking the lowest
      // byte twice and moving the whole int
      // down by one byte between each one.
      twoBytes[1] = (new Integer(i)).byteValue();
      i = i >> 8;
      twoBytes[0] = (new Integer(i)).byteValue();
      return(twoBytes);
    }

}
```

## Applying Data Storage to a Game

In this section, you'll see how the example game works. As I mentioned previously, the game involves a character (in fact, a princess) exploring a dungeon that's made up of a 16×16 grid (see Figure 5-1). To make it more interesting, the maze is a vertical cross-section of the dungeon, so the princess gets around by jumping up and falling down in addition to running around. Also, to add to the challenge, four keys on each board open eight locked doors. Each key is a different color and opens doors of the corresponding color. Each board has two doors of each color. The player can hold only one key at a time. The goal is to find a crown that's locked away somewhere in the maze.

*Figure 5-1. The game in action*

In this version, data storage comes into play because the user can save a game that's currently in progress and start again later from that point. All the saved game information is serialized and deserialized by the GameInfo class (see Listing 5-4). As you'll see in the code, the GameInfo class stores the number of the board that the player is currently on, the current location of the player, the current locations of the keys, the key (if any) that's currently in the player's hand, the doors that are already open, and the time on the clock. All the locations are in terms of their coordinates on a 16×16 grid, so they're integers from 0 to 15 (inclusive). Therefore, to save memory, I've stocked the coordinates two to a byte using the DataConverter class in Listing 5-3. The time on the clock, however, may be a very large number, so I use all 4 bytes to store it. Listing 5-4 shows the code for GameInfo.java.

*Listing 5-4.* GameInfo.java

```
package net.frog_parrot.dungeon;

import javax.microedition.lcdui.*;
import javax.microedition.lcdui.game.*;
import javax.microedition.rms.*;
```

```
import net.frog_parrot.util.DataConverter;

/**
 * This class contains the data for a game currently in progress.
 * used to store a game and to resume a stored game.
 *
 * @author Carol Hamer
 */
public class GameInfo {

  //---------------------------------------------------------
  //  fields

  /**
   * The name of the datastore.
   */
  public static final String STORE = "GameInfo";

  /**
   * This is set to true if an attempt is made to
   * read a game when no game has been saved.
   */
  private boolean myNoDataSaved;

  /**
   * The number that indicates which board the player
   * is currently on.
   */
  private int myBoardNum;

  /**
   * The amount of time that has passed.
   */
  private int myTime;

  /**
   * The coordinates of where the player is on the board.
   * coordinate values must be between 0 and 15.
   */
  private int[] myPlayerSquare;

  /**
   * The coordinates of where the keys are currently found.
   * MUST BE four sets of two integer coordinates.
```

```
 * coordinate values must be between 0 and 15.
 */
private int[][] myKeyCoords;

/**
 * The list of which doors are currently open.
 * 0 = open
 * 1 = closed
 * WARNING: this array MUST have length 8.
 */
private int[] myDoorsOpen;

/**
 * The number of the key that is currently being held
 * by the player.  if no key is held, then the value is -1.
 */
private int myHeldKey;

//----------------------------------------------------------
//   data gets/sets

/**
 * @return true if no saved game records were found.
 */
boolean getIsEmpty() {
  return(myNoDataSaved);
}

/**
 * @return The number that indicates which board the player
 * is currently on.
 */
int getBoardNum() {
  return(myBoardNum);
}

/**
 * @return The number of the key that is currently being held
 * by the player.  if no key is held, then the value is -1.
 */
int getHeldKey() {
  return(myHeldKey);
}
```

```java
/**
 * @return The amount of time that has passed.
 */
int getTime() {
  return(myTime);
}


/**
 * @return The coordinates of where the player is on the board.
 * coordinate values must be between 0 and 15.
 */
int[] getPlayerSquare() {
  return(myPlayerSquare);
}


/**
 * @return The coordinates of where the keys are currently found.
 * MUST BE four sets of two integer coordinates.
 * coordinate values must be between 0 and 15.
 */
int[][] getKeyCoords() {
  return(myKeyCoords);
}


/**
 * @return The list of which doors are currently open.
 * 0 = open
 * 1 = closed
 * WARNING: this array MUST have length 8.
 */
int[] getDoorsOpen() {
  return(myDoorsOpen);
}


//----------------------------------------------------------
// constructors

/**
 * This constructor records the game info of a game currently
 * in progress.
 */
GameInfo(int boardNum, int time, int[] playerSquare, int[][] keyCoords,
         int[] doorsOpen, int heldKey) throws Exception {
  myBoardNum = boardNum;
```

```
    myTime = time;
    myPlayerSquare = playerSquare;
    myKeyCoords = keyCoords;
    myDoorsOpen = doorsOpen;
    myHeldKey = heldKey;
    encodeInfo();
}


/**
 * This constructor reads the game configuration from memory.
 * This is used to reconstruct a saved game.
 */
GameInfo() {
  RecordStore store = null;
  try {
    // if the record store does not yet exist, don't
    // create it
    store = RecordStore.openRecordStore(STORE, false);
    if((store != null) && (store.getNumRecords() > 0)) {
      // the first record has id number 1
      // it should also be the only record since this
      // particular game stores only one game.
      byte[] data = store.getRecord(1);
      myBoardNum = data[0];
      myPlayerSquare = DataConverter.decodeCoords(data[1]);
      myKeyCoords = new int[4][];
      myKeyCoords[0] = DataConverter.decodeCoords(data[2]);
      myKeyCoords[1] = DataConverter.decodeCoords(data[3]);
      myKeyCoords[2] = DataConverter.decodeCoords(data[4]);
      myKeyCoords[3] = DataConverter.decodeCoords(data[5]);
      myDoorsOpen = DataConverter.decode8(data[6]);
      myHeldKey = data[7];
      byte[] fourBytes = new byte[4];
      System.arraycopy(data, 8, fourBytes, 0, 4);
      myTime = DataConverter.parseInt(fourBytes);
    } else {
      myNoDataSaved = true;
    }
  } catch(Exception e) {
    // this throws when the record store doesn't exist.
    // for that or any error, you assume no data is saved:
    myNoDataSaved = true;
  } finally {
    try {
```

```
        if(store != null) {
          store.closeRecordStore();
        }
      } catch(Exception e) {
        // if the record store is open this shouldn't throw.
      }
    }
  }
}


//----------------------------------------------------------
//  encoding method

/**
 * Turn the data into a byte array and save it.
 */
private void encodeInfo() throws Exception {
  RecordStore store = null;
  try {
    byte[] data = new byte[12];
    data[0] = (new Integer(myBoardNum)).byteValue();
    data[1] = DataConverter.encodeCoords(myPlayerSquare);
    data[2] = DataConverter.encodeCoords(myKeyCoords[0]);
    data[3] = DataConverter.encodeCoords(myKeyCoords[1]);
    data[4] = DataConverter.encodeCoords(myKeyCoords[2]);
    data[5] = DataConverter.encodeCoords(myKeyCoords[3]);
    data[6] = DataConverter.encode8(myDoorsOpen, 0);
    data[7] = (new Integer(myHeldKey)).byteValue();
    byte[] timeBytes = DataConverter.intToFourBytes(myTime);
    System.arraycopy(timeBytes, 0, data, 8, 4);
    // if the record store does not yet exist, the second
    // arg "true" tells it to create.
    store = RecordStore.openRecordStore(STORE, true);
    int numRecords = store.getNumRecords();
    if(numRecords > 0) {
      store.setRecord(1, data, 0, data.length);
    } else {
      store.addRecord(data, 0, data.length);
    }
  } catch(Exception e) {
    throw(e);
  } finally {
    try {
      if(store != null) {
        store.closeRecordStore();
```

```
        }
      } catch(Exception e) {
        // if the record store is open this shouldn't throw.
      }
    }
  }


}
```

In this version of the game, I'm not storing the floor plan of each board in memory records on the device. That's because the dungeons themselves aren't created by the user's interaction with the game; they're created in advance. In the next chapter, you'll use the same basic game, but you'll store the various boards in memory as the user downloads them from a game site. In this version, I've compacted all the information for the boards into bytes in anticipation of the next version in which the boards themselves will be downloaded and stored locally. Listing 5-5 shows the class that converts an array of bytes to a dungeon (BoardDecoder.java).

*Listing 5-5.* BoardDecoder.java

```java
package net.frog_parrot.dungeon;

import javax.microedition.lcdui.*;
import javax.microedition.lcdui.game.*;

import net.frog_parrot.util.DataConverter;

/**
 * This class contains the data for the map of the dungeon.
 *
 * @author Carol Hamer
 */
public class BoardDecoder {

  //----------------------------------------------------------
  //  fields

  /**
   * The coordinates of where the player starts on the map
   * in terms of the array indices.
   */
  private int[] myPlayerSquare;
```

```java
/**
 * The coordinates of the goal (crown).
 */
private int[] myGoalSquare;

/**
 * The coordinates of the doors.
 * the there should be two in a row of each color,
 * following the same sequence as the keys.
 */
private int[][] myDoors;

/**
 * The coordinates of the Keys.
 * they should be of each color,
 * following the same sequence as the doors.
 */
private int[][] myKeys;

/**
 * The coordinates of the stone walls of the maze,
 * encoded bit by bit.
 */
private TiledLayer myLayer;

/**
 * The data in bytes that gives the various boards.
 * This was created using EncodingUtils...
 * This is a two-dimensional array: Each of the four
 * main sections corresponds to one of the four
 * possible boards.
 */
private static byte[][] myData = {
    { 0, 0, -108, -100, -24, 65, 21, 58, 53, -54, -116, -58, -56,
      -84, 115, -118,
      -1, -1, -128, 1, -103, -15, -128, 25, -97, -127, -128, 79, -14,
      1, -126, 121, -122, 1, -113, -49, -116, 1, -100, -3, -124, 5,
      -25, -27, -128, 1, -1, -1 },
    { 0, 1, 122, 90, -62, 34, -43, 72, -59, -29, 56, -55, 98, 126,
      -79, 61,
      -1, -1, -125, 1, -128, 17, -26, 29, -31, 57, -72, 1, -128, -51,
      -100, 65, -124, 57, -2, 1, -126, 13, -113, 1, -97, 25, -127,
      -99, -8, 1, -1, -1 },
```

```
        { 0, 2, 108, -24, 18, -26, 102, 30, -58, 46, -28, -88, 34,
          -98, 97, -41,
          -1, -1, -96, 1, -126, 57, -9, 97, -127, 69, -119, 73, -127,
          1, -109, 59, -126, 1, -26, 103, -127, 65, -103, 115, -127,
          65, -25, 73, -128, 1, -1, -1 },
        { 0, 3, -114, 18, -34, 27, -39, -60, -76, -50, 118, 90, 82,
          -88, 34, -74,
          -1, -1, -66, 1, -128, 121, -26, 125, -128, -123, -103, 29,
          -112, 1, -109, 49, -112, 1, -116, -31, -128, 5, -122, 5,
          -32, 13, -127, -51, -125, 1, -1, -1 },
    };


    //----------------------------------------------------------
    //  initialization

    /**
     * Constructor fills data fields by interpreting
     * the data bytes.
     */
    public BoardDecoder(int boardNum) throws Exception {
      // you start by selecting the two dimensional
      // array corresponding to the desired board:
      byte[] data = myData[boardNum];
      // The first two bytes give the version number and
      // the board number, but you ignore them because
      // they are assumed to be correct.
      // The third byte of the first array is the first one
      // you read: it gives the player's starting coordinates:
      myPlayerSquare = DataConverter.decodeCoords(data[2]);
      // the next byte gives the coordinates of the crown:
      myGoalSquare = DataConverter.decodeCoords(data[3]);
      // the next 4 bytes give the coordinates of the keys:
      myKeys = new int[4][];
      for(int i = 0; i < myKeys.length; i++) {
        myKeys[i] = DataConverter.decodeCoords(data[i + 4]);
      }
      // the next 8 bytes give the coordinates of the doors:
      myDoors = new int[8][];
      for(int i = 0; i < myDoors.length; i++) {
        myDoors[i] = DataConverter.decodeCoords(data[i + 8]);
      }
      // now you create the TiledLayer object that is the
      // background dungeon map:
```

```
    myLayer = new TiledLayer(16, 16,
        Image.createImage("/images/stone.png"),
        DungeonManager.SQUARE_WIDTH, DungeonManager.SQUARE_WIDTH);
    // now you call an internal utility that reads the array
    // of data that gives the positions of the blocks in the
    // walls of this dungeon:
    decodeDungeon(data, myLayer, 16);
}


//----------------------------------------------------------
//  get/set data

/**
 * @return the number of boards currently stored in
 * this class.
 */
public static int getNumBoards() {
  return(myData.length);
}


/**
 * get the coordinates of where the player starts on the map
 * in terms of the array indices.
 */
public int[] getPlayerSquare() {
  return(myPlayerSquare);
}


/**
 * get the coordinates of the goal crown
 * in terms of the array indices.
 */
public int[] getGoalSquare() {
  return(myGoalSquare);
}


/**
 * get the tiled layer that gives the map of the dungeon.
 */
public TiledLayer getLayer() {
  return(myLayer);
}
```

```
/**
 * Creates the array of door sprites. (call this only once to avoid
 * creating redundant sprites).
 */
DoorKey[] createDoors() {
  DoorKey[] retArray = new DoorKey[8];
  for(int i = 0; i < 4; i++) {
    retArray[2*i] = new DoorKey(i, false, myDoors[2*i]);
    retArray[2*i + 1] = new DoorKey(i, false, myDoors[2*i + 1]);
  }
  return(retArray);
}


/**
 * Creates the array of key sprites. (call this only once to avoid
 * creating redundant sprites.)
 */
DoorKey[] createKeys() {
  DoorKey[] retArray = new DoorKey[4];
  for(int i = 0; i < 4; i++) {
    retArray[i] = new DoorKey(i, true, myKeys[i]);
  }
  return(retArray);
}


//------------------------------------------------------------
//   decoding utilities

/**
 * Takes a dungeon given as a byte array and uses it
 * to set the tiles of a tiled layer.
 *
 * The TiledLayer in this case is a 16x16 grid
 * in which each square can be either blank
 * (value of 0) or can be filled with a stone block
 * (value of 1). Therefore each square requires only
 * one bit of information.  Each byte of data in
 * the array called "data" records the frame indices
 * of eight squares in the grid.
 */
private static void decodeDungeon(byte[] data, TiledLayer dungeon,
      int offset) throws Exception {
  if(data.length + offset < 32) {
    throw(new Exception(
              "BoardDecoder.decodeDungeon-->not enough data!!!"));
```

```
    }
    // a frame index of zero indicates a blank square
    // (this is always true in a TiledLayer).
    // This TiledLayer has only one possible (nonblank)
    // frame, so a frame index of 1 indicates a stone block
    int frame = 0;
    // Each of the 32 bytes in the data array records
    // the frame indices of eight block in the 16x16
    // grid. Two bytes give one row of the dungeon,
    // so you have the array index go from zero to 16
    // to set the frame indices for each of the 16 rows.
    for(int i = 0; i < 16; i++) {
      // The flag allows you to look at each bit individually
      // to determine if it is one or zero. The number 128
      // corresponds to the highest bit of a byte, so you
      // start with that one.
      int flag = 128;
      // Here you check two bytes at the same time
      // (the two bytes together correspond to one row
      // of the dungeon). You use a loop that checks
      // the bytes bit by bit by performing a bitwise
      // and (&) between the data byte and a flag:
      for(int j = 0; j < 8; j++) {
        if((data[offset + 2*i] & flag) != 0) {
          frame = 1;
        } else {
          frame = 0;
        }
        dungeon.setCell(j, i, frame);
        if((data[offset + 2*i + 1] & flag) != 0) {
          frame = 1;
        } else {
          frame = 0;
        }
        dungeon.setCell(j + 8, i, frame);
        // move the flag down one bit so you can
        // check the next bit of data on the next pass
        // through the loop:
        flag = flag >> 1;
      }
    }
  }

}
```

In case you're wondering where the byte arrays in the previous class came from, Listing 5-6 shows the utility class I used to encode them. Keep in mind that this class is merely a tool I used to create the data for the game. Once the data has been created, this class is no longer used. It would certainly not be distributed to users with the game. Listing 5-6 shows EncodingUtils.java.

*Listing 5-6.* EncodingUtils.java

```
package net.frog_parrot.dungeon;

import   net.frog_parrot.util.DataConverter;

/**
 * This class contains the data for the map of the dungeon.
 * This is a utility class that allows a developer to write
 * the data for a board in a simple format, then this class
 * encodes the data in a format that the game can use.
 *
 * note that the data that this class encodes is hard-coded.
 * that is because this class is intended to be used only a
 * few times to encode the data. Once the board data has been
 * encoded, it never needs to be encoded again. The encoding
 * methods used in this class could be generalized to be used
 * to create a board editor that would allow a user to easily
 * create new boards, but that is an exercise for another day...
 *
 * @author Carol Hamer
 */
public class EncodingUtils {

  //-----------------------------------------------------------
  //   fields

  /**
   * data for which squares are filled and which are blank.
   * 0 = empty
   * 1 = filled
   */
  private int[][] mySquares = {
    { 1, 1, 1, 1, 1, 1, 1, 1, 1, 1, 1, 1, 1, 1, 1, 1 },
    { 1, 0, 0, 0, 0, 0, 1, 1, 0, 0, 0, 0, 0, 0, 0, 1 },
    { 1, 0, 0, 0, 0, 0, 0, 0, 0, 0, 0, 1, 0, 0, 0, 1 },
    { 1, 1, 1, 0, 0, 1, 1, 0, 0, 0, 0, 1, 1, 1, 0, 1 },
    { 1, 1, 1, 0, 0, 0, 0, 1, 0, 0, 1, 1, 1, 0, 0, 1 },
```

```
      { 1, 0, 1, 1, 1, 0, 0, 0, 0, 0, 0, 0, 0, 0, 0, 1 },
      { 1, 0, 0, 0, 0, 0, 0, 0, 1, 1, 0, 0, 1, 1, 0, 1 },
      { 1, 0, 0, 1, 1, 1, 0, 0, 0, 1, 0, 0, 0, 0, 0, 1 },
      { 1, 0, 0, 0, 0, 1, 0, 0, 0, 0, 1, 1, 1, 0, 0, 1 },
      { 1, 1, 1, 1, 1, 1, 1, 0, 0, 0, 0, 0, 0, 0, 0, 1 },
      { 1, 0, 0, 0, 0, 0, 1, 0, 0, 0, 0, 0, 1, 1, 0, 1 },
      { 1, 0, 0, 0, 1, 1, 1, 1, 0, 0, 0, 0, 0, 0, 0, 1 },
      { 1, 0, 0, 1, 1, 1, 1, 1, 0, 0, 0, 1, 1, 0, 0, 1 },
      { 1, 0, 0, 0, 0, 0, 0, 1, 1, 0, 0, 1, 1, 1, 0, 1 },
      { 1, 1, 1, 1, 1, 0, 0, 0, 0, 0, 0, 0, 0, 0, 0, 1 },
      { 1, 1, 1, 1, 1, 1, 1, 1, 1, 1, 1, 1, 1, 1, 1, 1 },
    };

    /**
     * The coordinates of where the player starts on the map
     * in terms of the array indices.
     */
    private int[] myPlayerSquare = { 7, 10 };

    /**
     * The coordinates of the goal (crown).
     */
    private int[] myGoalSquare = { 5, 10 };

    //-----------------------------------------------------------
    //   get/set data

    /**
     * Creates the array of door sprites. (call this only once to avoid
     * creating redundant sprites).
     */
    int[][] getDoorCoords() {
      int[][] retArray = new int[8][];
      for(int i = 0; i < retArray.length; i++) {
        retArray[i] = new int[2];
      }
      // red
      retArray[0][0] = 12;
      retArray[0][1] = 5;
      retArray[1][0] = 14;
      retArray[1][1] = 3;
      // green
      retArray[2][0] = 3;
      retArray[2][1] = 8;
```

```
    retArray[3][0] = 12;
    retArray[3][1] = 9;
    // blue
    retArray[4][0] = 6;
    retArray[4][1] = 2;
    retArray[5][0] = 7;
    retArray[5][1] = 14;
    // yellow
    retArray[6][0] = 11;
    retArray[6][1] = 1;
    retArray[7][0] = 3;
    retArray[7][1] = 13;
    return(retArray);
}


/**
 * Creates the array of key sprites. (call this only once to avoid
 * creating redundant sprites.)
 */
int[][] getKeyCoords() {
  int[][] retArray = new int[4][];
  for(int i = 0; i < retArray.length; i++) {
    retArray[i] = new int[2];
  }
  // red
  retArray[0][0] = 12;
  retArray[0][1] = 2;
  // green
  retArray[1][0] = 2;
  retArray[1][1] = 2;
  // blue
  retArray[2][0] = 13;
  retArray[2][1] = 5;
  // yellow
  retArray[3][0] = 4;
  retArray[3][1] = 8;
  return(retArray);
}


//-----------------------------------------------------------
//  encoding / decoding utilities
```

```java
/**
 * Encodes the entire dungeon.
 */
byte[][] encodeDungeon() {
  byte[][] retArray = new byte[2][];
  retArray[0] = new byte[16];
  // the first byte is the version number:
  retArray[0][0] = 0;
  // the second byte is the board number:
  retArray[0][1] = 0;
  // the player's start square:
  retArray[0][2] = DataConverter.encodeCoords(myPlayerSquare);
  // the goal (crown) square:
  retArray[0][3] = DataConverter.encodeCoords(myGoalSquare);
  //encode the keys:
  int[][] keyCoords = getKeyCoords();
  for(int i = 0; i < keyCoords.length; i++) {
    retArray[0][i + 4] = DataConverter.encodeCoords(keyCoords[i]);
  }
  //encode the doors:
  int[][] doorCoords = getDoorCoords();
  for(int i = 0; i < doorCoords.length; i++) {
    retArray[0][i + 8] = DataConverter.encodeCoords(doorCoords[i]);
  }
  //encode the maze:
  try {
    retArray[1] = encodeDungeon(mySquares);
  } catch(Exception e) {
    e.printStackTrace();
  }
  return(retArray);
}


/**
 * Takes a dungeon given in terms of an array of ones and zeros
 * and turns it into an array of bytes.
 * WARNING: the array MUST BE 16x16.
 */
static byte[] encodeDungeon(int[][] dungeonMap) throws Exception {
  if((dungeonMap.length != 16) || (dungeonMap[0].length != 16)) {
    throw(new Exception("EncodingUtils.encodeDungeon-->must be 16x16!!!"));
  }
  byte[] retArray = new byte[32];
  for(int i = 0; i < 16; i++) {
```

```
        retArray[2*i] = DataConverter.encode8(dungeonMap[i], 0);
        retArray[2*i + 1] = DataConverter.encode8(dungeonMap[i], 8);
    }
    return(retArray);
}


//----------------------------------------------------------
// main prints the bytes to standard out.
// (note that this class is not intended to be run as a MIDlet)

/**
 * Prints the byte version of the board to standard out.
 */
public static void main(String[] args) {
    try {
        EncodingUtils map = new EncodingUtils();
        byte[][] data = map.encodeDungeon();
        System.out.println("EncodingUtils.main-->dungeon encoded");
        System.out.print("{\n    " + data[0][0]);
        for(int i = 1; i < data[0].length; i++) {
            System.out.print(", " + data[0][i]);
        }
        for(int i = 1; i < data[1].length; i++) {
            System.out.print(", " + data[1][i]);
        }
        System.out.println("\n};");
    } catch(Exception e) {
        e.printStackTrace();
    }
}

}
```

## Creating the Complete Example Game

All the classes you've seen to encode and store data aren't much use without
a game to go with them. This section shows you the code for the fun part of the
game. I've discussed all the programming ideas used in this game in previous
chapters, so I'm leaving the explanation for the comments.

Listing 5-7 shows the code for the MIDlet subclass Dungeon.java.

*Listing 5-7.* Dungeon.java

```
package net.frog_parrot.dungeon;

import javax.microedition.midlet.*;
import javax.microedition.lcdui.*;

/**
 * This is the main class of the dungeon game.
 *
 * @author Carol Hamer
 */
public class Dungeon extends MIDlet implements CommandListener {

  //-------------------------------------------------------
  //     game object fields

  /**
   * The canvas that the dungeon is drawn on.
   */
  private DungeonCanvas myCanvas;

  /**
   * the thread that advances the game clock.
   */
  private GameThread myGameThread;

  //-------------------------------------------------------
  //     command fields

  /**
   * The button to exit the game.
   */
  private Command myExitCommand = new Command("Exit", Command.EXIT, 99);

  /**
   * The command to save the game in progress.
   */
  private Command mySaveCommand = new Command("Save Game", Command.SCREEN, 2);
```

```
/**
 * The command to restore a previously saved game.
 */
private Command myRestoreCommand
  = new Command("Restore Game", Command.SCREEN, 2);


/**
 * the command to start moving when the game is paused.
 */
private Command myGoCommand = new Command("Go", Command.SCREEN, 1);


/**
 * the command to pause the game.
 */
private Command myPauseCommand = new Command("Pause", Command.SCREEN, 1);


/**
 * the command to start a new game.
 */
private Command myNewCommand = new Command("Next Board", Command.SCREEN, 1);


//-------------------------------------------------------
//    initialization and game state changes

/**
 * Initialize the canvas and the commands.
 */
public Dungeon() {
  try {
    // create the canvas and set up the commands:
    myCanvas = new DungeonCanvas(this);
    myCanvas.addCommand(myExitCommand);
    myCanvas.addCommand(mySaveCommand);
    myCanvas.addCommand(myRestoreCommand);
    myCanvas.addCommand(myPauseCommand);
    myCanvas.setCommandListener(this);
  } catch(Exception e) {
    // if there's an error during creation, display it as an alert.
    errorMsg(e);
  }
}
```

```
/**
 * Switch the command to the play again command.
 * (removing other commands that are no longer relevant)
 */
void setNewCommand() {
  myCanvas.removeCommand(myPauseCommand);
  myCanvas.removeCommand(myGoCommand);
  myCanvas.addCommand(myNewCommand);
}

/**
 * Switch the command to the go command.
 * (removing other commands that are no longer relevant)
 */
void setGoCommand() {
  myCanvas.removeCommand(myPauseCommand);
  myCanvas.removeCommand(myNewCommand);
  myCanvas.addCommand(myGoCommand);
}

/**
 * Switch the command to the pause command.
 * (removing other commands that are no longer relevant)
 */
void setPauseCommand() {
  myCanvas.removeCommand(myNewCommand);
  myCanvas.removeCommand(myGoCommand);
  myCanvas.addCommand(myPauseCommand);
}

//-----------------------------------------------------------------
//  implementation of MIDlet
// these methods may be called by the application management
// software at any time, so you always check fields for null
// before calling methods on them.

/**
 * Start the application.
 */
public void startApp() throws MIDletStateChangeException {
  if(myCanvas != null) {
    if(myGameThread == null) {
      // create the thread and start the game:
      myGameThread = new GameThread(myCanvas);
```

```
        myCanvas.start();
        myGameThread.start();
      } else {
        // in case this gets called again after
        // the application has been started once:
        myCanvas.removeCommand(myGoCommand);
        myCanvas.addCommand(myPauseCommand);
        myCanvas.flushKeys();
        myGameThread.resumeGame();
      }
    }
  }


  /**
   * Stop the threads and throw out the garbage.
   */
  public void destroyApp(boolean unconditional)
      throws MIDletStateChangeException {
    myCanvas = null;
    if(myGameThread != null) {
      myGameThread.requestStop();
    }
    myGameThread = null;
    System.gc();
  }  .


  /**
   * Pause the game.
   */
  public void pauseApp() {
    if(myCanvas != null) {
      setGoCommand();
    }
    if(myGameThread != null) {
      myGameThread.pause();
    }
  }


  //------------------------------------------------------------------
  //  implementation of CommandListener

  /*
   * Respond to a command issued on the Canvas.
   * (reset, exit, or change size prefs).
   */
```

```
public void commandAction(Command c, Displayable s) {
  try {
    //myCanvas.setNeedsRepaint();
    if(c == myGoCommand) {
      myCanvas.setNeedsRepaint();
      myCanvas.removeCommand(myGoCommand);
      myCanvas.addCommand(myPauseCommand);
      myCanvas.flushKeys();
      myGameThread.resumeGame();
    } else if(c == myPauseCommand) {
      myCanvas.setNeedsRepaint();
      myCanvas.removeCommand(myPauseCommand);
      myCanvas.addCommand(myGoCommand);
      myGameThread.pause();
    } else if(c == myNewCommand) {
      myCanvas.setNeedsRepaint();
      // go to the next board and restart the game
      myCanvas.removeCommand(myNewCommand);
      myCanvas.addCommand(myPauseCommand);
      myCanvas.reset();
      myGameThread.resumeGame();
    } else if(c == Alert.DISMISS_COMMAND) {
      // if there was a serious enough error to
      // cause an alert, then we end the game
      // when the user is done reading the alert:
      // (Alert.DISMISS_COMMAND is the default
      // command that is placed on an Alert
      // whose timeout is FOREVER)
      destroyApp(false);
      notifyDestroyed();
    } else if(c == mySaveCommand) {
      myCanvas.setNeedsRepaint();
      myCanvas.saveGame();
    } else if(c == myRestoreCommand) {
      myCanvas.setNeedsRepaint();
      myCanvas.removeCommand(myNewCommand);
      myCanvas.removeCommand(myGoCommand);
      myCanvas.addCommand(myPauseCommand);
      myCanvas.revertToSaved();
    } else if(c == myExitCommand) {
      destroyApp(false);
      notifyDestroyed();
    }
```

```
    } catch(Exception e) {
      errorMsg(e);
    }
  }


  //--------------------------------------------------------
  //  error methods

  /**
   * Converts an exception to a message and displays
   * the message.
   */
  void errorMsg(Exception e) {
    if(e.getMessage() == null) {
      errorMsg(e.getClass().getName());
    } else {
      errorMsg(e.getClass().getName() + ":" + e.getMessage());
    }
  }


  /**
   * Displays an error message alert if something goes wrong.
   */
  void errorMsg(String msg) {
    Alert errorAlert = new Alert("error",
                                      msg, null, AlertType.ERROR);
    errorAlert.setCommandListener(this);
    errorAlert.setTimeout(Alert.FOREVER);
    Display.getDisplay(this).setCurrent(errorAlert);
  }

}
```

Listing 5-8 shows the code for the GameCanvas subclass DungeonCanvas.java.

*Listing 5-8.* DungeonCanvas.java

```
package net.frog_parrot.dungeon;

import javax.microedition.lcdui.*;
import javax.microedition.lcdui.game.*;

/**
 * This class is the display of the game.
 *
```

```
 * @author Carol Hamer
 */
public class DungeonCanvas extends GameCanvas {

  //----------------------------------------------------------
  //    dimension fields
  //    (constant after initialization)

  /**
   * the height of the black region below the play area.
   */
  static int TIMER_HEIGHT = 32;

  /**
   * the top-corner X coordinate according to this
   * object's coordinate system:
   */
  static final int CORNER_X = 0;

  /**
   * the top-corner Y coordinate according to this
   * object's coordinate system:
   */
  static final int CORNER_Y = 0;

  /**
   * the width of the portion of the screen that this
   * canvas can use.
   */
  static int DISP_WIDTH;

  /**
   * the height of the portion of the screen that this
   * canvas can use.
   */
  static int DISP_HEIGHT;

  /**
   * the height of the font used for this game.
   */
  static int FONT_HEIGHT;
```

```
/**
 * the font used for this game.
 */
static Font FONT;

/**
 * color constant
 */
public static final int BLACK = 0;

/**
 * color constant
 */
public static final int WHITE = 0xffffff;

//------------------------------------------------------------
//   game object fields

/**
 * a handle to the display.
 */
private Display myDisplay;

/**
 * a handle to the MIDlet object (to keep track of buttons).
 */
private Dungeon myDungeon;

/**
 * the LayerManager that handles the game graphics.
 */
private DungeonManager myManager;

/**
 * whether the game has ended.
 */
private static boolean myGameOver;

/**
 * The number of ticks on the clock the last time the
 * time display was updated.
 * This is saved to determine if the time string needs
 * to be recomputed.
 */
private int myOldGameTicks = 0;
```

```
/**
 * the number of game ticks that have passed since the
 * beginning of the game.
 */
private int myGameTicks = myOldGameTicks;

/**
 * you save the time string to avoid re-creating it
 * unnecessarily.
 */
private static String myInitialString = "0:00";

/**
 * you save the time string to avoid re-creating it
 * unnecessarily.
 */
private String myTimeString = myInitialString;

//-------------------------------------------------------
//    gets/sets

/**
 * This is called when the game ends.
 */
void setGameOver() {
  myGameOver = true;
  myDungeon.pauseApp();
}

/**
 * Find out if the game has ended.
 */
static boolean getGameOver() {
  return(myGameOver);
}

/**
 * Tell the layer manager that it needs to repaint.
 */
public void setNeedsRepaint() {
  myManager.setNeedsRepaint();
}
```

```
//--------------------------------------------------------
//     initialization and game state changes

/**
 * Constructor sets the data, performs dimension calculations,
 * and creates the graphical objects.
 */
public DungeonCanvas(Dungeon midlet) throws Exception {
  super(false);
  myDisplay = Display.getDisplay(midlet);
  myDungeon = midlet;
  // calculate the dimensions
  DISP_WIDTH = getWidth();
  DISP_HEIGHT = getHeight();
  if((!myDisplay.isColor()) || (myDisplay.numColors() < 256)) {
    throw(new Exception("game requires full-color screen"));
  }
  if((DISP_WIDTH < 150) || (DISP_HEIGHT < 170)) {
    throw(new Exception("Screen too small"));
  }
  if((DISP_WIDTH > 250) || (DISP_HEIGHT > 250)) {
    throw(new Exception("Screen too large"));
  }
  // since the time is painted in white on black,
  // it shows up better if the font is bold:
  FONT = Font.getFont(Font.FACE_SYSTEM,
                          Font.STYLE_BOLD, Font.SIZE_MEDIUM);
  // calculate the height of the black region that the
  // timer is painted on:
  FONT_HEIGHT = FONT.getHeight();
  TIMER_HEIGHT = FONT_HEIGHT + 8;
  // create the LayerManager (where all the interesting
  // graphics go!) and give it the dimensions of the
  // region it is supposed to paint:
  if(myManager == null) {
    myManager = new DungeonManager(CORNER_X, CORNER_Y,
          DISP_WIDTH, DISP_HEIGHT - TIMER_HEIGHT, this);
  }
}

/**
 * This is called as soon as the application begins.
 */
```

```
void start() {
  myGameOver = false;
  myDisplay.setCurrent(this);
  setNeedsRepaint();
}


/**
 * sets all variables back to their initial positions.
 */
void reset() throws Exception {
  // most of the variables that need to be reset
  // are held by the LayerManager:
  myManager.reset();
  myGameOver = false;
  setNeedsRepaint();
}


/**
 * sets all variables back to the positions
 * from a previously saved game.
 */
void revertToSaved() throws Exception {
  // most of the variables that need to be reset
  // are held by the LayerManager, so we
  // prompt the LayerManager to get the
  // saved data:
  myGameTicks = myManager.revertToSaved();
  myGameOver = false;
  myOldGameTicks = myGameTicks;
  myTimeString = formatTime();
  setNeedsRepaint();
}


/**
 * save the current game in progress.
 */
void saveGame() throws Exception {
  myManager.saveGame(myGameTicks);
}


/**
 * clears the key states.
 */
```

```
void flushKeys() {
  getKeyStates();
}

/**
 * If the game is hidden by another app (or a menu)
 * ignore it since not much happens in this game
 * when the user is not actively interacting with it.
 * (you could pause the timer, but it's not important
 * enough to bother with when the user is just pulling
 * up a menu for a few seconds)
 */
protected void hideNotify() {
}

/**
 * When it comes back into view, just make sure the
 * manager knows that it needs to repaint.
 */
protected void showNotify() {
  setNeedsRepaint();
}

//----------------------------------------------------------
//   graphics methods

/**
 * paint the game graphics on the screen.
 */
public void paint(Graphics g) {
  // color the bottom segment of the screen black
  g.setColor(BLACK);
  g.fillRect(CORNER_X, CORNER_Y + DISP_HEIGHT - TIMER_HEIGHT,
             DISP_WIDTH, TIMER_HEIGHT);
  // paint the LayerManager (which paints
  // all the interesting graphics):
  try {
    myManager.paint(g);
  } catch(Exception e) {
    myDungeon.errorMsg(e);
  }
  // draw the time
  g.setColor(WHITE);
  g.setFont(FONT);
```

```
    g.drawString("Time: " + formatTime(), DISP_WIDTH/2,
                  CORNER_Y + DISP_HEIGHT - 4, g.BOTTOM|g.HCENTER);
    // write "Dungeon Completed" when the user finishes a board:
    if(myGameOver) {
      myDungeon.setNewCommand();
      // clear the top region:
      g.setColor(WHITE);
      g.fillRect(CORNER_X, CORNER_Y, DISP_WIDTH, FONT_HEIGHT*2 + 1);
      int goWidth = FONT.stringWidth("Dungeon Completed");
      g.setColor(BLACK);
      g.setFont(FONT);
      g.drawString("Dungeon Completed", (DISP_WIDTH - goWidth)/2,
                    CORNER_Y + FONT_HEIGHT, g.TOP|g.LEFT);
    }
  }


  /**
   * a simple utility to make the number of ticks look like a time...
   */
  public String formatTime() {
    if((myGameTicks / 16) != myOldGameTicks) {
      myTimeString = "";
      myOldGameTicks = (myGameTicks / 16) + 1;
      int smallPart = myOldGameTicks % 60;
      int bigPart = myOldGameTicks / 60;
      myTimeString += bigPart + ":";
      if(smallPart / 10 < 1) {
        myTimeString += "0";
      }
      myTimeString += smallPart;
    }
    return(myTimeString);
  }


  //----------------------------------------------------------
  //   game movements

  /**
   * update the display.
   */
  void updateScreen() {
    myGameTicks++;
    // paint the display
```

```
      try {
        paint(getGraphics());
        flushGraphics(CORNER_X, CORNER_Y, DISP_WIDTH, DISP_HEIGHT);
      } catch(Exception e) {
        myDungeon.errorMsg(e);
      }
    }


    /**
     * Respond to keystrokes.
     */
    public void checkKeys() {
      if(! myGameOver) {
        int vertical = 0;
        int horizontal = 0;
        // determine which moves the user would like to make:
        int keyState = getKeyStates();
        if((keyState & LEFT_PRESSED) != 0) {
          horizontal = -1;
        }
        if((keyState & RIGHT_PRESSED) != 0) {
          horizontal = 1;
        }
        if((keyState & UP_PRESSED) != 0) {
          vertical = -1;
        }
        if((keyState & DOWN_PRESSED) != 0) {
          // if the user presses the down key,
          // we put down or pick up a key object
          // or pick up the crown:
          myManager.putDownPickUp();
        }
        // tell the manager to move the player
        // accordingly if possible:
        myManager.requestMove(horizontal, vertical);
      }
    }

}
```

Listing 5-9 shows the code for the LayerManager subclass DungeonManager.java.

*Listing 5-9.* `DungeonManager.java`

```java
package net.frog_parrot.dungeon;

import javax.microedition.lcdui.*;
import javax.microedition.lcdui.game.*;

/**
 * This class handles the graphics objects.
 *
 * @author Carol Hamer
 */
public class DungeonManager extends LayerManager {

  //----------------------------------------------------------
  //    dimension fields
  //    (constant after initialization)

  /**
   * The X coordinate of the place on the game canvas where
   * the LayerManager window should appear, in terms of the
   * coordinates of the game canvas.
   */
  static int CANVAS_X;

  /**
   * The Y coordinate of the place on the game canvas where
   * the LayerManager window should appear, in terms of the
   * coordinates of the game canvas.
   */
  static int CANVAS_Y;

  /**
   * The width of the display window.
   */
  static int DISP_WIDTH;

  /**
   * The height of this object's visible region.
   */
  static int DISP_HEIGHT;
```

```
/**
 * the (right or left)  distance the player
 * goes in a single keystroke.
 */
static final int MOVE_LENGTH = 8;

/**
 * The width of the square tiles that this game is divided into.
 * This is the width of the stone walls as well as the princess and
 * the ghost.
 */
static final int SQUARE_WIDTH = 24;

/**
 * The jump index that indicates that no jump is
 * currently in progress.
 */
static final int NO_JUMP = -6;

/**
 * The maximum speed for the player's fall.
 */
static final int MAX_FREE_FALL = 3;

//----------------------------------------------------------
//    game object fields

/**
 * the handle back to the canvas.
 */
private DungeonCanvas myCanvas;

/**
 * the background dungeon.
 */
private TiledLayer myBackground;

/**
 * the player.
 */
private Sprite myPrincess;
```

```
/**
 * the goal.
 */
private Sprite myCrown;

/**
 * the doors.
 */
private DoorKey[] myDoors;

/**
 * the keys.
 */
private DoorKey[] myKeys;

/**
 * the key currently held by the player.
 */
private DoorKey myHeldKey;

/**
 * The leftmost X coordinate that should be visible on the
 * screen in terms of this objects internal coordinates.
 */
private int myViewWindowX;

/**
 * The top Y coordinate that should be visible on the
 * screen in terms of this objects internal coordinates.
 */
private int myViewWindowY;

/**
 * Where the princess is in the jump sequence.
 */
private int myIsJumping = NO_JUMP;

/**
 * Whether the screen needs to be repainted.
 */
private boolean myModifiedSinceLastPaint = true;
```

```
/**
 * Which board we're playing on.
 */
private int myCurrentBoardNum = 0;


//-------------------------------------------------------
//    gets/sets

/**
 * Tell the layer manager that it needs to repaint.
 */
public void setNeedsRepaint() {
  myModifiedSinceLastPaint = true;
}


//-------------------------------------------------------
//    initialization
//    set up or save game data.

/**
 * Constructor merely sets the data.
 * @param x The X coordinate of the place on the game canvas where
 * the LayerManager window should appear, in terms of the
 * coordinates of the game canvas.
 * @param y The Y coordinate of the place on the game canvas where
 * the LayerManager window should appear, in terms of the
 * coordinates of the game canvas.
 * @param width the width of the region that is to be
 * occupied by the LayoutManager.
 * @param height the height of the region that is to be
 * occupied by the LayoutManager.
 * @param canvas the DungeonCanvas that this LayerManager
 * should appear on.
 */
public DungeonManager(int x, int y, int width, int height,
                         DungeonCanvas canvas) throws Exception {
    myCanvas = canvas;
    CANVAS_X = x;
    CANVAS_Y = y;
    DISP_WIDTH = width;
    DISP_HEIGHT = height;
    // create a decoder object that creates the dungeon and
    // its associated Sprites from data.
    BoardDecoder decoder = new BoardDecoder(myCurrentBoardNum);
```

```
// get the background TiledLayer
myBackground = decoder.getLayer();
// get the coordinates of the square that the princess
// starts on.
int[] playerCoords = decoder.getPlayerSquare();
// create the player sprite
myPrincess = new Sprite(Image.createImage("/images/princess.png"),
                        SQUARE_WIDTH, SQUARE_WIDTH);
myPrincess.setFrame(1);
// you define the reference pixel to be in the middle
// of the princess image so that when the princess turns
// from right to left (and vice versa) she does not
// appear to move to a different location.
myPrincess.defineReferencePixel(SQUARE_WIDTH/2, 0);
// the dungeon is a 16x16 grid, so the array playerCoords
// gives the player's location in terms of the grid, and
// then you multiply those coordinates by the SQUARE_WIDTH
// to get the precise pixel where the player should be
// placed (in terms of the LayerManager's coordinate system)
myPrincess.setPosition(SQUARE_WIDTH * playerCoords[0],
                        SQUARE_WIDTH * playerCoords[1]);
// you append all the Layers (TiledLayer and Sprite)
// so that this LayerManager will paint them when
// flushGraphics is called.
append(myPrincess);
// get the coordinates of the square where the crown
// should be placed.
int[] goalCoords = decoder.getGoalSquare();
myCrown = new Sprite(Image.createImage("/images/crown.png"));
myCrown.setPosition((SQUARE_WIDTH * goalCoords[0]) + (SQUARE_WIDTH/4),
                    (SQUARE_WIDTH * goalCoords[1]) + (SQUARE_WIDTH/2));
append(myCrown);
// The decoder creates the door and key sprites and places
// them in the correct locations in terms of the LayerManager's
// coordinate system.
myDoors = decoder.createDoors();
myKeys = decoder.createKeys();
for(int i = 0; i < myDoors.length; i++) {
  append(myDoors[i]);
}
for(int i = 0; i < myKeys.length; i++) {
  append(myKeys[i]);
}
// append the background last so it will be painted first.
```

```
        append(myBackground);
        // this sets the view screen so that the player is
        // in the center.
        myViewWindowX = SQUARE_WIDTH * playerCoords[0]
          - ((DISP_WIDTH - SQUARE_WIDTH)/2);
        myViewWindowY = SQUARE_WIDTH * playerCoords[1]
          - ((DISP_HEIGHT - SQUARE_WIDTH)/2);
        // a number of objects are created in order to set up the game,
        // but they should be eliminated to free up memory:
        decoder = null;
        System.gc();
    }


    /**
     * sets all variables back to their initial positions.
     */
    void reset() throws Exception {
        // first get rid of the old board:
        for(int i = 0; i < myDoors.length; i++) {
            remove(myDoors[i]);
        }
        myHeldKey = null;
        for(int i = 0; i < myKeys.length; i++) {
            remove(myKeys[i]);
        }
        remove(myBackground);
        // now create the new board:
        myCurrentBoardNum++;
        // in this version you go back to the beginning if
        // all boards have been completed.
        if(myCurrentBoardNum == BoardDecoder.getNumBoards()) {
            myCurrentBoardNum = 0;
        }
        // you create a new decoder object to read and interpret
        // all the data for the current board.
        BoardDecoder decoder = new BoardDecoder(myCurrentBoardNum);
        // get the background TiledLayer
        myBackground = decoder.getLayer();
        // get the coordinates of the square that the princess
        // starts on.
        int[] playerCoords = decoder.getPlayerSquare();
        // the dungeon is a 16x16 grid, so the array playerCoords
        // gives the player's location in terms of the grid, and
        // then you multiply those coordinates by the SQUARE_WIDTH
```

```
    // to get the precise pixel where the player should be
    // placed (in terms of the LayerManager's coordinate system)
    myPrincess.setPosition(SQUARE_WIDTH * playerCoords[0],
                           SQUARE_WIDTH * playerCoords[1]);
    myPrincess.setFrame(1);
    // get the coordinates of the square where the crown
    // should be placed.
    int[] goalCoords = decoder.getGoalSquare();
    myCrown.setPosition((SQUARE_WIDTH * goalCoords[0]) + (SQUARE_WIDTH/4),
                        (SQUARE_WIDTH * goalCoords[1]) + (SQUARE_WIDTH/2));
    // The decoder creates the door and key sprites and places
    // them in the correct locations in terms of the LayerManager's
    // coordinate system.
    myDoors = decoder.createDoors();
    myKeys = decoder.createKeys();
    for(int i = 0; i < myDoors.length; i++) {
      append(myDoors[i]);
    }
    for(int i = 0; i < myKeys.length; i++) {
      append(myKeys[i]);
    }
    // append the background last so it will be painted first.
    append(myBackground);
    // this sets the view screen so that the player is
    // in the center.
    myViewWindowX = SQUARE_WIDTH * playerCoords[0]
      - ((DISP_WIDTH - SQUARE_WIDTH)/2);
    myViewWindowY = SQUARE_WIDTH * playerCoords[1]
      - ((DISP_HEIGHT - SQUARE_WIDTH)/2);
    // a number of objects are created in order to set up the game,
    // but they should be eliminated to free up memory:
    decoder = null;
    System.gc();
  }

/**
 * sets all variables back to the position in the saved game.
 * @return the time on the clock of the saved game.
 */
int revertToSaved() throws Exception {
  int retVal = 0;
  // first get rid of the old board:
  for(int i = 0; i < myDoors.length; i++) {
    remove(myDoors[i]);
```

```
      }
      myHeldKey = null;
      for(int i = 0; i < myKeys.length; i++) {
        remove(myKeys[i]);
      }
      remove(myBackground);
      // now get the info of the saved game
      // only one game is saved at a time, and the GameInfo object
      // will read the saved game's data from memory.
      GameInfo info = new GameInfo();
      if(info.getIsEmpty()) {
        // if no game has been saved, you start from the beginning.
        myCurrentBoardNum = 0;
        reset();
      } else {
        // get the time on the clock of the saved game.
        retVal = info.getTime();
        // get the number of the board the saved game was on.
        myCurrentBoardNum = info.getBoardNum();
        // create the BoradDecoder that gives the data for the
        // desired board.
        BoardDecoder decoder = new BoardDecoder(myCurrentBoardNum);
        // get the background TiledLayer
        myBackground = decoder.getLayer();
        // get the coordinates of the square that the princess
        // was on in the saved game.
        int[] playerCoords = info.getPlayerSquare();
        myPrincess.setPosition(SQUARE_WIDTH * playerCoords[0],
                               SQUARE_WIDTH * playerCoords[1]);
        myPrincess.setFrame(1);
        // get the coordinates of the square where the crown
        // should be placed (this is given by the BoardDecoder
        // and not from the data of the saved game because the
        // crown does not move during the game).
        int[] goalCoords = decoder.getGoalSquare();
        myCrown.setPosition((SQUARE_WIDTH * goalCoords[0]) + (SQUARE_WIDTH/4),
                            (SQUARE_WIDTH * goalCoords[1]) + (SQUARE_WIDTH/2));
        // The decoder creates the door and key sprites and places
        // them in the correct locations in terms of the LayerManager's
        // coordinate system.
        myDoors = decoder.createDoors();
        myKeys = decoder.createKeys();
        // get an array of ints that lists whether each door is
        // open or closed in the saved game
```

```
      int[] openDoors = info.getDoorsOpen();
      for(int i = 0; i < myDoors.length; i++) {
        append(myDoors[i]);
        if(openDoors[i] == 0) {
          // if the door was open, make it invisible
          myDoors[i].setVisible(false);
        }
      }
      // the keys can be moved by the player, so you get their
      // coordinates from the GameInfo saved data.
      int[][] keyCoords = info.getKeyCoords();
      for(int i = 0; i < myKeys.length; i++) {
        append(myKeys[i]);
        myKeys[i].setPosition(SQUARE_WIDTH * keyCoords[i][0],
                              SQUARE_WIDTH * keyCoords[i][1]);
      }
      // if the player was holding a key in the saved game,
      // you have the player hold that key and set it to invisible.
      int heldKey = info.getHeldKey();
      if(heldKey != -1) {
        myHeldKey = myKeys[heldKey];
        myHeldKey.setVisible(false);
      }
      // append the background last so it will be painted first.
      append(myBackground);
      // this sets the view screen so that the player is
      // in the center.
      myViewWindowX = SQUARE_WIDTH * playerCoords[0]
        - ((DISP_WIDTH - SQUARE_WIDTH)/2);
      myViewWindowY = SQUARE_WIDTH * playerCoords[1]
        - ((DISP_HEIGHT - SQUARE_WIDTH)/2);
      // a number of objects are created in order to set up the game,
      // but they should be eliminated to free up memory:
      decoder = null;
      System.gc();
    }
    return(retVal);
  }

  /**
   * save the current game in progress.
   */
  void saveGame(int gameTicks) throws Exception {
    int[] playerSquare = new int[2];
```

```
    // the coordinates of the player are given in terms of
    // the 16x16 dungeon grid. You divide the player's
    // pixel coordinates to get the right grid square.
    // If the player was not precisely aligned with a
    // grid square when the game was saved, the difference
    // will be shaved off.
    playerSquare[0] = myPrincess.getX()/SQUARE_WIDTH;
    playerSquare[1] = myPrincess.getY()/SQUARE_WIDTH;
    // save the coordinates of the current locations of
    // the keys, and if a key is currently held by the
    // player, we save the info of which one it was.
    int[][] keyCoords = new int[4][];
    int heldKey = -1;
    for(int i = 0; i < myKeys.length; i++) {
      keyCoords[i] = new int[2];
      keyCoords[i][0] = myKeys[i].getX()/SQUARE_WIDTH;
      keyCoords[i][1] = myKeys[i].getY()/SQUARE_WIDTH;
      if((myHeldKey != null) && (myKeys[i] == myHeldKey)) {
        heldKey = i;
      }
    }
    // save the information of which doors were open.
    int[] doorsOpen = new int[8];
    for(int i = 0; i < myDoors.length; i++) {
      if(myDoors[i].isVisible()) {
        doorsOpen[i] = 1;
      }
    }
    // take all the information you've gathered and
    // create a GameInfo object that will save the info
    // in the device's memory.
    GameInfo info = new GameInfo(myCurrentBoardNum, gameTicks,
                                 playerSquare, keyCoords,
                                 doorsOpen, heldKey);
  }


  //----------------------------------------------------------
  //  graphics methods

  /**
   * paint the game graphic on the screen.
   */
  public void paint(Graphics g) throws Exception {
    // only repaint if something has changed:
```

```
    if(myModifiedSinceLastPaint) {
      g.setColor(DungeonCanvas.WHITE);
      // paint the background white to cover old game objects
      // that have changed position since last paint.
      // here coordinates are given
      // with respect to the graphics (canvas) origin:
      g.fillRect(0, 0, DISP_WIDTH, DISP_HEIGHT);
      // here coordinates are given
      // with respect to the LayerManager origin:
      setViewWindow(myViewWindowX, myViewWindowY, DISP_WIDTH, DISP_HEIGHT);
      // call the paint function of the superclass LayerManager
      // to paint all the Layers
      paint(g, CANVAS_X, CANVAS_Y);
      // don't paint again until something changes:
      myModifiedSinceLastPaint = false;
    }
  }


//---------------------------------------------------------
//  game movements

/**
 * respond to keystrokes by deciding where to move
 * and then moving the pieces and the view window correspondingly.
 */
void requestMove(int horizontal, int vertical) {
  if(horizontal != 0) {
    // see how far the princess can move in the desired
    // horizontal direction (if not blocked by a wall
    // or closed door)
    horizontal = requestHorizontal(horizontal);
  }
  // vertical < 0 indicates that the user has
  // pressed the UP button and would like to jump.
  // therefore, if you're not currently jumping,
  // you begin the jump.
  if((myIsJumping == NO_JUMP) && (vertical < 0)) {
    myIsJumping++;
  } else if(myIsJumping == NO_JUMP) {
    // if you're not jumping at all, you need to check
    // if the princess should be falling:
    // you (temporarily) move the princess down and see if that
    // causes a collision with the floor:
    myPrincess.move(0, MOVE_LENGTH);
```

```
      // if the princess can move down without colliding
      // with the floor, then we set the princess to
      // be falling.  The variable myIsJumping starts
      // negative while the princess is jumping up and
      // is zero or positive when the princess is coming
      // back down. You therefore set myIsJumping to
      // zero to indicate that the princess should start
      // falling.
      if(! checkCollision()) {
        myIsJumping = 0;
      }
      // you move the princess Sprite back to the correct
      // position she was at before you (temporarily) moved
      // her down to see if she would fall.
      myPrincess.move(0, -MOVE_LENGTH);
    }
    // if the princess is currently jumping or falling,
    // you calculate the vertical distance she should move
    // (taking into account the horizontal distance that
    // she is also moving).
    if(myIsJumping != NO_JUMP) {
      vertical = jumpOrFall(horizontal);
    }
    // now that you've calculated how far the princess
    // should move, you move her. (this is a call to
    // another internal method of this method
    // suite, it is not a built-in LayerManager method):
    move(horizontal, vertical);
  }


  /**
   * Internal to requestMove.  Calculates what the
   * real horizontal distance moved should be
   * after taking obstacles into account.
   * @return the horizontal distance that the
   * player can move.
   */
  private int requestHorizontal(int horizontal) {
    // you (temporarily) move her to the right or left
    // and see if she hits a wall or a door:
    myPrincess.move(horizontal * MOVE_LENGTH, 0);
    if(checkCollision()) {
      // if she hits something, then she's not allowed
      // to go in that direction, so you set the horizontal
```

```
      // move distance to zero and then move the princess
      // back to where she was.
      myPrincess.move(-horizontal * MOVE_LENGTH, 0);
      horizontal = 0;
    } else {
      // if she doesn't hit anything then the move request
      // succeeds, but you still move her back to the
      // earlier position because this was just the checking
      // phase.
      myPrincess.move(-horizontal * MOVE_LENGTH, 0);
      horizontal *= MOVE_LENGTH;
    }
    return(horizontal);
}


/**
 * Internal to requestMove.  Calculates the vertical
 * change in the player's position if jumping or
 * falling.
 * this method should only be called if the player is
 * currently jumping or falling.
 * @return the vertical distance that the player should
 * move this turn. (negative moves up, positive moves down)
 */
private int jumpOrFall(int horizontal) {
    // by default you do not move vertically
    int vertical = 0;
    // The speed of rise or descent is computed using
    // the int myIsJumping. Since you are in a jump or
    // fall, you advance the jump by one (which simulates
    // the downward pull of gravity by slowing the rise
    // or accelerating the fall) unless the player is
    // already falling at maximum speed. (a maximum
    // free fall speed is necessary because otherwise
    // it is possible for the player to fall right through
    // the bottom of the maze...)
    if(myIsJumping <= MAX_FREE_FALL) {
        myIsJumping++;
    }
    if(myIsJumping < 0) {
        // if myIsJumping is negative, that means that
        // the princess is rising. You calculate the
        // number of pixels to go up by raising 2 to
        // the power myIsJumping (absolute value).
```

```
    // note that you make the result negative because
    // the up and down coordinates in Java are the
    // reverse of the vertical coordinates we learned
    // in math class: as you go up, the coordinate
    // values go down, and as you go down the screen,
    // the coordinate numbers go up.
    vertical = -(2<<(-myIsJumping));
} else {
    // if myIsJumping is positive, the princess is falling.
    // you calculate the distance to fall by raising 2
    // to the power of the absolute value of myIsJumping.
    vertical = (2<<(myIsJumping));
}
// now you temporarily move the princess the desired
// vertical distance (with the corresponding horizontal
// distance also thrown in), and see if she hits anything:
myPrincess.move(horizontal, vertical);
if(checkCollision()) {
    // here you're in the case where she did hit something.
    // you move her back into position and then see what
    // to do about it.
    myPrincess.move(-horizontal, -vertical);
    if(vertical > 0) {
        // in this case the player is falling.
        // so you need to determine precisely how
        // far she can fall before she hit the bottom
        vertical = 0;
        // you temporarily move her the desired horizontal
        // distance while calculating the corresponding
        // vertical distance.
        myPrincess.move(horizontal, 0);
        while(! checkCollision()) {
            vertical++;
            myPrincess.move(0, 1);
        }
        // now that you've calculated how far she can fall,
        // you move her back to her earlier position
        myPrincess.move(-horizontal, -vertical);
        // you subtract 1 pixel from the distance calculated
        // because once she has actually collided with the
        // floor, she's gone one pixel too far...
        vertical--;
        // now that she's hit the floor, she's not jumping
        // anymore.
```

```
      myIsJumping = NO_JUMP;
  } else {
    // in this case you're going up, so she
    // must have hit her head.
    // This next if is checking for a special
    // case where there's room to jump up exactly
    // one square. In that case you increase the
    // value of myIsJumping in order to make the
    // princess not rise as high. The details
    // of the calculation in this case were found
    // through trial and error:
    if(myIsJumping == NO_JUMP + 2) {
      myIsJumping++;
      vertical = -(2<<(-myIsJumping));
      // now you see if the special shortened jump
      // still makes her hit her head:
      // (as usual, temporarily move her to test
      // for collisions)
      myPrincess.move(horizontal, vertical);
      if(checkCollision()) {
        // if she still hits her head even
        // with this special shortened jump,
        // then she was not meant to jump...
        myPrincess.move(-horizontal, -vertical);
        vertical = 0;
        myIsJumping = NO_JUMP;
      } else {
        // now that you've checked for collisions,
        // you move the player back to her earlier
        // position:
        myPrincess.move(-horizontal, -vertical);
      }
    } else {
      // if she hit her head, then she should not
      // jump up.
      vertical = 0;
      myIsJumping = NO_JUMP;
    }
  }
} else {
  // since she didn't hit anything when you moved
  // her, then all you have to do is move her back.
  myPrincess.move(-horizontal, -vertical);
}
```

```
    return(vertical);
  }


  /**
   * Internal to requestMove. Once the moves have been
   * determined, actually perform the move.
   */
  private void move(int horizontal, int vertical) {
    // repaint only if you actually change something:
    if((horizontal != 0) || (vertical != 0)) {
      myModifiedSinceLastPaint = true;
    }
    // if the princess is moving left or right, you set
    // her image to be facing the right direction:
    if(horizontal > 0) {
      myPrincess.setTransform(Sprite.TRANS_NONE);
    } else if(horizontal < 0) {
      myPrincess.setTransform(Sprite.TRANS_MIRROR);
    }
    // if she's jumping or falling, you set the image to
    // the frame where the skirt is inflated:
    if(vertical != 0) {
      myPrincess.setFrame(0);
      // if she's just running, you alternate between the
      // two frames:
    } else if(horizontal != 0) {
      if(myPrincess.getFrame() == 1) {
        myPrincess.setFrame(0);
      } else {
        myPrincess.setFrame(1);
      }
    }
    // move the position of the view window so that
    // the player stays in the center:
    myViewWindowX += horizontal;
    myViewWindowY += vertical;
    // after all that work, you finally move the
    // princess for real!!!
    myPrincess.move(horizontal, vertical);
  }


  //----------------------------------------------------------
  //  sprite interactions
```

```
/**
 * Drops the currently held key and picks up another.
 */
void putDownPickUp() {
  // you do not want to allow the player to put
  // down the key in the air, so you verify that
  // you're not jumping or falling first:
  if((myIsJumping == NO_JUMP) &&
     (myPrincess.getY() % SQUARE_WIDTH == 0)) {
    // since you're picking something up or putting
    // something down, the display changes and needs
    // to be repainted:
    setNeedsRepaint();
    // if the thing you're picking up is the crown,
    // you're done, the player has won:
    if(myPrincess.collidesWith(myCrown, true)) {
      myCanvas.setGameOver();
      return;
    }
    // keep track of the key you're putting down in
    // order to place it correctly:
    DoorKey oldHeld = myHeldKey;
    myHeldKey = null;
    // if the princess is on top of another key,
    // that one becomes the held key and is hence
    // made invisible:
    for(int i = 0; i < myKeys.length; i++) {
      // you check myHeldKey for null because you don't
      // want to accidentally pick up two keys.
      if((myPrincess.collidesWith(myKeys[i], true)) &&
         (myHeldKey == null)) {
        myHeldKey = myKeys[i];
        myHeldKey.setVisible(false);
      }
    }
    if(oldHeld != null) {
      // place the key you're putting down in the princess's
      // current position and make it visible:
      oldHeld.setPosition(myPrincess.getX(), myPrincess.getY());
      oldHeld.setVisible(true);
    }
  }
}
```

```
/**
 * Checks of the player hits a stone wall or a door.
 */
boolean checkCollision() {
  boolean retVal = false;
  // the "true" arg means to check for a pixel-level
  // collision (so merely an overlap in image
  // squares does not register as a collision)
  if(myPrincess.collidesWith(myBackground, true)) {
    retVal = true;
  } else {
    // Note: it is not necessary to synchronize
    // this block because the thread that calls this
    // method is the same as the one that puts down the
    // keys, so there's no danger of the key being put down
    // between the moment you check for the key and
    // the moment you open the door:
    for(int i = 0; i < myDoors.length; i++) {
      // if she's holding the right key, then open the door
      // otherwise bounce off
      if(myPrincess.collidesWith(myDoors[i], true)) {
        if((myHeldKey != null) &&
           (myDoors[i].getColor() == myHeldKey.getColor())) {
          setNeedsRepaint();
          myDoors[i].setVisible(false);
        } else {
          // if she's not holding the right key, then
          // she has collided with the door just the same
          // as if she had collided with a wall:
          retVal = true;
        }
      }
    }
  }
  return(retVal);
}

}
```

The princess and the crown Sprites were too simple to warrant making
whole subclasses for them (similarly I didn't bother to subclass TiledLayer for the
background this time). But for the doors and keys, I wanted to store their colors
in the Sprite object itself, so I created a subclass, DoorKey.java (see Listing 5-10).

*Listing 5-10.* `DoorKey.java`

```
package net.frog_parrot.dungeon;

import javax.microedition.lcdui.*;
import javax.microedition.lcdui.game.*;

/**
 * This class represents doors and keys.
 *
 * @author Carol Hamer
 */
public class DoorKey extends Sprite {

  //------------------------------------------------------------
  //    fields

  /**
   * The image file shared by all doors and keys.
   */
  public static Image myImage;

  /**
   * A code int that indicates the door or key's color.
   */
  private int myColor;

  //------------------------------------------------------------
  //    get/set data

  /**
   * @return the door or key's color.
   */
  public int getColor() {
    return(myColor);
  }

  //------------------------------------------------------------
  //    constructor and initializer

  static {
    try {
      myImage = Image.createImage("/images/keys.png");
    } catch(Exception e) {
```

```
        throw(new RuntimeException(
            "DoorKey.<init>-->failed to load image, caught "
            + e.getClass() + ": " + e.getMessage()));
    }
}


/**
 * Standard constructor sets the image to the correct frame
 * (according to whether this is a door or a key and what
 * color it should be) and then puts it in the correct location.
 */
public DoorKey(int color, boolean isKey, int[] gridCoordinates) {
    super(myImage, DungeonManager.SQUARE_WIDTH, DungeonManager.SQUARE_WIDTH);
    myColor = color;
    int imageIndex = color * 2;
    if(isKey) {
        imageIndex++;
    }
    setFrame(imageIndex);
    setPosition(gridCoordinates[0] * DungeonManager.SQUARE_WIDTH,
                gridCoordinates[1] * DungeonManager.SQUARE_WIDTH);
}


}
```

And, of course, you don't want to forget about the Thread subclass
GameThread.java (see Listing 5-11).

*Listing 5-11.* GameThread.java

```
package net.frog_parrot.dungeon;

/**
 * This class contains the loop that keeps the game running.
 *
 * @author Carol Hamer
 */
public class GameThread extends Thread {


    //-----------------------------------------------------------
    //    fields

    /**
     * Whether the main thread would like this thread
```

```
 * to pause.
 */
private boolean myShouldPause;


/**
 * Whether the main thread would like this thread
 * to stop.
 */
private static boolean myShouldStop;


/**
 * A handle back to the graphical components.
 */
private DungeonCanvas myDungeonCanvas;


//------------------------------------------------------------
//    initialization

/**
 * standard constructor.
 */
GameThread(DungeonCanvas canvas) {
  myDungeonCanvas = canvas;
}


//------------------------------------------------------------
//    actions

/**
 * pause the game.
 */
void pause() {
  myShouldPause = true;
}


/**
 * restart the game after a pause.
 */
synchronized void resumeGame() {
  myShouldPause = false;
  notify();
}
```

```
/**
 * stops the game.
 */
synchronized void requestStop() {
  myShouldStop = true;
  this.notify();
}


/**
 * start the game..
 */
public void run() {
  // flush any keystrokes that occurred before the
  // game started:
  myDungeonCanvas.flushKeys();
  myShouldStop = false;
  myShouldPause = false;
  while(true) {
    if(myShouldStop) {
      break;
    }
    myDungeonCanvas.checkKeys();
    myDungeonCanvas.updateScreen();
    // you do a very short pause to allow the other thread
    // to update the information about which keys are pressed:
    synchronized(this) {
      try {
        wait(1);
      } catch(Exception e) {}
    }
    if(myShouldPause) {
      synchronized(this) {
        try {
          wait();
        } catch(Exception e) {}
      }
    }
  }
}
```

Storing your data locally on the device isn't the only application of transforming your object data into byte arrays (and later converting it back). You can use the same functions that prepare your data to be stored to prepare your data to be transmitted over a network, and you can use the functions that interpret the bytes of data without modification to interpret data that the device receives from a server. In the next chapter, you'll see how to add a little bit of communications code to this same example game to allow a remote server to update the data used by the game.

# CHAPTER 6

# Communicating over a Network

IT SEEMS LIKE everything in the Java 2 Micro Edition (J2ME) is a limited, simplified version of what you can do in the Java 2 Standard Edition (J2SE) or Java 2 Enterprise Edition (J2EE), and communicating over a network is no exception. As you may guess, the Connected Limited Device Configuration (CLDC) has no Java Remote Method Invocation (RMI). (And don't even think about running an Enterprise JavaBean on a cell phone!) So instead of writing a completely object-oriented program in which the client can transparently call object methods on the server, as a J2ME programmer you have to write the client-server messages by hand.

Unfortunately, a great potential for errors and miscommunication exists when you write methods to read and write custom data. So, programs that communicate over data sockets can be harder to debug and harder to maintain than programs that use RMI. Instead of having the compiler verify for you that all your communications messages are correct and well-formed, you have to analyze carefully that both the client and the server are sending and interpreting the data correctly in every possible case. That's not to suggest that programming and debugging with Java RMI is trivial—the problems that arise from distributed, dynamic code loading for RMI can create their own headaches. But it doesn't really matter what your personal preference may be with respect to exchanging raw data versus using distributed objects since CLDC doesn't give you a choice. The overhead needed for RMI is too costly in a small device. So, if you want your game to communicate with another machine, you'll have to write the code to create and parse the data yourself.

## Understanding the Types of Network Communication in MIDP

The one protocol that's always available to you with the Mobile Internet Device Profile (MIDP) is Hypertext Transfer Protocol (HTTP). In MIDP 1.0, HTTP is the only protocol that all implementations are required to support. In MIDP 2.0, secure HTTP (HTTPS) is also required, allowing you to exchange HTTPS messages (see Chapter 7 for more details on using HTTPS). Since HTTP is the one protocol you can always use, the first example game in this chapter will illustrate a simple use of HTTP. The example will be a continuation of the dungeon example from the previous chapter with the addition of code that fetches new dungeons from a server.

In addition to HTTP, several other protocols may optionally be supported. Some of the most useful for games include User Datagram Protocol (UDP) and plain Transfer Control Protocol (TCP) sockets. UDP is an asynchronous one-way protocol, which means that once the data is sent, the sender doesn't receive any information about whether it was correctly received. The advantage to UDP is speed, which is a big deal for games. The application doesn't have to go through the entire process of establishing a two-way connection before sending the data, and it sends the message immediately instead of buffering it and sending it in bursts. This advantage often outweighs the inconvenience of writing the extra error-handling code to deal with lost messages. With a plain socket, on the other hand, you sacrifice a little bit of speed in the beginning in order to have assured two-way communications. The advantage to using plain sockets over HTTP and UDP in a game situation is that you have a continuous back-and-forth exchange of data instead of a request-response model like HTTP or a request-and-not-necessarily-any-response model like UDP. (The sidebar "Deciding When to Use HTTP and When to Use a Plain Socket" covers the disadvantages.)

In this chapter, the second example game will illustrate how to use plain socket communications with a two-player checkers game. Notice that even though the classes that correspond to plain TCP sockets aren't present in the MIDP 1.0 Javadoc, they're available in some MIDP 1.0 implementations.

All the different communication protocols used by MIDP are based on a single interface: `javax.microedition.io.Connection`. Regardless of which type of `Connection` you want to use, you get an instance of it by calling the static method `javax.microedition.io.Connector.open()` with the Uniform Resource Locator (URL) of the destination program as an argument. The application management software parses the URL to determine which subinterface of `Connection` to give you. The beginning of the URL gives the protocol. In this chapter, you'll see examples using `http://` and `socket://`. In the next chapter, you'll see how to use secure connections by starting the URLs with `https://` and `ssl://`.

You may be wondering why all the types of connections are represented by interfaces in the MIDP Application Programming Interface (API) rather than by classes. This is because the variation among CLDC devices makes it necessary for each device to provide its own implementation of the various types of `Connection`s. For this same reason, you as a developer don't have much say in how the `Connection` is created. The application management software assumes that it knows better than you do how all the connection parameters need to be set.

Once you have a handle to a `Connection` object, you can use it to get the `DataInputStream` to read data from and the `DataOutputStream` to write data to it. These are the same classes that were used as utilities to serialize data in the "Serializing More Complex Data Using Streams" section in Chapter 5, so they're easy to use. Each one has a series of methods (such as readInt() and readLong()) to read and write different types of data. The tricky part is to make certain the bytes that the server writes as a certain type will be read by the client device as the same type, and vice versa. Remember that once you write a value to the DataOutputStream, it's rendered as just a sequence of bytes— nothing indicates what type a given set of bytes used to be. So, you need to be careful to make sure the client and server are reading and writing the data in the same order. It's easy for the sending algorithm and the receiving algorithm to become misaligned by a few bytes, and when that happens, your data is toast! It's difficult to recover from such an error.

## Using HTTP

Using the interface javax.microedition.io.HttpConnection is probably the easiest way to use the MIDP API to communicate with a server. Listing 6-1 is a code segment that will create an instance of HttpConnection and use it to send a message to a server and read a response.

*Listing 6-1. Creating an Instance of* HttpConnection

```
/**
 * Makes a connection to the server and reads the data.
 */
public void run() {
  // you sync on the class because you don't want multiple
  // instances simultaneously attempting to download
  ContentConnection connection = null;
  DataInputStream dis = null;
  DataOutputStream dos = null;
  byte dataToSend = 3;
  try {
    // the method Connector.open() uses the URL argument
    // to decide what protocol to use (and hence what type
    // of Connection interface to return) in addition to
    // using the URL to determine the address of the
    // program to contact.
    connection = (ContentConnection)Connector.open(
            "http://frog-parrot.net:8080/servlet/ExampleServlet");
    ((HttpConnection)connection).setRequestMethod(HttpConnection.POST);
    dos = connection.openDataOutputStream();
    dos.write(dataToSend);
    // flush sends the message
    dos.flush();
```

```
    // some implementations give errors if you open the data input stream
    // without first reading the response code:
    int responseCode = ((HttpConnection)connection).getResponseCode();
    dis = connection.openDataInputStream();
    byte received = dis.readByte();
  } catch(Exception e) {
    // normally you would add some code here to send
    // the user an error message.
  } finally {
    // even if there is a communications error, you need
    // to close the connection and the streams:
    try {
      if(dis != null) {
        dis.close();
      }
      if(dos != null) {
        dos.close();
      }
      if(connection != null) {
        connection.close();
      }
    } catch(Exception e) {
      // normally you would add some code here to send
      // the user an error message.
    }
  }
}
```

Several points in Listing 6-1 require some further explanation. First, it wasn't an accident that I called the method run() as if the previous code were from a subclass of Thread. Since reading from a socket may cause the current thread to block, it's a good idea to spawn a new thread for communications rather than using the main thread. Another thing to notice is that I set the HTTP method to POST. I did this because the program sends data to the server (see the sidebar "GET, POST, and HEAD" for more explanation).

Another thing to notice in Listing 6-1 is that I read 1 byte of data from the stream regardless of how much data is available. If no data is available, the thread could block and stay blocked until the program terminates. It's a good idea to have the server set the Content-Length HTTP header so that your program will know precisely how much data to read from the stream. (You can get the value of the Content-Length header by calling getLength().) If your client program has to figure out for itself how much data to read, it's a good idea to call the read() method (with a byte array to read the data into). Unlike readFully(), read() won't block if it can't fill the whole array (although it will block if there's no data to read at all and the server hasn't yet closed the stream). As long as there's at least 1 byte of data to read, the method read() reads as many bytes of data as it can and then returns the number of bytes it read. To make sure you got all the data, you can call read() multiple times (specifying an offset to avoid overwriting the data you've already read) until the method returns a value of -1 to indicate it has reached the end of the stream. Another trick is to use the available() method of java.io.DataInputStream to determine how many bytes of data are available before reading them in. That way, you can call readFully() with no danger of blocking. The only problem with using available() is that in my tests I've found it has an annoying tendency to return zero even when there are bytes available to read, so I generally don't use it.

The corresponding server code for HTTP is also easy because most of the work has been done for you. All you need to do is write a Servlet and run it on a Web server that will direct the client to the Servlet (using the URL that was used when creating the HttpConnection).

If you don't have a Web server that will run Servlets, you can download Tomcat free from http://jakarta.apache.org/tomcat/. The download contains all of the information you need to configure and run the Tomcat Servlet container.

Don't forget that if you want to run your HTTP code on a real device, you'll need to have your Servlet running on a machine that can be accessed from the Internet. It's better to use a domain name (such as frog-parrot.net) instead of a numerical Internet Protocol (IP) address (such as 80.13.176.79) in the contact URL (sent as an argument to Connector.open()) because a numerical IP address can change. However, for testing it shouldn't be a problem to use a numerical IP address. If you don't know what your machine's IP address is, see the "Accessing the WML File and Downloading Applications" section in Chapter 1. If your test environment isn't connected to the Internet, you can still test your code with the emulator as long as the emulator and the Servlet container are running on the same network. That's how I did most of my debugging for the examples in this chapter. The emulator is perfectly willing to accept a URL that contains the local machine's name in place of a domain name or IP address.

Servlets aren't hard to write. If you want to know all of the theory behind them and all of the cool things you can do with them, there are whole books written on the subject (plenty of them). But if you're content with a simple Servlet, you can just follow the example in the section "Writing the Server Code for the Dungeon Example." As you can see from the example, all you need to do is implement the method doGet() if you want your Servlet to handle GET requests and implement the method doPost() if you want your Servlet to handle POST requests. Both of these methods receive Request and Response objects as arguments, which you can query to get input and output streams to use to read from and write to the client just as the client uses input and output streams to communicate with the server.

Of course, just because the server-side code can be taken care of with just a simple Servlet, that doesn't mean it's your only option. The server side can be quite elaborate for some applications. For example, Forum Nokia has produced a document called *Optimizing the Client/Server Communication for Mobile Applications Part 1* (http://ncsp.forum.nokia.com/downloads/nokia/documents/ Optimizing_client_server_part1.pdf) that describes various possibilities for MIDP client-server communications, including suggestions for using a proxy server to route HTTP messages to an Enterprise JavaBean (EJB) running on an application server. But since the focus of this book is on programming for the device itself, I'll keep the server side of the examples in this chapter as simple as possible.

## The Dungeon Example: Downloading the Next Board

As an example of how to use HTTP in a typical game situation, you'll now improve the dungeon example from the previous chapter. This time, instead of hard-coding the data that describes the various boards, you'll have only one hard-coded board ship with the game and have the user download the other boards. That way, the number of possible boards for the game is unlimited because you can always add more boards to your Servlet. Plus, this example shows one way to implement the business model in which you freely distribute the first segment of the game, and then the users who like it can pay to download more (see the sidebar "Using Secure Connections While Selling Your Game" in Chapter 7 for more about that marketing strategy).

Now I'll go over in detail the changes necessary to make the dungeon game use HTTP to download board data.

## Writing the Client Code for the Dungeon Example

The biggest change to the client program is the addition of the class BoardReader, which contacts a server and downloads the data for the remaining boards that the user doesn't have yet and stores them in the device's memory.

Here's how it works: First, you add a command to the MIDlet subclass (Dungeon) to allow the user to tell the game to contact the server to download boards. This means that in the command fields section of the Dungeon class, you add the following command:

```
/**
 * The command to download new boards.
 */
private Command myDownloadCommand
  = new Command("Download boards", Command.SCREEN, 10);
```

Second, of course, you need to add the new command to Canvas, so you should change the constructor of Dungeon to the following:

```
/**
 * Initialize the canvas and the commands.
 */
public Dungeon() {
  try {
    // create the canvas and set up the commands:
    myCanvas = new DungeonCanvas(this);
    myCanvas.addCommand(myExitCommand);
    myCanvas.addCommand(myDownloadCommand);
    myCanvas.addCommand(mySaveCommand);
    myCanvas.addCommand(myRestoreCommand);
    myCanvas.addCommand(myPauseCommand);
    myCanvas.setCommandListener(this);
  } catch(Exception e) {
    // if there's an error during creation, display it as an alert.
    errorMsg(e);
  }
}
```

Finally, when the user selects Download Boards from the command menu, the program needs to create an instance of the new BoardReader class and start it up. So, in the commandAction() method of the Dungeon class, you need to add the following additional else if block to the list of else if blocks:

```
} else if(c == myDownloadCommand) {
  // spawn a new BoardReader thread to
  // connect and download new boards:
  BoardReader br = new BoardReader(this, myCanvas);
  br.start();
```

In the previous code block, you call br.start() because BoardReader is a subclass of Thread, as discussed in the "Using HTTP" section. When the BoardReader starts (in the run() method), the first thing it does is open a connection to the server. Then it checks the local record store to see how many boards are currently stored on the device. BoardReader opens the output stream and tells the server how many boards the device already has. The server then sends the data for the boards that the client doesn't have yet. Then BoardReader reads the data from the Connection's output stream and stores it locally in a series of records. Each record contains all the data needed to construct one board.

Most of the action of BoardReader takes place in the run() method, but also some helper methods store and retrieve the boards from local memory. I made all the local memory methods static since other classes may call them even if the user doesn't download any boards in a given game session. Making them static avoids instantiating Thread objects that won't be used.

Listing 6-2 shows the code for BoardReader.java.

*Listing 6-2.* `BoardReader.java`

```
package net.frog_parrot.dungeon;

import java.io.*;
import javax.microedition.io.*;
import javax.microedition.lcdui.*;
import javax.microedition.rms.*;

import net.frog_parrot.util.DataConverter;

/**
 * This class contacts a remote server in order to
 * download data for new game boards and stores
 * them locally.
 *
 * @author Carol Hamer
 */
public class BoardReader extends Thread {

  //------------------------------------------------------------
  //  fields

  /**
   * This is the name of the local datastore on the CLDC device.
   */
  public static final String LOCAL_DATASTORE = "BoardData";

  /**
   * This is the URL to contact.
   * IMPORTANT: change the domain name in the following URL
   * from "frog-parrot.net" to the domain name of the
   * server that the corresponding servlet is running on!!!!
   * (The "/games/DungeonDownload" part of the URL
   * may also need to be changed, depending on how servlet
   * URLs are configured on the Web server.)
   */
  public static final String SERVER_URL
    = "http://frog-parrot.net:8080/games/DungeonDownload";

  /**
   * This is the size of the byte array containing
   * all the info for one board.
   */
  public static final int DATA_LENGTH = 48;
```

```
//-----------------------------------------------------------
//  instance fields
//  these are used by the thread when downloading
//  boards to display a possible error message.

/**
 * The MIDlet subclass, used to set the Display
 * in the case where an error message needs to be sent.
 */
private Dungeon myDungeon;

/**
 * The Canvas subclass, used to set the Display
 * in the case where an error message needs to be sent.
 */
private DungeonCanvas myCanvas;


//-----------------------------------------------------------
//  initialization

/**
 * Constructor is used only when the program wants
 * to spawn a data-fetching thread, not for merely
 * reading local data with static methods.
 */
BoardReader(Dungeon dungeon, DungeonCanvas canvas) {
  myDungeon = dungeon;
  myCanvas = canvas;
}


//-----------------------------------------------------------
//  local data methods
//  note that these methods are static and do
//  not run on a separate thread even though this
//  class is a subclass of Thread

/**
 * @return the number of boards currently stored in the
 * device memory. (this does not include the hard-coded board)
 */
static int getNumBoards() {
  RecordStore store = null;
  int retVal = 0;
```

```
      try {
        // if the record store does not yet exist, don't
        // create it
        store = RecordStore.openRecordStore(LOCAL_DATASTORE, false);
        if(store != null) {
          retVal = store.getNumRecords();
        }
      } catch(Exception e) {
      } finally {
        try {
          if(store != null) {
            store.closeRecordStore();
          }
        } catch(Exception e) {
          // if the record store is open, this shouldn't throw.
        }
      }
      return(retVal);
    }


    /**
     * @return the byte array that gives the board that
     * has the number boardNum (if it is found). returns null
     * if there is no board in memory that has the given number.
     */
    static byte[] getBoardData(int boardNum) {
      RecordStore store = null;
      byte[] retArray = null;
      try {
        // if the record store does not yet exist, don't
        // create it
        store = RecordStore.openRecordStore(LOCAL_DATASTORE, false);
        if((store != null) && (store.getNumRecords() >= boardNum)) {
          retArray = store.getRecord(boardNum);
        }
      } catch(Exception e) {
      } finally {
        try {
          if(store != null) {
            store.closeRecordStore();
          }
        } catch(Exception e) {
          // if the record store is open, this shouldn't throw.
        }
      }
```

```
      return(retArray);
    }


    /**
     * Saves the data of a board being downloaded from the Internet
     */
    static void saveBoardData(byte[] data) throws Exception {
      RecordStore store = null;
      try {
        // if the record store does not yet exist,
        // create it
        store = RecordStore.openRecordStore(LOCAL_DATASTORE, true);
        store.addRecord(data, 0, data.length);
      } finally {
        try {
          if(store != null) {
            store.closeRecordStore();
          }
        } catch(Exception e) {
          // if the record store is open, this shouldn't throw.
        }
      }
    }


    //-----------------------------------------------------------
    //  download methods

    /**
     * Makes a HTTP connection to the server and gets data
     * for more boards.
     */
    public void run() {
      // you sync on the class because you don't want multiple
      // instances simultaneously attempting to download
      synchronized(this.getClass()) {
        ContentConnection connection = null;
        DataInputStream dis = null;
        DataOutputStream dos = null;
        try {
          connection = (ContentConnection)Connector.open(SERVER_URL);
          // send the number of local boards to the server
          // so the server will know which boards to send:
          int numBoards = getNumBoards();
          dos = connection.openDataOutputStream();
```

```
    // munBoards is an int but it is transferred as a
    // byte.  It should therefore not be more than 15.
    dos.write(numBoards);
    // flush to send the message:
    dos.flush();
    // connection.getLength() returns the value of the
    // content-length header, not the number of bytes
    // available to read.  The server must set this header
    // if the client wants to use it.
    // Here numBoards is the number
    // of boards that will be read from the downloaded data.
    numBoards = ((int)connection.getLength())/DATA_LENGTH;
    int responseCode = ((HttpConnection)connection).getResponseCode();
    dis = connection.openDataInputStream();
    for(int i = 0; i < numBoards; i++) {
      byte[] data = new byte[DATA_LENGTH];
      dis.readFully(data);
      saveBoardData(data);
    }
} catch(Exception e) {
  // if this fails, it is almost undoubtedly
  // a communication problem (server down, etc.)
  // you need to give the right message to the user:
  Alert alert = new Alert("download failed",
                 "please try again later", null, AlertType.INFO);
  // You set the timeout to forever so this Alert will
  // have a default dismiss command. When the user
  // presses the Alert.DISMISS_COMMAND, the displayable
  // myCanvas will become current (see setCurrent() below):
  alert.setTimeout(Alert.FOREVER);
  myCanvas.setNeedsRepaint();
  // the second arg tells the Display to go to
  // myCanvas when the user dismisses the alert
  Display.getDisplay(myDungeon).setCurrent(alert, myCanvas);
} finally {
  try {
    if(dis != null) {
      dis.close();
    }
    if(dos != null) {
      dos.close();
    }
    if(connection != null) {
      connection.close();
    }
```

```
    } catch(Exception e) {
      // if this throws, at least you made your best effort
      // to close everything up.
    }
  }
 }
}
```

```
}
```

To use the BoardReader class, you have to make a couple of other small changes in other parts of the code. Most of the rest of the changes are in the BoardDecoder. Essentially, you change BoardDecoder so that it no longer reads the board data from an internal (hard-coded) data array but rather calls BoardReader to get the board data from memory. The changes are pretty small compared to the size of the class, so I'll list just the changes rather than listing the whole class and having you search for the differences. First, you eliminate the parts that are related to the local data storage, namely, the field myData and the method getNumBoards(). Instead, you store only the data for the first board by adding the following field:

```
/**
 * This is the array of bytes for just the first board.
 * encodes where to place the various items
 * in the dungeon and the placement of the walls.
 */
static byte[] myFirstBoard = {
    0, 0, -108, -100, -24, 65, 21, 58, 53, -54, -116, -58, -56,
    -84, 115, -118,
    -1, -1, -128, 1, -103, -15, -128, 25, -97, -127, -128, 79, -14,
    1, -126, 121, -122, 1, -113, -49, -116, 1, -100, -3, -124, 5,
    -25, -27, -128, 1, -1, -1,
};
```

Second, in the beginning of the BoardDecoder constructor, you consult the BoardReader class to get the board data by replacing the following line:

```
byte[] data = myData[boardNum];
```

with these lines:

```
byte[] data = null;
if(boardNum < 1) {
  data = myFirstBoard;
} else {
  data = BoardReader.getBoardData(boardNum);
}
```

The final change that's needed to make this example work is to have DungeonManager consult BoardReader instead of BoardDecoder to get the number of possible boards by changing the following line:

```
if(myCurrentBoardNum == BoardDecoder.getNumBoards()) {
```

to the following:

```
if(myCurrentBoardNum >= BoardReader.getNumBoards()) {
```

With these changes, the dungeon example will run just as before except that now a potentially unlimited number of boards could be downloaded for the game instead of just using the boards that came with the original jar file.

## Writing the Server Code for the Dungeon Example

The other half of a client-server exchange is of course the server. Since you're using HTTP, the easiest way to implement the server side is to write a Servlet and run it on a Web server. I've written a simple Servlet called DungeonDownload. In my tests I ran the Servlet on a Tomcat server.

DungeonDownload first redirects all requests to the doPost() method and handles the requests from there. If you followed the client half of the conversation in the previous section, you should be able to guess what the server needs to do in this exchange. It reads the data from the client's message. The data consists of an integer that gives the number of boards currently stored locally on the client. If the server has more game boards than the client has, the server sends the remaining boards to the client. Before sending the data, the server determines precisely how many bytes of data it will send and passes this information along to the client by calling setContentLength().

Listing 6-3 shows the code for DungeonDownload.java.

*Listing 6-3.* DungeonDownload.java

```
package net.frog_parrot.servlet;

import java.io.*;
import javax.servlet.*;
import javax.servlet.http.*;

/**
 * This is the servlet that a small device running the
 * dungeon game can call to download more boards for the game.
 *
```

```
  * @author Carol Hamer
  */
public class DungeonDownload extends HttpServlet {

  //----------------------------------------------------------
  //   data

  /**
   * The data in bytes that gives the various boards.
   * no more than 127 boards should be sent to the device
   * in this version because the value that gives the
   * number of remote boards in the transaction is
   * stored in a byte.  If the value is greater than
   * 127, there will be errors when transforming it to a byte.
   */
  static byte[][] myData = {
    { 0, 1, 122, 90, -62, 34, -43, 72,
      -59, -29, 56, -55, 98, 126, -79, 61,
      -1, -1, -125, 1, -128, 17, -26, 29, -31, 57, -72, 1, -128, -51,
      -100, 65, -124, 57, -2, 1, -126, 13, -113, 1, -97, 25, -127,
      -99, -8, 1, -1, -1 },
    { 0, 2, 108, -24, 18, -26, 102, 30, -58, 46, -28, -88, 34,
      -98, 97, -41,
      -1, -1, -96, 1, -126, 57, -9, 97, -127, 69, -119, 73, -127,
      1, -109, 59, -126, 1, -26, 103, -127, 65, -103, 115, -127,
      65, -25, 73, -128, 1, -1, -1 },
    { 0, 3, -114, 18, -34, 27, -39, -60, -76, -50, 118, 90, 82,
      -88, 34, -74,
      -1, -1, -66, 1, -128, 121, -26, 125, -128, -123, -103, 29,
      -112, 1, -109, 49, -112, 1, -116, -31, -128, 5, -122, 5,
      -32, 13, -127, -51, -125, 1, -1, -1 },
  };

  //----------------------------------------------------------
  //   implementation of servlet

  /**
   * send the doPut requests to doPost.
   */
  public void doPut(HttpServletRequest request, HttpServletResponse response)
      throws ServletException, IOException {
    doPost(request, response);
  }
```

```java
/**
 * send the doGet requests to doPost.
 */
public void doGet(HttpServletRequest request, HttpServletResponse response)
    throws ServletException, IOException {
  doPost(request, response);
}


/**
 * send the data..
 */
public void doPost(HttpServletRequest request, HttpServletResponse response)
  throws ServletException, IOException {
  try {
    InputStream is = request.getInputStream();
    // read the number of boards currently on the device.
    int remoteBoards = is.read();
    OutputStream os = response.getOutputStream();
    // use the number of remote boards to decide how many
    // boards to send:
    if(myData.length > remoteBoards) {
      response.setContentLength(
          myData[0].length*(myData.length - remoteBoards));
      for(int i = remoteBoards; i < myData.length; i++) {
        os.write(myData[i]);
      }
    } else {
      response.setContentLength(0);
    }
    // send the message
    os.close();
    response.flushBuffer();
    // if this fails, you try to send the client as much info
    // as possible about what the failure might have been:
    // (The numerical arguments in the sendError() method
    // below are HTTP error codes.)
  } catch(EOFException eofe) {
    System.err.println("DungeonDownload.doPost-->caught " + eofe.getClass()
                       + ": " + eofe.getMessage());
    eofe.printStackTrace();
    response.sendError(408, eofe.getMessage());
  } catch(IOException ioe) {
    System.err.println("DungeonDownload.doPost-->caught " + ioe.getClass()
                       + ": " + ioe.getMessage());
```

```
      ioe.printStackTrace();
      response.sendError(500, ioe.getClass() + ": " + ioe.getMessage());
    } catch(Exception e) {
      System.err.println("DungeonDownload.doPost-->caught " + e.getClass()
                          + ": " + e.getMessage());
      e.printStackTrace();
      response.sendError(500, e.getClass() + ": " + e.getMessage());
    }
  }

}
```

## Get, Post, and Head

When you use the class HttpConnection, you can choose which HTTP request method to use by calling the method setRequestMethod(). Your choices are GET, POST, and HEAD. Which one to use depends on what you need to do.

HEAD is the most limited. The idea of the HEAD request is to ask the server for just the HTTP headers from the URL. A Servlet can't even handle a HEAD request in a custom way since there's no doHead() method in the Servlet class. It'll merely return the headers that would be returned by a GET request without returning the content.

GET and POST are similar. They both allow the client to transmit data to the server and receive the server's response data. The difference is how the client's message is encoded as it's sent to the server. As the names of the methods suggest, the purpose of the GET method is to merely request (get) data from the server whereas POST is used when the client wants to send (post) data to the server (and receive a response from the server). Behind the scenes, a client GET request has no body. Any data sent to the server must be encoded in the URL (which limits the type and amount of data that can be sent). In a POST request, the client can fill the body of the message with whatever data it wants to send to the server. So, if the client needs to send data to the server, it's better to go with POST. Otherwise, you can just stick with the default method, which is GET.

## Using Plain Sockets

If you're interested in a more complex exchange than a simple data download, you may want to use a SocketConnection. Plain sockets give you a little more freedom than HTTP-protocol sockets, and consequently they're a little more difficult.

The main difference between the two is that a connection using HTTP is sending a bit of extra information behind the scenes (a command with parameters and a list of header information), but with a SocketConnection, you write all of the data to the stream yourself. Additionally, on a single SocketConnection the client and server can exchange multiple messages back and forth whereas an HttpConnection requires the client to complete its message before reading server's response, and after the client has started reading the response, no more data can be sent to the server on that connection.

One advantage of HttpConnection is that it provides a special header line in which the server can specify the length of the data body of the message being sent. And even if the server fails to provide that information, the client can just keep reading in data from the server until it gets to the end, indicated by the read() method returning a value of -1. With a SocketConnection, the client and server have to be a little more carefully synchronized. Since the connection isn't normally closed between each burst of data, neither side can just read all the data until read() returns a value of -1. So each side has to know how much data to read and when to read it. If the length of the messages may vary, it makes sense to send the length of the message with the message. But this time you don't have a convenient method such as setContentLength() to put the length in. You have to write the length to the stream yourself. And if you do that, the recipient needs to expect it and needs to know precisely which bytes (and how many bytes) of the message should be interpreted as the length. In my example game I got around the question of sending the length by always having each message be exactly 4 bytes long, as you'll see in the next section.

The basics of the client code will look the same whether you use plain sockets or HTTP. Either way, you get a handle to the Connection by calling Connector.open(). Which type of Connection you receive depends on what kind of URL you send as an argument. To get a SocketConnection, send a URL that starts with socket://.

The code on the server side is going to look quite a bit different, however, since you can't just use a Servlet if you're not using HTTP! You have to write a program that will listen on a ServerSocket. Server programs can vary quite a lot in complexity. In the example server code the section "Writing the Server Code for the Checkers Example," I wrote the simplest most basic server code I could come up with so that you could see the essential points without getting mired in the details.

## Creating a Multiplayer Game Example: Checkers

The example application that illustrates using the SocketConnection interface is a simple game of checkers. Two players compete by having their respective devices call a central server, which routes the game messages from one player to the other.

Figure 6-1 shows what the game looks like.

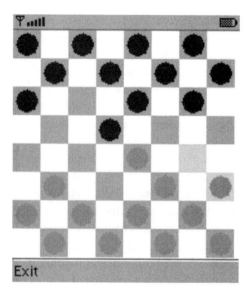

*Figure 6-1. The checkers game. In this figure, the local player is in the process of moving a piece on the right side of the screen.*

## Writing the Client Code for the Checkers Example

The checkers game itself is simple. The interesting part is the interaction between the client and the server. All of the interaction on the client side is done by the class Communicator, which extends Thread just like the BoardReader class from the previous example.

Once the Communicator thread starts, the first thing it does is attempt to contact the server. It first sets a message on the Canvas to warn the user that this may take some time because the connection itself may take a few seconds, and after that the local player will have to wait for another player to either join the game or make a move. Then it opens the Connection and the corresponding input and output streams.

Throughout the game, the client and server send each other data in 4-byte segments. This data consists of either the coordinate information for how to move a game piece (2 bytes for the original coordinates of the piece to move and 2 bytes for the destination) or a flag that gives a message such as "game over" or "end turn." If the data consists of a message flag, the flag itself is contained in the first byte of the four, but I always send 4 bytes anyway since neither side knows in advance whether it'll receive a move or just a simple message. It'd be possible to write the program in such a way that 4 bytes are sent when the data contains a move and only 1 byte is sent when it's just a message flag. In that case, the client could read the first byte and then read three more only if the byte isn't a message flag. (It's easy to tell them apart since the coordinates of a move are always positive, and looking at the static fields section in Listing 6-4 you'll notice that my message flags are all negative.) But as I mentioned previously, keeping the client and server aligned in terms of interpreting the data on a socket is already difficult. In this case, the savings in data transmission that would be gained by shortening some of the messages is outweighed by the confusion that would be created by allowing variable-length transmissions. It's better to keep the code and data clear and simple than try to do something complex and fancy for such a small savings. That said, it is of course also important in general to minimize the size of the messages sent from and received by a small device. Choosing how to encode the data sent along a socket is probably the hardest part of socket programming for a small device because of the delicate balance between efficiency and simplicity.

The run() method is unfortunately a little long, so it's easy to lose track of what's happening. It has two main parts: the initial exchange and then the loop that handles all subsequent data exchanges. The initial exchange starts with the client reading 4 bytes from the server just to make sure everything is in order. Then the client waits for a message indicating what the other player is going to do. The readFully() method causes the Communicator thread to block until the message from the other player arrives. The message will be a move from the other player (in the case where the other player had contacted the server first), or the message will be a message flag to signal the local player to make the first move (in the case where the local player contacted the server first). This initial exchange happens outside the main loop because the client doesn't know in advance which of the two players will get to go first. If the connection between the client and server is somehow cut off before the client reads the bytes it wants from the stream, the method readFully() will throw an Exception. Also, I have the client code itself throw an exception in the case where the message is a flag signaling that the game is over. (The "game over" flag is sent at this point only if another player had joined the game but has disconnected before the local player could make a move.) Either one of these Exceptions will be caught by the catch block in the middle of the method, which gives the user an error message and then ends the game.

After the initial exchange has ended, the run() method enters its main loop. The first thing that the Communicator does on entering the main loop is wait. In this case, the thread is waiting for the local player to make a move. A different thread handles keystrokes, so this thread waits until the other thread sets the keystroke information by calling one of the command-related methods of the Communicator class: endGame(), endTurn(), or move(). All three of these methods end by notifying the Communicator thread to stop waiting and act on the user's command. Since the user could press Exit at any time, I check the myShouldStop field after every call to wait() to see if I should break out of the loop and end the game. (If you break out of the loop, you can see further down that the result is that, in the finally block, the program will send the "game over" flag to notify the server that the local user is quitting, and then the connection and corresponding streams are closed.) Once the user has made a move, the Communicator sends the move data to the server, which passes the data along to the other player.

The next step after sending the move data is to allow the possibility that the local user may move again before the end of the turn. This can happen in a game of checkers if the player has the opportunity to make a double (or triple, and so on) jump. Looking over this example game, you'll notice that almost all of the complexity arises because of the possibility of multiple jumps. It's because the local player may make multiple jumps that the Communicator class needs a separate endTurn() method instead of just having the turn end as soon as the user is done making a move. It's also because of the possibility of multiple jumps that it was necessary to create the END_TURN_FLAG message flag to indicate that the player is done.

Once the local player is done making a move and the program has sent the end turn flag, the opponent's turn starts. Again the Communicator thread waits while the player is selecting the move to make, but this time instead of using the wait() method, the thread blocks on the readFully() method waiting for the server to send the opponent's move. (At this point a really professional game may display a message or even a little animation to indicate to the local player that the remote player is thinking about what move to make.) When the message arrives, the program reads in all the move data and moves the opponent's piece accordingly. After verifying that the game hasn't ended, the Communicator ends this pass through the loop by prompting the Canvas to repaint itself (showing where the opponent's piece has moved to), and then the loop begins again.

Listing 6-4 shows the code for Communicator.java.

*Listing 6-4.* Communicator.java

```
package net.frog_parrot.checkers;

import java.io.*;
import javax.microedition.io.*;
import javax.microedition.lcdui.*;
import javax.microedition.rms.*;

import net.frog_parrot.util.DataConverter;

/**
 * This class contacts a remote server in order to
 * play a game of checkers against an opponent.
 *
 * @author Carol Hamer
 */
public class Communicator extends Thread {

  //-----------------------------------------------------------
  //  static fields
```

```java
/**
 * This is the URL to contact.
 * IMPORTANT: before compiling, the following URL
 * must be changed to the correct URL of the
 * machine running the server code.
 */
public static final String SERVER_URL
  = "socket://frog-parrot.net:8007";

/**
 * The int to signal that the game is to begin.
 */
public static final byte START_GAME_FLAG = -4;

/**
 * The byte to signal that the game is to end.
 */
public static final byte END_GAME_FLAG = -3;

/**
 * The byte to signal the end of a turn.
 */
public static final byte END_TURN_FLAG = -2;

//---------------------------------------------------------
//  game instance fields

/**
 * The MIDlet subclass, used to set the Display
 * in the case where an error message needs to be sent.
 */
private Checkers myCheckers;

/**
 * The Canvas subclass, used to set the Display
 * in the case where an error message needs to be sent.
 */
private CheckersCanvas myCanvas;

/**
 * The game logic class that you send the opponent's
 * moves to.
 */
private CheckersGame myGame;
```

```java
/**
 * Whether the MIDlet class has requested the
 * game to end.
 */
private boolean myShouldStop;

//----------------------------------------------------------
//   data exchange instance fields

/**
 * The data from the local player that is to
 * be sent to the opponent.
 */
private byte[] myMove;

/**
 * Whether the current turn is done and
 * should be sent.
 */
private boolean myTurnIsDone = true;

//----------------------------------------------------------
//   initialization

/**
 * Constructor is used only when the program wants
 * to spawn a data-fetching thread, not for merely
 * reading local data with static methods.
 */
Communicator(Checkers checkers, CheckersCanvas canvas,
             CheckersGame game) {
  myCheckers = checkers;
  myCanvas = canvas;
  myGame = game;
}

//----------------------------------------------------------
//   methods called by CheckersGame to send move
//      information to the opponent.

/**
 * Stop the game entirely.  Notify the servlet that
 * the user is exiting the game.
 */
```

```
synchronized void endGame() {
  myShouldStop = true;
  if(myGame != null) {
    myGame.setGameOver();
  }
  notify();
}


/**
 * This is called when the player moves a piece.
 */
synchronized void move(byte sourceX, byte sourceY, byte destinationX,
                  byte destinationY) {
  myMove = new byte[4];
  myMove[0] = sourceX;
  myMove[1] = sourceY;
  myMove[2] = destinationX;
  myMove[3] = destinationY;
  myTurnIsDone = false;
  notify();
}


/**
 * This is called when the local player's turn is over.
 */
synchronized void endTurn() {
  myTurnIsDone = true;
  notify();
}


//---------------------------------------------------------
//  main communication method

/**
 * Makes a connection to the server and sends and receives
 * information about moves.
 */
public void run() {
  DataInputStream dis = null;
  DataOutputStream dos = null;
  SocketConnection conn = null;
  byte[] fourBytes = new byte[4];
  try {
    // tell the user the game waiting for the other player to join:
    myCanvas.setWaitScreen(true);
```

```
    myCanvas.repaint();
    myCanvas.serviceRepaints();
    // now make the connection:
    conn = (SocketConnection)Connector.open(SERVER_URL);
    conn.setSocketOption(SocketConnection.KEEPALIVE, 1);
    dos = conn.openDataOutputStream();
    dis = conn.openDataInputStream();
    // you read 4 bytes to make sure the connection works.
    dis.readFully(fourBytes);
    if(fourBytes[0] != START_GAME_FLAG) {
      throw(new Exception("server-side error"));
    }
    // On this line it will block waiting for another
    // player to join the game or make a move:
    dis.readFully(fourBytes);
    // if the server sends the start game flag again,
    // that means you start with the local player's turn.
    // Otherwise, you read the other player's first move from the
    // stream:
    if(fourBytes[0] != START_GAME_FLAG) {
      // verify that the other player sent a move
      // and not just a message ending the game.
      if(fourBytes[0] == END_GAME_FLAG) {
        throw(new Exception("other player quit"));
      }
      // you move the opponent on the local screen.
      // then you read from the opponent again,
      // in case there's a double-jump:
      while(fourBytes[0] != END_TURN_FLAG) {
        myGame.moveOpponent(fourBytes);
        dis.readFully(fourBytes);
      }
    }
    // now signal the local game that the opponent is done
    // so the board must be updated and the local player
    // prompted to make a move:
    myGame.endOpponentTurn();
    myCanvas.setWaitScreen(false);
    myCanvas.repaint();
    myCanvas.serviceRepaints();
    // begin main game loop:
    while(! myShouldStop) {
      // now it's the local player's turn.
      // wait for the player to move a piece:
```

```
synchronized(this) {
  wait();
}
// after every wait, you check if the game
// ended while you were waiting...
if(myShouldStop) {
  break;
}
while(! myTurnIsDone) {
  // send the current move:
  if(myMove != null) {
    dos.write(myMove, 0, myMove.length);
    myMove = null;
  }
  // If the player can continue the move with a double
  // jump, you wait for the player to do it:
  synchronized(this) {
    // make sure the turn isn't done before you start waiting
    // (the end turn notify might accidentally be called
    // before you start waiting...)
    if(! myTurnIsDone) {
      wait();
    }
  }
}
// after every wait, you check if the game
// ended while you were waiting...
if(myShouldStop) {
  break;
}
// now you tell the other player that this player's
// turn is over:
fourBytes[0] = END_TURN_FLAG;
dos.write(fourBytes, 0, fourBytes.length);
// now that you've sent the move, you wait for a response:
dis.readFully(fourBytes);
while((fourBytes[0] != END_TURN_FLAG) &&
      (fourBytes[0] != END_GAME_FLAG) && (!myShouldStop)) {
  // you move the opponent on the local screen.
  // then you read from the opponent again,
  // in case there's a double jump:
  myGame.moveOpponent(fourBytes);
  dis.readFully(fourBytes);
}
```

```
        // if the other player has left the game, you tell the
        // local user that the game is over.
        if((fourBytes[0] == END_GAME_FLAG) || (myShouldStop)) {
          endGame();
          break;
        }
        myGame.endOpponentTurn();
        myCanvas.repaint();
        myCanvas.serviceRepaints();
      } // end while loop
    } catch(Exception e) {
      // if there's an error, you display its messsage and
      // end the game.
      myCheckers.errorMsg(e.getMessage());
    } finally {
      // now you send the information that you're leaving the game,
      // then close up and delete everything.
      try {
        if(dos != null) {
          dos.write(END_GAME_FLAG);
          dos.close();
        }
        if(dis != null) {
          dis.close();
        }
        if(conn != null) {
          conn.close();
        }
        dis = null;
        dos = null;
        conn = null;
      } catch(Exception e) {
        // if this throws, at least you made your best effort
        // to close everything up.
      }
    }
    // one last paint job to display the "Game Over"
    myCanvas.repaint();
    myCanvas.serviceRepaints();
  }

}
```

Now you'll look at the logic behind the game, which is implemented in the CheckersGame class. Nothing in this class is specifically MIDP related. This class could easily be used to keep track of all the pieces on a checkerboard for a checkers game written for J2SE and/or a game in which the opponent is the computer (in the form of some additional class) rather than having a remote opponent.

One important consideration I had to think about before writing this code was how the user interface would work. More precisely, how will the player decide which piece to move and where to move it? There's no one correct answer to this question, but I came up with a relatively intuitive system. In the beginning of the turn (triggered by the method endOpponentTurn()), the program finds a square that contains one of the player's pieces that's capable of making a move and marks the square as selected. Then, by pressing the left and right keys, the user can select a different square. The methods rightPressed() and leftPressed() find the next square to the left (or respectively to the right) that contains one of the local player's pieces that has possible moves to make. Once the user has finalized the choice of which piece to move, he presses the up key. As soon as the up key is pressed, then the next thing to select is the destination square. Choosing the destination square works in the same way. One of the possible moves starts out appearing selected, and the user moves the selection frame through the list of possible moves by using the right and left keys. To finalize the selection of the destination square, the user presses the up key again. If the user selects a piece to move but then changes his mind before choosing a destination square, he can deselect the piece to move by pressing the down key. It sounds rather complicated when I write it out in words, but in practice the system is simple to use. Behind the scenes, the square selection algorithm required quite a number of methods working together. The methods leftPressed, rightPressed, upPressed, deselect, fixSelection, selectNext, and selectPrevious, as well as some of the internal utilities, all work together just to allow the user to choose a move.

A few additional points in the game of checkers required a little extra thought. The first one was that the game is played only on the dark squares. So even though a checkerboard is an 8×8 square, if you look only at the dark squares, it ends up being eight rows of four columns each. (That's why in the code after the value of X_LENGTH is 4, and the value of Y_LENGTH is 8.) But if you represent it that way, the columns aren't really lined up. Which other squares you can move a given piece to depends on whether the piece is on an even row or an odd row. That's why I needed to write some rather complicated methods near the bottom (getCornerCoordinates() and getMoves()) to figure out all of the possible moves for each piece.

Another point that required some extra effort was dealing with the fact that usually a player can move only once, but if the player jumps, he may be allowed to jump again, possibly multiple times. Dealing with a turn consisting of multiple moves is what motivated a large portion of the code. Most of the move() method is devoted to dealing with what happens when the player can jump again, and as I mentioned in the discussion of the Communicator class, double jumps are what made me create separate functions to end the players' turns rather than just having the turn end as soon as the player has moved.

Aside from the points mentioned, the workings of the CheckersGame are straightforward. The class has a two-dimensional array myGrid that keeps track of where all the pieces are on the checkerboard. The remote player can update this internal set of data through the Communicator calling the methods moveOpponent() and endOpponentTurn(). And the local player can also update the data (taking turns correctly, of course!) by pressing keys to select moves to make.

Listing 6-5 shows the code for CheckersGame.java.

*Listing 6-5.* CheckersGame.java

```java
package net.frog_parrot.checkers;

import java.util.Vector;

/**
 * This class takes care of the underlying logic and data of
 * the checkers game being played. That includes where
 * all of the pieces are on the board and where it is okay
 * for them to move to.
 *
 * @author Carol Hamer
 */
public class CheckersGame {

  //----------------------------------------------------------
  //    static fields

  /**
   * The length of the checkerboard in the X direction.
   */
  public static final byte X_LENGTH = 4;

  /**
   * The length of the checkerboard in the Y direction.
   */
  public static final byte Y_LENGTH = 8;

  //----------------------------------------------------------
  //    instance fields

  /**
   * a handle to the communications class that exchanges
   * data with the server.
   */
  private Communicator myCommunicator;
```

```
/**
 * This array represents the black squares of the
 * checkerboard. The two dimensions of the array
 * represent the two dimensions of the checkerboard.
 * The value represents what type of piece is on
 * the square.
 * 0 = empty
 * 1 = local player's piece
 * 2 = local player's king
 * -1 = remote player's piece
 * -2 = remote player's king
 */
private byte[][] myGrid;

/**
 * If the user has currently selected a piece to move,
 * this is its X grid coordinate. (-1 if none selected)
 */
private byte mySelectedX = -1;

/**
 * If the user has currently selected a piece to move,
 * this is its Y grid coordinate. (-1 if none selected)
 */
private byte mySelectedY = -1;

/**
 * If the user has currently selected a possible
 * destination square for a move, this is its X coordinate.
 * (-1 if none selected)
 */
private byte myDestinationX = -1;

/**
 * If the user has currently selected a possible
 * destination square for a move, this is its Y coordinate.
 * (-1 if none selected)
 */
private byte myDestinationY = -1;

/**
 * This Vector contains the coordinates of all of the
 * squares that the player could currently move to.
 */
private Vector myPossibleMoves = new Vector(4);
```

```
/**
 * Whether the currently displayed checkers have
 * been completed.
 */
private boolean myGameOver = false;

/**
 * Whether it is currently this player's turn.
 */
private boolean myTurn = false;

/**
 * This is true if the player has just jumped and can
 * jump again.
 */
private boolean myIsJumping = false;

//----------------------------------------------------------
//   get/set data

/**
 * get the piece on the given grid square.
 */
byte getPiece(byte x, byte y) {
  return(myGrid[x][y]);
}

/**
 * This is called by CheckersCanvas to determine if
 * the square is currently selected (as containing
 * a piece to move or a destination square).
 */
boolean isSelected(byte x, byte y) {
  boolean retVal = false;
  if((x == mySelectedX) && (y == mySelectedY)) {
    retVal = true;
  } else if((x == myDestinationX) && (y == myDestinationY)) {
    retVal = true;
  }
  return(retVal);
}

/**
 * This tells whether the keystrokes should currently
 * be taken into account.
```

```
   */
  boolean isMyTurn() {
    boolean retVal = false;
    if((!myGameOver) && ((myTurn) || (myIsJumping))) {
      retVal = true;
    }
    return(retVal);
  }


  /**
   * This tells whether the game has ended.
   */
  boolean getGameOver () {
    return(myGameOver);
  }


  /**
   * tell the CheckersGame that the other player has ended the game.
   */
  void setGameOver() {
    myGameOver = true;
  }


  /**
   * set the communicator object.
   */
  void setCommunicator(Communicator comm) {
    myCommunicator = comm;
  }


  //---------------------------------------------------------
  //   initialization

  /**
   * Constructor puts the pieces in their initial positions:
   */
  CheckersGame() {
    myGrid = new byte[X_LENGTH][];
    for(byte i = 0; i < myGrid.length; i++) {
      myGrid[i] = new byte[Y_LENGTH];
      for(byte j = 0; j < myGrid[i].length; j++) {
        if(j < 3) {
          // fill the top of the board with remote players
          myGrid[i][j] = -1;
```

```
      } else if(j > 4) {
        // fill the bottom of the board with local players
        myGrid[i][j] = 1;
      }
    }
  }
}


/**
 * This is called just before the player makes the
 * first move.
 */
void start() {
  mySelectedX = 0;
  mySelectedY = 5;
  myTurn = true;
  getMoves(mySelectedX, mySelectedY, myPossibleMoves, false);
}


//-----------------------------------------------------------
//    move the opponent
// to be called by Communicator

/**
 * This is called when the opponent wants to move
 * its piece.
 * @param moveData an array of four bytes:
 * moveData[0] = opponent's initial X coordinate
 * moveData[1] = opponent's initial Y coordinate
 * moveData[2] = opponent's destination X coordinate
 * moveData[3] = opponent's destination Y coordinate
 */
void moveOpponent(byte[] moveData) {
  // since both players appear on their own screens
  // as the red side (bottom of the screen), you need
  // to invert the opponent's move:
  moveData[0] = (new Integer(X_LENGTH - moveData[0] - 1)).byteValue();
  moveData[2] = (new Integer(X_LENGTH - moveData[2] - 1)).byteValue();
  moveData[1] = (new Integer(Y_LENGTH - moveData[1] - 1)).byteValue();
  moveData[3] = (new Integer(Y_LENGTH - moveData[3] - 1)).byteValue();
  myGrid[moveData[2]][moveData[3]]
    = myGrid[moveData[0]][moveData[1]];
  myGrid[moveData[0]][moveData[1]] = 0;
  // deal with an opponent's jump:
```

```
            if((moveData[1] - moveData[3] > 1) ||
               (moveData[3] - moveData[1] > 1)) {
              int jumpedY = (moveData[1] + moveData[3])/2;
              int jumpedX = moveData[0];
              int parity = moveData[1] % 2;
              if((parity > 0) && (moveData[2] > moveData[0])) {
                jumpedX++;
              } else if((parity == 0) && (moveData[0] > moveData[2])) {
                jumpedX--;
              }
              myGrid[jumpedX][jumpedY] = 0;
            }
            // if the opponent reaches the far side,
            // make him a king:
            if(moveData[3] == Y_LENGTH - 1) {
              myGrid[moveData[2]][moveData[3]] = -2;
            }
          }


  /**
   * This is called when the opponent's turn is over.
   * Note that the turn doesn't automatically end after
   * the opponent moves because the opponent may make
   * a double or triple jump.
   */
  void endOpponentTurn() {
    myTurn = true;
    // Now begin the local player's turn:
    // First select the first local piece that can be
    // moved. (rightPressed will select an appropriate
    // piece or end the game if the local player has
    // no possible moves to make)
    mySelectedX = 0;
    mySelectedY = 0;
    myDestinationX = -1;
    myDestinationY = -1;
    rightPressed();
    // the local player's thread has been waiting
    // for the opponent's turn to end.
    synchronized(this) {
      notify();
    }
  }
```

```
//-----------------------------------------------------------
//    handle keystrokes
// to be called by CheckersCanvas


/**
 * if the left button is pressed, this method takes
 * the correct course of action depending on the situation.
 */
void leftPressed() {
  // in the first case the user has not yet selected a
  // piece to move:
  if(myDestinationX == -1) {
    // find the next possible piece (to the left)
    // that can move:
    selectPrevious();
    // if selectPrevious fails to fill myPossibleMoves, that
    // means that the local player cannot move, so the game
    // is over:
    if(myPossibleMoves.size() == 0) {
      myCommunicator.endGame();
    }
  } else {
    // if the user has already selected a piece to move,
    // you give the options of where the piece can move to:
    for(byte i = 0; i < myPossibleMoves.size(); i++) {
      byte[] coordinates = (byte[])myPossibleMoves.elementAt(i);
      if((coordinates[0] == myDestinationX) &&
        (coordinates[1] == myDestinationY)) {
        i++;
        i = (new Integer(i % myPossibleMoves.size())).byteValue();
        coordinates = (byte[])myPossibleMoves.elementAt(i);
        myDestinationX = coordinates[0];
        myDestinationY = coordinates[1];
        break;
      }
    }
  }
}

/**
 * if the right button is pressed, this method takes
 * the correct course of action depending on the situation.
 */
void rightPressed() {
```

```
      // in the first case the user has not yet selected a
      // piece to move:
      if(myDestinationX == -1) {
        // find the next possible piece that can
        // move:
        selectNext();
        // if selectNext fails to fill myPossibleMoves, that
        // means that the local player cannot move, so the game
        // is over:
        if(myPossibleMoves.size() == 0) {
          myCommunicator.endGame();
        }
      } else {
        // if the user has already selected a piece to move,
        // you give the options of where the piece can move to:
        for(byte i = 0; i < myPossibleMoves.size(); i++) {
          byte[] coordinates = (byte[])myPossibleMoves.elementAt(i);
          if((coordinates[0] == myDestinationX) &&
             (coordinates[1] == myDestinationY)) {
            i++;
            i = (new Integer(i % myPossibleMoves.size())).byteValue();
            coordinates = (byte[])myPossibleMoves.elementAt(i);
            myDestinationX = coordinates[0];
            myDestinationY = coordinates[1];
            break;
          }
        }
      }
    }

  /**
   * If no piece is selected, you select one. If a piece
   * is selected, you move it.
   */
  void upPressed() {
    // in the first case the user has not yet selected a
    // piece to move:
    if(myDestinationX == -1) {
      fixSelection();
    } else {
      // if the source square and destination square
      // have been chosen, you move the piece:
      move();
    }
  }
```

```
/**
 * If the user decided not to move the selected piece
 * (and instead wants to select again), this undoes
 * the selection. This corresponds to pressing the
 * DOWN key.
 */
void deselect() {
  // if the player has just completed a jump and
  // could possibly jump again but decides not to
  // (i.e. deselects), then the turn ends:
  if(myIsJumping) {
    mySelectedX = -1;
    mySelectedY = -1;
    myDestinationX = -1;
    myDestinationY = -1;
    myIsJumping = false;
    myTurn = false;
    myCommunicator.endTurn();
  } else {
    // setting the destination coordinates to -1
    // is the signal that the the choice of which
    // piece to move can be modified:
    myDestinationX = -1;
    myDestinationY = -1;
  }
}


//-----------------------------------------------------------
//    internal square selection methods

/**
 * When the player has decided that the currently selected
 * square contains the piece he really wants to move, this
 * is called. This method switches to the mode where
 * the player selects the destination square of the move.
 */
private void fixSelection() {
  byte[] destination = (byte[])myPossibleMoves.elementAt(0);
  // setting the destination coordinates to valid
  // coordinates is the signal that the user is done
  // selecting the piece to move and now is choosing
  // the destination square:
  myDestinationX = destination[0];
  myDestinationY = destination[1];
}
```

```
/**
 * This method starts from the currently selected square
 * and finds the next square that contains a piece that
 * the player can move.
 */
private void selectNext() {
  // Test the squares one by one (starting from the
  // currently selected square) until you find a square
  // that contains one of the local player's pieces
  // that can move:
  byte testX = mySelectedX;
  byte testY = mySelectedY;
  while(true) {
    testX++;
    if(testX >= X_LENGTH) {
      testX = 0;
      testY++;
      testY = (new Integer(testY % Y_LENGTH)).byteValue();
    }
    getMoves(testX, testY, myPossibleMoves, false);
    if((myPossibleMoves.size() != 0) ||
        ((testX == mySelectedX) && (testY == mySelectedY))) {
      mySelectedX = testX;
      mySelectedY = testY;
      break;
    }
  }
}

/**
 * This method starts from the currently selected square
 * and finds the next square (to the left) that contains
 * a piece that the player can move.
 */
private void selectPrevious() {
  // Test the squares one by one (starting from the
  // currently selected square) until you find a square
  // that contains one of the local player's pieces
  // that can move:
  byte testX = mySelectedX;
  byte testY = mySelectedY;
  while(true) {
    testX--;
```

```
      if(testX < 0) {
        testX += X_LENGTH;
        testY--;
        if(testY < 0) {
          testY += Y_LENGTH;
        }
      }
      getMoves(testX, testY, myPossibleMoves, false);
      if((myPossibleMoves.size() != 0) ||
         ((testX == mySelectedX) && (testY == mySelectedY))) {
        mySelectedX = testX;
        mySelectedY = testY;
        break;
      }
    }
  }
}


//----------------------------------------------------------
//   internal utilities

/**
 * Once the user has selected the move to make, this
 * updates the data accordingly.
 */
private void move() {
  // the piece that was on the source square is
  // now on the destination square:
  myGrid[myDestinationX][myDestinationY]
    = myGrid[mySelectedX][mySelectedY];
  // the source square is emptied:
  myGrid[mySelectedX][mySelectedY] = 0;
  if(myDestinationY == 0) {
    myGrid[myDestinationX][myDestinationY] = 2;
  }
  // tell the communicator to inform the other player
  // of this move:
  myCommunicator.move(mySelectedX, mySelectedY,
                      myDestinationX, myDestinationY);
  // deal with the special rules for jumps::
  if((mySelectedY - myDestinationY > 1) ||
     (myDestinationY - mySelectedY > 1)) {
    int jumpedY = (mySelectedY + myDestinationY)/2;
    int jumpedX = mySelectedX;
```

```
        int parity = mySelectedY % 2;
        // the coordinates of the jumped square depend on
        // what row you're in:
        if((parity > 0) && (myDestinationX > mySelectedX)) {
          jumpedX++;
        } else if((parity == 0) && (mySelectedX > myDestinationX)) {
          jumpedX--;
        }
        // remove the piece that was jumped over:
        myGrid[jumpedX][jumpedY] = 0;
        // now get ready to jump again if possible:
        mySelectedX = myDestinationX;
        mySelectedY = myDestinationY;
        myDestinationX = -1;
        myDestinationY = -1;
        // see if another jump is possible.
        // The "true" argument tells the program to return
        // only jumps because the player can go again ONLY
        // if there's a jump:
        getMoves(mySelectedX, mySelectedY, myPossibleMoves, true);
        // if there's another jump possible with the same piece,
        // allow the player to continue jumping:
        if(myPossibleMoves.size() != 0) {
          myIsJumping = true;
          byte[] landing = (byte[])myPossibleMoves.elementAt(0);
          myDestinationX = landing[0];
          myDestinationY = landing[1];
        } else {
          myTurn = false;
          myCommunicator.endTurn();
        }
      } else {
        // since it's not a jump, you just end the turn
        // by deselecting everything.
        mySelectedX = -1;
        mySelectedY = -1;
        myDestinationX = -1;
        myDestinationY = -1;
        myPossibleMoves.removeAllElements();
        myTurn = false;
        // tell the other player you're done:
        myCommunicator.endTurn();
      }
    }
  }
```

```
/**
 * Given a square on the grid, get the coordinates
 * of one of the adjoining (diagonal) squares.
 * 0 = top left
 * 1 = top right
 * 2 = bottom left
 * 3 = bottom right.
 * @return the coordinates or null if the desired corner
 * is off the board.
 */
private byte[] getCornerCoordinates(byte x, byte y, byte corner) {
  byte[] retArray = null;
  if(corner < 2) {
    y--;
  } else {
    y++;
  }
  // Where the corner is on the grid depends on
  // whether this is an odd row or an even row:
  if((corner % 2 == 0) && (y % 2 != 0)) {
    x--;
  } else if((corner % 2 != 0) && (y % 2 == 0)) {
    x++;
  }
  try {
    if(myGrid[x][y] > -15) {
      // you don't really care about the value; this
      // if statement is just there to get it to
      // throw if the coordinates aren't on the board.
      retArray = new byte[2];
      retArray[0] = x;
      retArray[1] = y;
    }
  } catch(ArrayIndexOutOfBoundsException e) {
    // this throws if the coordinates do not correspond
    // to a square on the board. It's not a problem,
    // so you do nothing--you just return null instead
    // of returning coordinates since no valid
    // coordinates correspond to the desired corner.
  }
  return(retArray);
}
```

```java
/**
 * Determines where the piece in the given
 * grid location can move. Clears the Vector
 * and fills it with the locations that
 * the piece can move to.
 * @param jumpsOnly if you should return only moves that
 *          are jumps.
 */
private void getMoves(byte x, byte y, Vector toFill, boolean jumpsOnly) {
  toFill.removeAllElements();
  // if the square does not contain one of the local player's
  // pieces, then there are no corresponding moves and you just
  // return an empty vector.
  if(myGrid[x][y] <= 0) {
    return;
  }
  // check each of the four corners to see if the
  // piece can move there:
  for(byte i = 0; i < 4; i++) {
    byte[] coordinates = getCornerCoordinates(x, y, i);
    // if the coordinate array is null, then the corresponding
    // corner is off the board and you don't deal with it.
    // The later two conditions in the following if statement
    // ensure that either the move is a forward move or the
    // current piece is a king:
    if((coordinates != null) &&
        ((myGrid[x][y] > 1) || (i < 2))) {
      // if the corner is empty (and you're not looking
      // for just jumps), then this is a possible move
      // so you add it to the vector of moves:
      if((myGrid[coordinates[0]][coordinates[1]] == 0) && (! jumpsOnly)) {
        toFill.addElement(coordinates);
        // if the space is occupied by an opponent, see if you can jump it:
      } else if(myGrid[coordinates[0]][coordinates[1]] < 0) {
        byte[] jumpLanding = getCornerCoordinates(coordinates[0],
                                                  coordinates[1], i);
        // if the space on the far side of the opponent's piece
        // is on the board and is unoccupied, then a jump
        // is possible, so you add it to the vector of moves:
        if((jumpLanding != null) &&
            (myGrid[jumpLanding[0]][jumpLanding[1]] == 0)) {
          toFill.addElement(jumpLanding);
        }
      }
    }
```

```
      }
    } // end for loop
  }


}
```

The CheckersCanvas class is a standard application of the Canvas class (see the "Using the Graphics and Canvas Classes" section in Chapter 2 for details about how you use the Canvas class). For this game, I didn't even bother to use GameCanvas since the graphics are simple, and I don't need to synchronize the keystroke queries with any game animations.

The part that's unique to the checkers game is in the paint() method. You can see that there are two possibilities: Either it just writes a message and returns or it paints the whole checkerboard. To make it a little easier on the eyes, I made the checkerboard gray and white, rather than red and black, and then made the pieces themselves red and black. (I made a point to verify that the color scheme looks OK on a grayscale screen.) Then whichever square is currently selected is painted a slightly lighter shade of gray than the other dark squares. The only point that may require some explanation is the use of the local variable offset. This variable keeps track of the fact that in every other row of the grid the set of dark squares shifts over one square. So, when painting the grid, you first determine whether you're in an even row or an odd row and (keeping track of it in offset) to determine which four squares should be colored of the eight squares in the row.

Also notice that I always have the local player be the red pieces that start on the bottom half of the screen. So when you're playing, it'll look to you like you moved a red piece, but on your opponent's cell phone it'll appear that you moved one of the black pieces. I can get away with this since the board is symmetric.

Listing 6-6 shows the code for CheckersCanvas.java.

*Listing 6-6.* CheckersCanvas.java

```
package net.frog_parrot.checkers;

import javax.microedition.lcdui.*;

/**
 * This class is the display of the game.
 *
 * @author Carol Hamer
 */
public class CheckersCanvas extends Canvas {

  //-----------------------------------------------------------
  //    static fields
```

```java
/**
 * color constant
 */
public static final int BLACK = 0;

/**
 * color constant
 */
public static final int WHITE = 0xffffff;

/**
 * color constant.
 * (not quite bright red)
 */
public static final int RED = 0xf96868;

/**
 * color constant
 */
public static final int GREY = 0xc6c6c6;

/**
 * color constant
 */
public static final int LT_GREY = 0xe5e3e3;

/**
 * how many rows and columns the display is divided into.
 */
public static final int GRID_WIDTH = 8;

//----------------------------------------------------------
//    instance fields

/**
 * The black crown to draw on the red pieces.
 */
private Image myBlackCrown;

/**
 * The red crown to draw on the black pieces.
 */
private Image myWhiteCrown;
```

```
/**
 * a handle to the display.
 */
private Display myDisplay;

/**
 * a handle to the object that stores the game logic
 * and game data.
 */
private CheckersGame myGame;

/**
 * checkers dimension: the width of the squares of the checkerboard.
 */
private int mySquareSize;

/**
 * checkers dimension: the minimum width possible for the
 * checkerboard squares.
 */
private int myMinSquareSize = 15;

/**
 * whether you're waiting for another player to join
 * the game.
 */
private boolean myIsWaiting;

//----------------------------------------------------------
//     gets / sets

/**
 * @return a handle to the class that holds the logic of the
 * checkers game.
 */
CheckersGame getGame() {
  return(myGame);
}

/**
 * Display a screen to inform the player that you're
 * waiting for another player.
 */
void setWaitScreen(boolean wait) {
```

```
  myIsWaiting = wait;
}


//-------------------------------------------------------
//    initialization and game state changes

/**
 * Constructor performs size calculations.
 * @throws Exception if the display size is too
 *            small to make a checkers.
 */
CheckersCanvas(Display d) throws Exception {
  myDisplay = d;
  myGame = new CheckersGame();
  // a few calculations to make the right checkerboard
  // for the current display.
  int width = getWidth();
  int height = getHeight();
  // get the smaller dimension of the two possible
  // screen dimensions in order to determine how
  // big to make the checkerboard.
  int screenSquareWidth = height;
  if(width < height) {
    screenSquareWidth = width;
  }
  mySquareSize = screenSquareWidth / GRID_WIDTH;
  // if the display is too small to make a reasonable checkerboard,
  // then you throw an Exception
  if(mySquareSize < myMinSquareSize) {
    throw(new Exception("Display too small"));
  }
  // initialize the crown images:
  myBlackCrown = Image.createImage("/images/blackCrown.png");
  myWhiteCrown = Image.createImage("/images/whiteCrown.png");
}

/**
 * This is called as soon as the application begins.
 */
void start() {
  myDisplay.setCurrent(this);
  // prepare the game data for the first move:
  myGame.start();
}
```

```
//---------------------------------------------------------
//  graphics methods

/**
 * Repaint the checkerboard.
 */
protected void paint(Graphics g) {
  int width = getWidth();
  int height = getHeight();
  g.setColor(WHITE);
  // clear the board (including the region around
  // the board, which can get menu stuff and other
  // garbage painted onto it...)
  g.fillRect(0, 0, width, height);
  // If you need to wait for another player to join the
  // game before you can start, this displays the appropriate
  // message:
  if(myIsWaiting) {
    // perform some calculations to place the text correctly:
    Font font = g.getFont();
    int fontHeight = font.getHeight();
    int fontWidth = font.stringWidth("waiting for another player");
    g.setColor(WHITE);
    g.fillRect((width - fontWidth)/2, (height - fontHeight)/2,
                       fontWidth + 2, fontHeight);
    // write in black
    g.setColor(BLACK);
    g.setFont(font);
    g.drawString("waiting for another player", (width - fontWidth)/2,
                 (height - fontHeight)/2,
                       g.TOP|g.LEFT);
    return;
  }
  // now draw the checkerboard:
  // first the black squares:
  byte offset = 0;
  for(byte i = 0; i < 4; i++) {
    for(byte j = 0; j < 8; j++) {
      if(j % 2 != 0) {
        offset = 1;
      } else {
        offset = 0;
      }
      // now if this is a selected square, you draw it lighter:
```

```
        if(myGame.isSelected(i, j)) {
          g.setColor(LT_GREY);
          g.fillRect((2*i + offset)*mySquareSize, j*mySquareSize,
                      mySquareSize, mySquareSize);
        } else {
          g.setColor(GREY);
          g.fillRect((2*i + offset)*mySquareSize, j*mySquareSize,
                      mySquareSize, mySquareSize);
        }
        // now put the pieces in their places:
        g.setColor(RED);
        int piece = myGame.getPiece(i, j);
        int circleOffset = 2;
        int circleSize = mySquareSize - 2*circleOffset;
        if(piece < 0) {
          // color the piece in black
          g.setColor(BLACK);
          g.fillRoundRect((2*i + offset)*mySquareSize + circleOffset,
                          j*mySquareSize + circleOffset,
                    circleSize, circleSize, circleSize, circleSize);
          // if the player is a king, draw a crown on:
          if(piece < -1) {
            g.drawImage(myWhiteCrown,
                        (2*i + offset)*mySquareSize + mySquareSize/2,
                        j*mySquareSize + 1 + mySquareSize/2,
                        Graphics.VCENTER|Graphics.HCENTER);
          }
        } else if(piece > 0) {
          // color the piece in red
          g.fillRoundRect((2*i + offset)*mySquareSize + circleOffset,
                          j*mySquareSize + circleOffset,
                    circleSize, circleSize, circleSize, circleSize);
          // if the player is a king, draw a crown on:
          if(piece > 1) {
            g.drawImage(myBlackCrown,
                        (2*i + offset)*mySquareSize + mySquareSize/2,
                        j*mySquareSize + 1 + mySquareSize/2,
                        Graphics.VCENTER|Graphics.HCENTER);
          }
        }
      }
    }
    // now the blank squares:
    g.setColor(WHITE);
```

```
    for(int i = 0; i < 4; i++) {
      for(int j = 0; j < 8; j++) {
        if(j % 2 == 0) {
          offset = 1;
        } else {
          offset = 0;
        }
        g.fillRect((2*i + offset)*mySquareSize, j*mySquareSize,
                    mySquareSize, mySquareSize);
      }
    }
    // if the player has reached the end of the game,
    // you display the end message.
    if(myGame.getGameOver()) {
      // perform some calculations to place the text correctly:
      Font font = g.getFont();
      int fontHeight = font.getHeight();
      int fontWidth = font.stringWidth("Game Over");
      g.setColor(WHITE);
      g.fillRect((width - fontWidth)/2, (height - fontHeight)/2,
                     fontWidth + 2, fontHeight);
      // write in black
      g.setColor(BLACK);
      g.setFont(font);
      g.drawString("Game Over", (width - fontWidth)/2,
                    (height - fontHeight)/2,
                        g.TOP|g.LEFT);
    }
  }

//---------------------------------------------------------
//  handle keystrokes

/**
 * Move the player.
 */
public void keyPressed(int keyCode) {
  if(myGame.isMyTurn()) {
    int action = getGameAction(keyCode);
    switch (action) {
    case LEFT:
      myGame.leftPressed();
      break;
```

```
        case RIGHT:
          myGame.rightPressed();
          break;
        case UP:
          myGame.upPressed();
          break;
        case DOWN:
          myGame.deselect();
          break;
        }
        repaint();
        serviceRepaints();
      }
    }

}
```

For completeness I'm including the MIDlet subclass (called Checkers in this case), but it hardly requires comment since it's nearly identical to the MIDlet subclass in all the earlier examples.

Listing 6-7 shows the code for Checkers.java.

*Listing 6-7.* Checkers.java

```java
package net.frog_parrot.checkers;

import javax.microedition.midlet.*;
import javax.microedition.lcdui.*;

/**
 * This is the main class of the checkers game.
 *
 * @author Carol Hamer
 */
public class Checkers extends MIDlet implements CommandListener {

  //--------------------------------------------------------
  //    game object fields

  /**
   * The canvas that the checkerboard is drawn on.
   */
  private CheckersCanvas myCanvas;
```

```
/**
 * The class that makes the http connection.
 */
private Communicator myCommunicator;


//-------------------------------------------------------
//     command fields

/**
 * The button to exit the game.
 */
private Command myExitCommand = new Command("Exit", Command.EXIT, 99);


//-------------------------------------------------------
//     initialization and game state changes

/**
 * Initialize the canvas and the commands.
 */
public Checkers() {
  try {
    //create the canvas and set up the commands:
    myCanvas = new CheckersCanvas(Display.getDisplay(this));
    myCanvas.addCommand(myExitCommand);
    myCanvas.setCommandListener(this);
    CheckersGame game = myCanvas.getGame();
    myCommunicator = new Communicator(this, myCanvas, game);
    game.setCommunicator(myCommunicator);
  } catch(Exception e) {
    // if there's an error during creation, display it as an alert.
    errorMsg(e);
  }
}


//-------------------------------------------------------------------
//   implementation of MIDlet
//   these methods may be called by the application management
//   software at any time, so you always check fields for null
//   before calling methods on them.

/**
 * Start the application.
 */
```

```
public void startApp() throws MIDletStateChangeException {
  // tell the canvas to set up the game data and paint the
  // checkerboard.
  if(myCanvas != null) {
    myCanvas.start();
  }
  // tell the communicator to start its thread and make a
  // connection.
  if(myCommunicator != null) {
    myCommunicator.start();
  }
}


/**
 * Throw out the garbage.
 */
public void destroyApp(boolean unconditional)
    throws MIDletStateChangeException {
  // tell the communicator to send the end game
  // message to the other player and then disconnect:
  if(myCommunicator != null) {
    myCommunicator.endGame();
  }
  // throw the larger game objects in the garbage:
  myCommunicator = null;
  myCanvas = null;
  System.gc();
}


/**
 * Pause the game.
 * This method merely ends the game because this
 * version of the Checkers game does not support
 * reentering a game that is in play. A possible
 * improvement to the game would be to allow
 * a player to disconnect and leave a game and then
 * later return to it, using some sort of session
 * token to find the correct game in progress on
 * the server side.
 */
public void pauseApp() {
  try {
    destroyApp(false);
    notifyDestroyed();
```

```
    } catch (MIDletStateChangeException ex) {
    }
}


//------------------------------------------------------------------
//   implementation of CommandListener

/*
 * Respond to a command issued on the Canvas.
 */
public void commandAction(Command c, Displayable s) {
  if((c == myExitCommand) || (c == Alert.DISMISS_COMMAND)) {
    try {
      destroyApp(false);
      notifyDestroyed();
    } catch (MIDletStateChangeException ex) {
    }
  }
}


//--------------------------------------------------------------
//   error methods

/**
 * Converts an exception to a message and displays
 * the message.
 */
void errorMsg(Exception e) {
  e.printStackTrace();
  if(e.getMessage() == null) {
    errorMsg(e.getClass().getName());
  } else {
    errorMsg(e.getMessage());
  }
}


/**
 * Displays an error message alert if something goes wrong.
 */
void errorMsg(String msg) {
  Alert errorAlert = new Alert("error",
                                 msg, null, AlertType.ERROR);
  errorAlert.setCommandListener(this);
  errorAlert.setTimeout(Alert.FOREVER);
```

```
        Display.getDisplay(this).setCurrent(errorAlert);
    }

}
```

## Writing the Server Code for the Checkers Example

As I mentioned, the server-side code you need to write when using a plain socket is a bit more complicated than just writing a Servlet. But it's not so terrible. For this example I've tried to write a minimal server so you can see clearly what the essential points are. (One obvious place where the following code could use improvement is that instead of creating a new thread for every pair of clients, the server should arrange the threads in a thread pool. If you know a bit about server-side programming, you can probably find other optimizations you could make.)

The server for the checkers game consists of two classes: SocketListener and ServerGame. SocketListener's job is to listen for client connections and handle them. For each pair of client players, the SocketListener class creates a new instance of ServerGame, which is a thread. It passes both clients to the instance of ServerGame and then starts up the thread. Once two clients have connected and have been delegated to an instance of ServerGame, the SocketListener class has nothing more to do with those clients, so it lets go of the current instance of ServerGame and listens for further clients to start checkers games. Notice that this means one Java Virtual Machine (JVM) can handle multiple simultaneous checkers games.

The ServerGame class is simple. All it does is read in the data for the first player's move and pass it along to the second player. Then for the second player's turn, it collects up the data and passes it in the other direction. The only complexity is the use of one-byte message flags to indicate when the game is starting or ending and to indicate the end of the turn. I explained the message flags in the "Writing the Client Code for the Checkers Example" section when explaining the Communicator class. (Obviously it's important that the values of the message flags be identical in the client code and the server code.)

If you look in the SocketListener class, you'll see that I chose to have this program listen on port number 8007. I chose this number more or less at random although I put it above 8000 in keeping with my system administrator's security guidelines. You can essentially pick any port number you want as long as no other program is using the port in question, but you'll probably want to discuss the choice of port with whomever is in charge of the host machine to see if there are any restrictions. And don't forget that the port number must appear in the URL that the client uses to contact the server (see the URL in the top of the Communicator class in Listing 6-7).

Listing 6-8 shows the code for SocketListener.java.

*Listing 6-8.* SocketListener.java

```
package net.frog_parrot.server;

import java.io.*;
import java.net.*;
import java.util.Vector;

/**
 * This class is a simple example of a server that
 * can communicate with the checkers game.
 *
 * @author Carol Hamer
 */

public class SocketListener {

//----------------------------------------------------------------
//        static fields

  /**
   * The port number to listen on.
   */
  static int myPortNum = 8007;

//----------------------------------------------------------------
//            instance fields

  /**
   * Variable to tell the Web server to stop.
   */
  private boolean myShouldStop = false;

  /**
   * If another player is currently waiting,
   * this is a handle to the other player's
   * game.
   */
  private ServerGame myCurrentServerGame;

//----------------------------------------------------------------------
//    business methods
```

```java
/**
 * Start listening.
 */
public void listen() {
  try {
    ServerSocket ss;
    ss = new ServerSocket(myPortNum);
    System.out.println("SocketListener.run-->listening on port "
                          + myPortNum);
    while(! myShouldStop) {
      Socket client = ss.accept();
      System.out.println("SocketListener.run-->accepted client socket");
      client.setKeepAlive(true);
      // The following block of code does not
      // need to be synchronized because all
      // calls to this method take place on
      // the same thread.
      if(myCurrentServerGame == null) {
        myCurrentServerGame = new ServerGame(client);
      } else {
        myCurrentServerGame.setSecondPlayer(client);
        myCurrentServerGame.start();
        // note that even though you're setting the
        // handle to null, it won't be garbage
        // collected because it's a live thread.
        // When the game terminates, the thread's run()
        // method will return and then the class will
        // be garbage collected.
        myCurrentServerGame = null;
      }
    }
  } catch(Exception ioe) {
    System.out.println("SocketListener.run-->caught Exception: "
        + ioe.getMessage());
  }
}


//---------------------------------------------------------------------
//   main

/**
 * main starts the server.
 */
public static void main(String[] args) {
```

```
    try {
      SocketListener sl = new SocketListener();
      sl.listen();
    } catch(Exception e) {
      e.printStackTrace();
      System.out.println("SocketListener.main-->"
          + "caught " + e.getClass() + ": " + e.getMessage());
    }
  }

}
```

Listing 6-9 shows the code for ServerGame.java.

*Listing 6-9.* ServerGame.java

```
package net.frog_parrot.server;

import java.io.*;
import java.net.*;

/**
 * This class handles the communications between
 * two players who are playing a game of checkers
 * against each other.
 *
 * @author Carol Hamer
 */
public class ServerGame extends Thread {

  //-----------------------------------------------------------
  //  static fields

  /**
   * The int to signal that the game is to begin.
   */
  public static final byte START_GAME_FLAG = -4;

  /**
   * The int to signal that the game is to end.
   */
  public static final byte END_GAME_FLAG = -3;
```

```java
/**
 * The int to signal the end of a turn.
 */
public static final byte END_TURN_FLAG = -2;


//--------------------------------------------------------------
//              instance fields

/**
 * The socket that the server uses to communicate
 * with the first player.
 */
private Socket myPlayerSocket1;

/**
 * The stream you write to when communicating with the
 * first player.
 */
private OutputStream myOutput1;

/**
 * The stream you read from when communicating with the
 * first player.
 */
private InputStream myInput1;

/**
 * The socket that the server uses to communicate
 * with the second player.
 */
private Socket myPlayerSocket2;

/**
 * The stream you write to when communicating with the
 * second player.
 */
private OutputStream myOutput2;

/**
 * The stream you read from when communicating with the
 * second player.
 */
private InputStream myInput2;
```

```
/**
 * Messages are sent and received in sets of 4 bytes.
 */
private byte[] myData = new byte[4];


//--------------------------------------------------------------
//                 initialization

/**
 * Constructor sets the first player and waits for
 * the second.
 */
ServerGame(Socket player1) {
  System.out.println("ServerGame.ServerGame");
  try {
    // start communications with the first player:
    myPlayerSocket1 = player1;
    myInput1 = player1.getInputStream();
    myOutput1 = player1.getOutputStream();
    // test the communications by sending an initial
    // set of four bytes:
    myData[0] = START_GAME_FLAG;
    myOutput1.write(myData);
    System.out.println("ServerGame.ServerGame-->wrote to player 1");
  } catch(Exception e) {
    e.printStackTrace();
  }
}


/**
 * Add a second player to the game.
 */
void setSecondPlayer(Socket player2) {
  try {
    // start communications with the second player:
    myPlayerSocket2 = player2;
    myInput2 = player2.getInputStream();
    myOutput2 = player2.getOutputStream();
    // test the communications by sending an initial
    // set of 4 bytes:
    myData[0] = START_GAME_FLAG;
    myOutput2.write(myData);
    System.out.println("ServerGame.setSecondPlayer-->"
                        + "wrote back to player 2");
```

```
        } catch(Exception e) {
          e.printStackTrace();
        }
      }


//---------------------------------------------------------------
//              business methods

/**
 * play the game.
 */
public void run() {
  try {
    // you write and tell the first player to go:
    myData[0] = START_GAME_FLAG;
    myOutput1.write(myData);
    // the main loop receives move information from
    // one player and passes it along to the other player,
    // then does the same thing in reverse:
    while(true) {
      readFour(myInput1);
      if(myData[0] == END_GAME_FLAG) {
        break;
      }
      while(myData[0] != END_TURN_FLAG) {
        System.out.println("ServerGame.run-->read from player 1: "
                            + myData[0] + ", "  + myData[1] + " to "
                            +  myData[2] +", "  + myData[3]);
        myOutput2.write(myData);
        readFour(myInput1);
      }
      // since the turn is over, you write the end turn flag:
      myOutput2.write(myData);
      System.out.println("ServerGame.run-->player 1 done, wrote: "
                          + myData[0]);
      // now it's the second player's turn:
      readFour(myInput2);
      if(myData[0] == END_GAME_FLAG) {
        break;
      }
      while(myData[0] != END_TURN_FLAG) {
        System.out.println("ServerGame.run-->read from player 2: "
                            + myData[0] +", "  + myData[1] + " to "
                            +  myData[2] +", "  + myData[3]);
```

```
      myOutput1.write(myData);
      readFour(myInput2);
    }
    // since the turn is over, you write the end turn flag:
    myOutput1.write(myData);
    System.out.println("ServerGame.run-->player 2 done, wrote: "
                       + myData[0]);
  }
} catch(Exception e) {
  // here you print the stack trace for information even
  // though often the Exception just indicates that one
  // player has left the game and is not an error...
  e.printStackTrace();
} finally {
  // regardless of what knocked you out of the main
  // game loop, you need to
  // tell everyone that the game is over and then close
  // up all of the streams and sockets.
  myData[0] = END_GAME_FLAG;
  try {
    myOutput1.write(myData);
    System.out.println("ServerGame.run-->"
                       + "sent end game to player 1, wrote: " +
                                                    myData[0]);
  } catch(Exception ie) {
    // this will throw if player 1 has left the game,
    // but it's not an error, so you don't bother with it.
  }
  try {
    myOutput2.write(myData);
    System.out.println("ServerGame.run-->"
                       + "sent end game to player 2, wrote: " +
                                                    myData[0]);
  } catch(Exception ie) {
    // this will throw if player 2 has left the game,
    // but it's not an error, so you don't bother with it.
  }
  // even if you fail to write to one of
  // the players, you want to close the sockets and streams.
  try {
    myOutput1.close();
    myOutput2.close();
    myInput1.close();
    myInput2.close();
```

```
            myPlayerSocket1.close();
            myPlayerSocket2.close();
        } catch(Exception ie) {
            ie.printStackTrace();
        }
    }
}


//-------------------------------------------------------------
//                  internal utilities

/**
 * This method reads exactly 4 bytes off the stream
 * and puts them in the array myData. This method is
 * used because I know that in this game the client
 * always sends sets of 4 bytes, but the method
 * read may return without reading all of them.
 * @throws Exception when the player corresponding
 * to the InputStream disconnects.
 */
private void readFour(InputStream istream) throws Exception {
    int total = 0;
    int numRead = 0;
    while(total < 4) {
        numRead = istream.read(myData, total, myData.length - total);
        if(numRead >= 0) {
            total += numRead;
            System.out.println("ServerGame.readFour-->read " + total + " bytes");
        } else {
            throw(new Exception("player ended game"));
        }
    }
}



}
```

## Handling Errors

Throughout the checkers game example I've been a little bit severe in terms of
how errors are handled. If you look over the code, you'll notice that essentially if
any unexpected error occurs, the game gives an error message and then terminates. That sort of behavior is appropriate in situations where the only Exceptions

possible would be generated by bugs in the code itself (and in that case you should have tested and debugged your production code well enough that a live user will never see an error message). But network communications code can easily throw Exceptions that have nothing to do with bugs in the code. In a professional game you may want to attempt to recover from a communications-related Exception if possible.

The most fundamental error you must be ready to deal with is what to do if the connection between a client and the server is unexpectedly broken. When a connection is broken the server should be able to tell whether the client broke the connection intentionally (by exiting the game) or whether the loss of contact was because of a communication problem. The MIDlet's destroyApp() should send a message back to the server before closing the connection. So when the server receives such a message it knows it should tell the other player that the game is over and terminate their game. On the other hand, if the server notices that the socket has closed before the client sent the "game over" message, then the server should assume that the communications got interrupted accidentally and allow for the possibility that the client may attempt to reconnect. Similarly, if the client notices that the socket has closed without receiving a "game over" message from the server, then the client should probably try to reconnect to the server. Implementing the possibility of reconnects would have the added advantage of allowing the client to disconnect when the user pauses the game and then reconnect later when the user unpauses it. A call to pauseApp() could send a particular message to the server before closing the connection so that the server knows to wait for that client to call back. (In theory, the game could hold open the connection with the server even when the game is paused, but this isn't recommended because a MIDlet is expected to release all scarce resources when pauseApp() is called. If the MIDlet fails to do so, the application management software may close the socket for the MIDlet, which could potentially cause errors if the MIDlet isn't prepared to deal with being disconnected.)

Since the game server will probably be programmed to serve multiple simultaneous game groups, allowing players to reconnect to a game in progress would require the server to keep handles to the games in progress. In the checkers game, the server creates an instance of ServerGame for each pair of players and then doesn't bother to maintain a handle to the instance after the game has started. But if the server maintained a Hashtable of active games, then the server could redirect a client to the correct game if the client reconnects. In fact, the server doesn't really even need to maintain a Hashtable of all active games; it could just hold onto those that have temporarily lost a player. When a game accidentally loses contact with one player, it could call up the main class of the game server and register itself to be put on the "lost and found" Hashtable. To direct an errant client back to the correct game in progress would require all of the clients to have some sort of identifying token. This could be a standard session token (in other words, invented by the server at the beginning of the session and passed back to the client), or it could even be a string chosen by the user. (In the latter case, the program needs to do a little extra work to make sure each client's handle is unique.) Letting the users choose handles could also be used for an additional improvement to the checkers game, namely allowing the users to select their opponents. In the current version of the checkers game, if you call up the server and someone is already waiting to play, then you'll be paired with that person. If you call up and no one is waiting to play, then you'll play against the next person who calls up. Instead, when the user connects, the server could send back a list of the handles of the players who are currently waiting for opponents, and then the user could choose to play against one of the people on the list or choose to wait for someone else.

Another type of error that should probably be dealt with is what to do in the case where one of the players attempts to make an illegal move. In the current version of the checkers game, if one player tells the other he wants to move a piece to some faraway square that he shouldn't normally be allowed to jump to in a single move, the game will permit it and obediently move the piece to the requested location. I didn't bother to deal with such a situation because it's unlikely to happen in practice (except by accident if the program has a bug). But in theory a user could write a new checkers client that acts just like the standard checkers client except that it allows the player to cheat. This would be a problem if your business model is to allow users to subscribe to the service of using your server to play against other users. Your customers would be annoyed if they discover that sometimes their opponents can cheat. So, in a production version of the game, it may be a good idea to have the client analyze the opponent's moves and have the possibility to refuse any moves that are illegal or have the server analyze them and refuse to pass illegal moves to the other player(s).

## Setting Networking Permissions

If you want to communicate over a plain socket instead of using HTTP, you need to be aware of one more step: You need to ask for permission. The way an application requests permission to use a restricted resource (such as a socket) is by adding a permission name to the `MIDlet-permissions` property in the applications jad file and `MANIFEST.MF`. (The "Building an Application for MIDP" section in Chapter 1 covers the syntax of these files.) The permission name to add if you'd like to use a plain socket such as the checkers game is `javax.microedition.io.Connector.socket`. If your program would like to have a certain permission but can run without it, then instead of listing the permission in the `MIDlet-permissions` property, you should list it in the `MIDlet-Permissions-Opt` property. An example of an optional permission would be a game that can be played against other players on a network but could also be played locally against the computer.

If your application has requested a permission, the user decides whether to grant the permission by creating a protection domain. The "Creating Protection Domains" section in Chapter 7 covers protection domains.

Note that the emulator isn't at all picky about verifying that permission requests appear in the descriptor files. So I was able to test the checkers game on the emulator without even adding the permission request to my jad and MANIFEST.MF files. But a real device won't be so lenient.

Throughout this chapter, all of the network communications I've illustrated have been written to pass through the Internet without any encryption or other protection. This is usually OK for noncommercial applications since most of the time no one is going to bother to intercept or interfere with your personal communications. But for commercial applications you'll probably be interested in having a little more protection for your data transmissions. The next chapter gives some explanation of how to make your game more secure.

## Deciding When to Use HTTP and When to Use a Plain Socket

In my example checkers game, I had the clients communicate with the server using plain sockets (class SocketConnection), but it would've been possible to write the same game using HttpConnection instead. The first question that should come to your mind is, why would you want to do that? In fact, you get some advantages when using HttpConnection instead of SocketConnection. The main advantage is portability. Every MIDP device can communicate using HTTP, including devices that are compatible only with MIDP 1.0. A device that uses MIDP 1.0 doesn't always have the possibility of communicating on a plain socket (using SocketConnection), and even for MIDP 2.0 devices, providing an implementation of SocketConnection is optional whereas HttpConnection is required. And even if you're sure that all your target devices are capable of using SocketConnection, HttpConnection is still more portable. That's because the user has to specially grant the program permission to use a SocketConnection (see the "Setting Networking Permissions" section) whereas HttpConnection is always allowed as long as the user OKs it when queried by the application management software. Additionally, on the server end, writing a Servlet to communicate with the game in HTTP may be easier and more familiar for many developers than writing a program that communicates on a plain socket.

HTTP has another big portability advantage--namely, it's more firewall-friendly. Even if your own server is willing to accept socket connections on the port you've chosen, a phone's message will be routed by an operator that likely has strict rules about what types of communication it will allow. An HTTP exchange will usually be allowed to pass through whereas a TCP message directed at another port will in many cases be blocked.

The class HttpConnection has some limitations, however. The most serious limitation in HttpConnection for an interactive game is that an instance of HttpConnection allows exactly one request and one response. This means that in a game such as the checkers example, you'd have to open the HttpConnection, send the local player's move, receive the remote player's move as a response, throw away that HttpConnection, and then create a new one for the next move (unlike a SocketConnection where you can send as many messages as you like in either direction and in any order without creating a new instance). HttpConnection's single request/response limitation creates a couple of problems in addition to the fact that it wastes memory by creating numerous temporary objects. One problem is that depending on the implementation, the connection may time out before the opponent's move is received. Having the server set a "Connection: Keep-Alive" header should take care of that problem. Another problem to deal with is how to hook the player up with the right game in progress if the server is handling more than one game. This problem can be easily handled with session tokens as follows: When the client game first connects and starts a game, the server sends the client a token (a string or a number associated with the client's session) and then stores all of the games in progress in a Hashtable using the tokens as keys. Then for each subsequent connection, the client sends its session token so that the server can send the client's message to the right game.

Clearly, using HTTP as the communication protocol for a multiplayer game would work best in the case of games where the players take turns (such as a card game or checkers) and not for a game where multiple players may be moving at once. But HTTP is an option to keep in mind for simple games on low-end devices.

# CHAPTER 7

# Securing Your Applications

IN THIS CHAPTER you'll see how to use the security features of the Mobile Information Device Profile (MIDP) to secure your games. You'll improve both of the games from the previous chapter by using secure connections to transmit the game data. You'll also learn about other aspects of the MIDP security system such as permissions and protection domains.

## Understanding How Security Works in MIDP

Effective security is one of the main selling points of Java. Java offers consumers the assurance that an untrusted program won't damage their devices, and Java offers developers the use of a wide array of security tools that can be easily integrated into an application. The security features offered by Java 2 Micro Edition (J2ME) with MIDP follow the same basic strategies and philosophy as the security features of other Java editions, albeit somewhat simplified.

## Understanding the Differences Between MIDP Security and Security in Other Java Versions

The MIDP security model has two main components: built-in Java (sandbox) security and end-to-end security for communications.

End-to-end security for communications just means that an application has the option of using a secure protocol when communicating with a server. A secure protocol allows the client to not only verify the identity of the server but also to encrypt the data being transmitted so that it can't be intercepted and read or modified by a third party. The "Setting Up Secure Connections" section covers how to use a secure connection with MIDP.

Java's built-in security is based on a Java application that's run by a virtual machine that prevents the application from breaking certain security rules. Essentially, the virtual machine allows each Java application access to its own data only, unlike a C program that can more or less read and modify any data anywhere on the machine. The virtual machine's bytecode verifier ensures that the Java application won't get out if its memory area by cheating and adding or removing the wrong data from the stack.

In addition to restricting access to memory, the virtual machine protects the real machine from a potentially malicious application by restricting access to protected resources. A `MIDlet` (like an `Applet`) is run in a "sandbox," which is essentially a place where it has enough room to run around and have fun but can't get out and make trouble. The application management software that runs the `MIDlet` decides which protected resources the `MIDlet` can access.

The user can determine which protected resources a given `MIDlet` suite will have access to by setting up a protection domain. See the "Creating Protection Domains" section for more details.

MIDP is missing some of the advanced security features found in standard Java. As usual, the missing items are features that wouldn't really be appropriate on a small device anyway. For example, MIDP has no `SecurityManager` class. But remember that the job of the `SecurityManager` class is to allow different sets of privileges to code loaded from different codebases (which essentially means different `jar` files). But aside from classes that are built into the MIDP implementation, a `MIDlet` can access classes only from its own `jar`. (By built-in classes I mean classes from the MIDP Application Programming Interface [API] and any proprietary classes installed by the device manufacturer.) So once you've assigned privileges to the `MIDlet` through its protection domain, there's no need for further fine-tuning with a `SecurityManager`. You aren't allowed to use a custom `Classloader` for approximately the same reason. In MIDP, the MIDP classes (and the proprietary classes) must be loaded from their preinstalled places in memory, and all of the `MIDlet`'s classes must be loaded from the `MIDlet`'s `jar` file. So a custom `Classloader` would have no use in a `MIDlet`.

## Using Digital Certificates

The MIDP security system is largely based on the X.509 Public Key Infrastructure (PKI). The public key infrastructure is integral to the creation of secure connections, and it's also used in the creation of protection domains. Since the user is more likely to trust a `jar` that has been digitally signed with an X.509 digital certificate, you can place such a `jar` in a protection domain that allows access to restricted resources.

A *digital certificate* is a set of data containing cryptographic information that allows you to encrypt messages and verify the identity of the sender. Since anyone can create a digital certificate containing any name they want, a certificate must be recognized in order to be useful for identification purposes. For limited applications you could load the same certificate onto the client and server to ensure that the client will recognize the server's certificate. But if you have a server that needs to securely communicate with a large number of unknown clients, the server's certificate needs to be signed by a recognized Certificate Authority (CA) in order to be trusted by the clients. The CA is a third party that both the client and server trust that can guarantee the server is who it says it is. Some widely accepted CAs include VeriSign, Thawte, and Baltimore Technologies.

If you just need a certificate for testing, you can create a self-signed certificate using the keytool utility that comes with the Java Software Development Kit (SDK). The following is an example of the command I used to create a certificate for my local testing:

```
keytool -genkey -alias tomcat -keyalg RSA
```

This command creates a digital certificate in the default keystore (`~/.keystore`) using the RSA algorithm. I gave the certificate an alias of `tomcat` because this is the certificate I used to create secure HTTP (HTTPS) connections on my Tomcat server. When you enter the command to create the certificate, keytool will prompt you to enter a name ("What is your first and last name?"). Don't be thrown off because it's asking for a first and last name—the name it really wants is the domain name (or the name of the host machine) that will be used in the host's Uniform Resource Locator (URL). It's important to enter the correct name if you want the client to accept the certificate.

If you'd like to get your certificate signed by a CA, you need to contact the CA to find out how to do it. It's not completely simple (because the CA needs to verify your identity), and unfortunately it's not free. Plus you'll need to renew the certificate regularly, which also costs money. But if you need to allow customers to securely contact you, you have no way around this.

## Protecting the Client

The focus of the MIDP security model is really on protecting the client (the client's device and the client's data) rather than on protecting the application provider. Obviously, this makes sense since the client's device is the one running MIDP. The advantage you gain from having a well-protected client is that it makes it easier for you to create a product that a customer will trust.

### Creating Protection Domains

The client decides which permissions to grant to which MIDlet suites by creating *protection domains*. A protection domain is just a set of permissions that may be granted to a MIDlet suite. You can mark the permissions in the protection domain as either *User* or *Allowed*. A User permission is one where the MIDlet suite can access the protected functionality but the application's management software first notifies the user and gets confirmation that it's OK. An Allowed permission is one where the MIDlet suite can access the protected functionality without first querying the user.

All of the permissions defined for MIDP 2.0 relate to making connections
of various types. A complete list of the permissions is as follows:

- `javax.microedition.io.Connector.http`

- `javax.microedition.io.Connector.https`

- `javax.microedition.io.Connector.datagram`

- `javax.microedition.io.Connector.datagramreceiver`

- `javax.microedition.io.Connector.socket`

- `javax.microedition.io.Connector.serversocket`

- `javax.microedition.io.Connector.ssl`

- `javax.microedition.io.Connector.comm`

Note that `MIDlet` suites that are untrusted are allowed to make HTTP and HTTPS
connections with explicit user permission. In other words, the protection domain for
untrusted `MIDlets` contains the permissions `javax.microedition.io.Connector.http`
and `javax.microedition.io.Connector.https` as User-level permissions. Devices with
built-in proprietary classes may have additional permissions defined for them.

Precisely how your `MIDlet` suite gets attached to a protection domain is
between the user and the device. It's a device-dependent procedure. By signing
your jar file (see the "Signing the jar" section), you can help to convince the user
to grant your `MIDlet` suite the permissions it needs. (In some implementations,
a jar that's signed with certain recognized certificates may be automatically placed
in the corresponding protection domain, and/or some protection domains may be
defined and managed by the telephone operator rather than by the end user.)

It isn't possible to define a fine-grained custom protection domain for the
emulator, but the emulator does have some built-in protection domains in
which an application can be tested. The possibilities are `trusted` (allow all permissions), `untrusted` (all permissions are set to User), `minimum` (all permissions are
denied), and `maximum` (same as trusted). To set the protection domain when running the emulator, you merely add the option `-Xdomain` to the command that's
used to run the emulator. The following is an example of a command to run the
emulator with a protection domain specified (all on one line):

```
./bin/emulator -Xdomain:minimum
-Xdescriptor:/home/carol/j2me/book/ch01/bin/hello.jad
```

If your game needs to be allowed certain permissions, then it needs to
request them in the descriptor (jad) file and in the manifest (`MANIFEST.MF`) file.
The permission requests that appear in these two files must be identical, or the
program will not run. You should place any permission that's critical for the program to run in the `MIDlet-Permissions` attribute, and you should place any
permission that the program would like to have but isn't critical in the `MIDlet-
Permissions-Opt` attribute. The following is an example of a manifest file with
some permission requests:

```
MIDlet-1: TestMessage, /images/crown.png, net.frog_parrot.http.Messenger
MIDlet-Description: A program that makes some connections for testing
MIDlet-Name: Test Message
MIDlet-Permissions: javax.microedition.io.Connector.socket
MIDlet-Permissions-Opt: javax.microedition.io.Connector.ssl
MIDlet-Vendor: frog-parrot.net
MIDlet-Version: 2.0
MicroEdition-Configuration: CLDC-1.0
MicroEdition-Profile: MIDP-2.0
```

If your MIDlet suite requires a permission that the user has denied to your MIDlet suite's protection domain, then the application management software won't load and run the MIDlet suite. If the MIDlet is running and is denied a permission, then the protected method will throw a SecurityException. This will happen if the permission was listed as optional and the protection domain denies it or if the user was queried for permission and refused. Your code needs to be prepared to handle a SecurityException when calling methods that may throw one. Of course, since the protected methods almost all have the risk of throwing an IOException, you'll probably naturally have some Exception-handling code in place.

## Signing the jar

To let your customers know that your application is trustworthy (or at least to be sure of the identity of whom to blame if it's not), you can add a digital certificate to the jad file and a signature to the jar and jad files. MIDP requires its implementations to support X.509 certificates. (Other types of certificates may optionally be supported.)

The toolkit provides a MIDlet suite signing utility called JADTool. The procedure takes a few steps, but it isn't hard. The first thing to do is to create and store a key pair (consisting of a public and a private key). You do this with keytool, which is a utility that comes with Java 2 Standard Edition (J2SE) or Java 2 Enterprise Edition (J2EE). I discussed this step previously in the "Using Digital Certificates" section. Once you have the keys to use, you need to add a certificate to the jad file using JADTool. The following is an example of a command that would work in my case (using the key pair generated in the "Using Digital Certificates" section):

```
java -jar JadTool.jar -addcert -alias tomcat
-storepass changeit -inputjad book.jad -outputjad book.jad
```

Of course, you should enter this command all on one line. It takes the certificate with alias tomcat from the default keystore (~/.keystore) and adds it to the jad file called book.jad.

The next step is to sign the jar file and add the jar file's signature to the jad file. The following is an example of a command to do that (again all on one line):

```
java -jar JadTool.jar -addjarsig -jarfile book.jar
-keypass changeit -alias tomcat -storepass changeit
-inputjad book.jad -outputjad book.jad
```

For further information and options for the JADTool utility, consult the toolkit's Hypertext Markup Language (HTML) documentation or run JADTool with the -help option.

You can also accomplish the whole procedure of signing the jar and jad files simply from KToolbar by selecting File ➤ Utilities ➤ Sign MIDlet. (See the "Using KToolbar" section in Chapter 1 for more information about running KToolbar.)

## Setting Up Secure Connections

Secure connections are extremely easy to program with MIDP because all the work is done behind the scenes for you. The idea is that the application developer doesn't really need to be concerned with the details of how the underlying secure socket is created; it's enough to know you want to use one and then leave the details to the application management software.

To use a secure connection, you need to get an instance of HttpsConnection instead of HttpConnection or get an instance of SecureConnection instead of SocketConnection. To get the right connection, all you need to do is send the right URL to the method Connector.open(). It couldn't be simpler. Once you have a handle to the Connection, you can get information about it by calling getSecurityInfo() to get the corresponding SecurityInfo object. The SecurityInfo object will give you more details about the protocol, the cipher suites, and the server's certificate.

### Using HTTPS

HTTPS is the standard protocol that most browsers use for communicating securely. It's just the same as HTTP except that communication takes place over a secure connection using the SSL protocol.

Because of MIDP's generic connection framework, switching a game from using HTTP to HTTPS is really just as simple as changing the URL. On the client side, that's the only change you need to make. The MIDP classes will take care of creating the right type of connection for you as long as the URL is right. Generally you need to change the http:// at the beginning of the URL to https:// and change the port number if the server listens for HTTP and HTTPS messages on different ports. (Consult your server configuration to find out what port it's listening on for

HTTPS connections.) In my test version of the dungeon game from the previous chapter, the URL changed from `http://frog-parrot.net:8080/games/DungeonDownload` to `https://frog-parrot.net:8443/games/DungeonDownload`. And that was the only change I needed to make in my client code. (Remember to use your own domain name or Internet Protocol [IP] address instead of `frog-parrot.net` when testing because my `Servlet` isn't usually running on this site.)

On the server side, the code doesn't need to change at all. A `Servlet` doesn't care if it's being served over HTTP or HTTPS. It's just a question of configuring your server to use HTTPS. (Consult the documentation; it shouldn't be very hard.)

The hardest part is setting up the certificate. If you're planning to communicate with real clients over the Internet using HTTPS, then you'll need a real certificate. See the earlier "Using Digital Certificates" section for more information.

If you'd like to test locally, then you can just create your own certificate. This is also discussed in the "Using Digital Certificates" section. You have one additional step to perform when using HTTPS with the emulator and a self-signed certificate: You must import the server's certificate into the emulator's keystore. If you don't do this, the emulator won't recognize the server's certificate and will refuse to connect (unless it's a real certificate from a CA and not just a self-signed certificate).

To import the server's certificate into the emulator's keystore, you can use the MEKeytool utility that comes with the MIDP toolkit. With my configuration, the command I used was the following (all on one line):

```
java -jar ~/j2me/WTK2.0/bin/MEKeyTool.jar
-import -alias tomcat -MEkeystore ~/j2me/WTK2.0/appdb/_main.ks
-storepass changeit
```

This command is loaded with options, but most of them are self-explanatory. The beginning (`java -jar ~/j2me/WTK2.0/bin/MEKeyTool.jar`) merely tells the machine to run MEKeytool. The `-import` option gives the command to import a certificate. Since I didn't include the option `-keystore`, MEKeytool assumes that the certificate should be read from the default keystore at `~/.keystore`. The `-alias tomcat` option tells it to use the certificate that has the alias `tomcat`. (The certificate has that alias because it's the certificate that my Tomcat server is using). The `-MEkeystore ~/j2me/WTK2.0/appdb/_main.ks` option tells MEKeytool that the destination keystore is `~/j2me/WTK2.0/appdb/_main.ks`, which is the default keystore for the emulator (assuming that the toolkit was installed in the directory `~/j2me/`). Then, obviously, the option `-storepass changeit` gives the password needed to read from the server's keystore. You'll almost certainly have to modify the options a bit if you run this command on your own system, but if the modifications you need to make aren't obvious, the toolkit's HTML documentation covers MEKeytool.

## Using Secure Connections While Selling Your Game

Let's face it: If you're giving your game away for free, you probably don't need to worry much about security. But unless you're lucky enough to have an infinite amount of free time for writing games, you're probably writing your games with the intention of making some money from them. The security features of MIDP can help you do that. Unfortunately, it's hard to prevent people from playing your game for free if they're determined to do so. But assuming you're an independent programmer distributing your game yourself or that you're running a small game business, this sidebar contains some suggestions on how to encourage your customers to pay for your game if they play it.

The simplest business model is to distribute the game completely free but have it somewhere contain a message that says, "If you like this game, please send $5 to the following address." Since most people are basically honest, you can actually get a fair amount of money from your game this way. Of course, that technique is mostly for hobbyists since a good portion of your customers definitely won't send in the money.

The next most simple business model is to place your `jar` file on a secure server and limit access to who can download it. The disadvantage of this one is that it's too easy for one paying customer to give away your game free to others. If the game is good, it will likely start popping up for free download on sites all over the Internet, and it's hard to get all of the unofficial distributors to cut it out.

Probably the most effective way to get paid for your game is to distribute it freely and then require it to call your server at some point. This works especially well if you have a part of the game that can be played for free and another segment that requires payment. That way, the "Napster instinct" that motivates users to share the free portion of your game works in your favor as the game acts as its own advertisement.

Two principal strategies exist for writing games with a free part and a paying part. The easiest is to put the entire game in the `jar` and just write the game in such a way that part of it won't play until the user calls up your server to unlock it. To "unlock" the game, all you need to do is instruct the game to create a special `RecordStore` when the game calls your `Servlet`, and then later, when the user would like to play the paid part of the game, have the program check that the required `RecordStore` exists before allowing the user to access that part of the game. The other strategy is to do as I did in the dungeon game, where you write a game in which the various levels or game boards are read from data, and you have the users call you up to download more boards. I'm partial to this second approach because it's flexible. If your game is well written, you can have one game keep bringing in more money just by writing more boards for it. Plus, your game can be elaborate and long running without wasting precious memory on your clients' devices because you can have the program replace the completed boards in memory with the new ones.

Whichever strategy you choose, MIDP makes it convenient for you to require the game to call your server at some point.

Here's a standard scenario: The first step is to run a `Servlet` on an HTTPS Web server with a real digital certificate from a CA. Then include a command in your game's command menu that leads to an instruction screen that indicates how to contact your company to purchase the right to play the rest of the game. Most likely you should instruct the user to visit your (secure) Web site with a regular browser in order to give you credit card information in exchange for a single-use password-type string. Otherwise, you could instruct your customers to conduct this transaction with you over the phone or by fax. Then the user can access a screen on the game to key in the password and call your server. The game should have the correct URL to use to contact your server already built in. Your `Servlet` should read in the password and mark it as used (so that further users can't download again using the same password) and send back either the game data or the instruction to unlock the paying part of the game. Note that it's certainly possible to have the user key his credit card information directly into the device and have the device send that information to your `Servlet` in the same transaction where the `Servlet` sends the data to the device. This has the advantage of simplicity, and it eliminates the step of creating a temporary password. The only disadvantage is that the user may not be accustomed to sending his credit card information that way and hence might hesitate to do it.

The device is using HTTPS to communicate with you, which will ensure that the user (or someone else) isn't just spoofing your site. If you use standard HTTP, a hacker could read all the data being transferred in both directions from a session between your server and a paying customer and then spoof your site and write a `Servlet` that returns the same data your `Servlet` returns. Then non-paying customers could go around you and get the complete game from the hacker. Such a hack is unlikely to happen or to steal much of your business in practice, but using HTTPS makes it nearly impossible to use such a hack. For additional security, you can have the program examine the site's certificate to make sure it's the right one (see the "Using SSL" section for information on how to do that), but with HTTPS it's not really necessary because the application management software verifies the name of certificate for you.

You may worry that once a user has downloaded the data or "unlocked" the game by contacting you, he may be able to distribute just the data or distribute an unlocked version of the game. This unfortunately is the weak point in the security model. Once the data is on the user's device, the user has access to it for good or for bad. It's true that when a `MIDlet` creates a `RecordStore`, no other `MIDlet` suite can access that `RecordStore` unless the `MIDlet` suite that created the `RecordStore` explicitly grants access to it to other `MIDlets` (to do this, use `RecordStore.setMode()` or create the `RecordStore` with the versions of `RecordStore.openRecordStore()` that takes the argument `authmode`). So you may think that then you could create a `RecordStore` containing secret data that the user can't read or alter. Unfortunately, this isn't possible since the user can read your `MIDlet`'s data and pass data to your `MIDlet` by performing phony updates.

To take advantage of the MIDlet suite update function, all the user has to do is create a new MIDlet suite and give it the same vendor name and MIDlet name as your MIDlet suite (since the vendor name and the MIDlet name are the parameters that the device uses to identify the owner of a RecordStore). If the user's goal is to read the data your program created, he can write a MIDlet that will list all the RecordStores and their contents. If the user has already installed your MIDlet suite on a device and then tries to install another MIDlet with the same name and vendor name, the device will view it as an update and ask the user if he wants to make the existing RecordStores available to the new version. Thus, the user can give the new (fake) version access to the old (real) version's data even if the URLs that the versions were downloaded from are completely different. Even signing the jar file isn't sufficient because the user can update a signed jar with a jar signed by someone else and still grant the new version access to the earlier version's data. So, a hacker could download your game, pay to download the additional data, and then read the data by "updating" the MIDlet suite with a RecordStore reading MIDlet that has the same name and vendor name as your MIDlet. He could then write a RecordStore writing MIDlet (again with the same name and vendor name as your MIDlet), which will create exactly the RecordStores that your MIDlet would normally create after calling your server. The hacker can distribute the RecordStore writing MIDlet and then tell people to run it once (to create and populate the RecordStore) and then "update" it with a copy of your game. In this way a hacker can grant users access to a cracked version of your game. Unfortunately, you have no way to prevent hackers from cracking your game in this manner. All you can really do is hope that it's too much of bother for a hacker to do and that you won't lose too much business to this exploit.

In addition to the trick using "update," some implementations of MIDP allow the user direct access to the MIDP RecordStores. According to the rules of MIDP, a record store that's private can't be accessed by MIDlet suites other than the MIDlet suite that created it. But it's possible to have an implementation that would allow the user to read and modify the MIDP RecordStores using a non-Java application such as a text editor! This is probably not typical, but on a MIDP device with this behavior, there's no simple way to keep a nonpaying user from unlocking his game by copying the RecordStores from the device of a paying user.

The only sure way to obligate users to pay for a game is to force the game to contact your server every time it runs. The disadvantage to such a strategy is that this will annoy your users a great deal, especially if they have to pay for Wireless Application Protocol (WAP) access, which they typically do. In the case of a distributed game (such as the example in the following section), the user won't mind connecting every time since it's obvious they can't play against other users without connecting. That's why hosting multiplayer games is a good business model. Using HTTPS you can ensure that the game will contact only your server, and by having the game send you some sort of ID or handle for each player, you can keep track of how much each user is playing (for billing purposes).

On the other hand, if you're a freelance programmer working from home and the question of securely distributing your game seems daunting, plenty of companies will distribute your games for you and give you a percentage of the profits. Some examples include Handango (http://www.handango.com) and In-Fusio (http://developer.in-fusio.com).

-----

## Using SSL

Switching your MIDP client program from using a SocketConnection to using a SecureConnection (in other words, switching from using a plain socket to using SSL) is almost as trivial as switching from HTTP to HTTPS. In fact, just as with HTTP vs. HTTPS, it's sufficient to just change the URL. (In this case, switch the beginning of the URL from socket:// to ssl://, and change the port number if necessary.)

Even though setting the right URL is all that's required for creating a SecureConnection, you should probably also programmatically verify that the certificate that the server is using is the right one. When you create a SecureConnection, the application management software will accept any valid certificate (as long as it's from a recognized CA). This means that unless you verify the name on the certificate yourself, you still may be making an SSL connection with the wrong host even though the host has a real certificate.

Checking the certificate is quite easy. To demonstrate, I've written a verification method to add to the Communicator class from the checkers game (see Listing 7-1).

*Listing 7-1. Verification Method*

```
/**
 * This takes a secure connection and makes sure that
 * the corresponding certificate is the right one.
 * @throws SecurityException if the certificate isn't
 * issued to the correct entity.
 */
private void verifyCertificate(SecureConnection conn)
    throws Exception {
  SecurityInfo info = conn.getSecurityInfo();
  Certificate cert = info.getServerCertificate();
  String sub = cert.getSubject();
  // the subject should end with CN=DOMAIN_NAME where
  // DOMAIN_NAME is the name of the domain that you
```

```
    // expect to be communicating with.
    if(! sub.endsWith("CN=" + DOMAIN_NAME)) {
      // you'll give it one more chance in case the CN
      // attribute wasn't the last attribute in the list:
      if(sub.indexOf("CN=" + DOMAIN_NAME + ";") == -1) {
        // if it fails both these tests, then the certificate
        // isn't the right one...
        throw(new SecurityException("Certificate CN wrong"));
      }
    }
  }
}
```

(To compile the `Communicator` class with this new addition, you must also add a statement to import the interface `javax.microedition.pki.Certificate`.) To understand Listing 7-1, keep in mind that the method `getSubject()` (of the `Certificate` interface) returns the name of the certificate owner in Lightweight Directory Access Protocol (LDAP) format. This means that the subject string will look something like this: `C=US;O=Any Company, Inc.;CN=www.anycompany.com`. The part of the subject you probably want to verify is the value of the `CN` attribute. This should be the URL of the site that owns the certificate. Technically it doesn't have to be, but in practice it usually is. The `CN` attribute should appear at the end of the subject string. That's why I used the method `endsWith()` to check if the `CN` of the certificate is right. If the end of the subject string isn't what I expected, then the certificate owner is probably the wrong one. In Listing 7-1 I give the certificate a second chance to have the correct `CN` somewhere in it (by using the method `indexOf()` to determine if the correct `CN` is present). In a professional game you may want to be so lenient.

To use Listing 7-1 in the `Communicator` class of the checkers game, you need to make a couple of additional changes. First, you need to define the field `DOMAIN_NAME` and set it equal to the domain name to which the certificate should be issued. Second, you need to call the method in Listing 7-1 from inside the `Communicator`'s `run()` method. Listing 7-2 shows the beginning of the `run()` method with a call to `verifyCertificate()` added.

*Listing 7-2. Calling* `verifyCertificate()`

```
public void run() {
  DataInputStream dis = null;
  DataOutputStream dos = null;
  SecureConnection conn = null;
  byte[] fourBytes = new byte[4];
  try {
    // tell the user you're waiting for the other player to join:
    myCanvas.setWaitScreen(true);
    myCanvas.repaint();
```

```
myCanvas.serviceRepaints();
// now make the connection:
conn = (SecureConnection)Connector.open(SERVER_URL);
verifyCertificate(conn);
conn.setSocketOption(SocketConnection.KEEPALIVE, 1);
```

Note that in Listing 7-2 I also changed the class of the `comm` variable from `SocketConnection` to `SecureConnection`. Since `SecureConnection` extends `SocketConnection`, I could just use the interface `SocketConnection` for some SSL applications. But in this case I use `SecureConnection` because I want to be able to get the associated `SecurityInfo` object.

Even though the return value of `verifyCertificate()` is void, the method is doing its job. If the certificate is wrong, the method will throw a `SecurityException` that will be caught by the `run()` method with the result of closing the connection, giving an appropriate error message to the user, and ending the game.

The changes necessary on the server side are a little more complicated because you need to construct an `SSLServerSocket` instead of just a `ServerSocket`, and the connection-related classes in standard Java aren't as simple as the connection-related classes in MIDP.

As before, I won't go into too much detail to explain the server code because I assume you're using this simple server code mainly for testing and that you'll do further server-side research before writing an SSL server that's optimized for your particular situation.

Listing 7-3 shows the method I added to the `SocketListener` class of the server for the checkers game.

*Listing 7-3. Creating a Secure Socket*

```
/**
 * get a secure server socket.
 */
private static SSLServerSocket getSecureServerSocket() {
  SSLServerSocket retObj = null;
  try {
    // initialize the key manager
    KeyManagerFactory kmf = KeyManagerFactory.getInstance("SunX509");
    // read the keys into the keystore and initialize the context:
    KeyStore ks = KeyStore.getInstance("JCEKS");
    char[] passphrase = "changeit".toCharArray();
    ks.load(new FileInputStream("/home/carol/.keystore"), passphrase);
    kmf.init(ks, passphrase);
    SSLContext context = SSLContext.getInstance("TLS");
    context.init(kmf.getKeyManagers(), null, null);
    // get the factory and use it to create the socket:
```

```
      SSLServerSocketFactory ssf = context.getServerSocketFactory();
      retObj = (SSLServerSocket)(ssf.createServerSocket(myPortNum));
    } catch (Exception e) {
      e.printStackTrace();
    }
    return(retObj);
}
```

Note that I precisely specify the keystore to use in the argument to the init() method of the KeyManagerFactory in Listing 7-3. For my tests I had this class use the same keystore as my Tomcat server was using for the dungeon example, which means that to run both examples I had to import only one certificate into the emulator's keystore. (Remember that when using a self-signed certificate for local testing, you must import the server's certificate into the emulator's keystore. If you haven't done that, see the earlier "Using HTTPS" section for how to do it.) If you're hosting a game server for real customers, you'll need to use a real certificate from a certificate authority (see the "Using Digital Certificates" section).

For the SocketListener class to use the new getSecureServerSocket() method, you need to make a few small additional changes to the code. First, you need to import the relevant classes that are needed to create the SSLServerSocket. Just add the following two lines to the top part of the file:

```
import javax.net.ssl.*;
import java.security.KeyStore;
```

If you're running the server using Java 1.4, the SSL-related classes should be built in. If not, you may have to download the Java Secure Socket Extensions (JSSE) package (version 1.0.2 or later) from http://java.sun.com/products/jsse/. To install JSSE, you need to copy the three jar files (jcert.jar, jnet.jar, and jsse.jar) into your $JAVA_HOME/jre/lib/ext directory.

Second, the other change to make to the SocketListener class is that instead of creating a ServerSocket, you call the method getSecureServerSocket() to get an SSLServerSocket. In other words, you replace the following line:

```
ss = new ServerSocket(myPortNum);
```

with this line:

```
ss = getSecureServerSocket();
```

With those few changes, the checkers server will use a secure socket instead of a plain socket and will be able to connect to the SecureSocket version of the checkers client.

If you're planning to host a game such as checkers, you probably want to add one more feature to the code. To make sure the clients connecting are authorized, you should probably have the client program send an ID string or a handle to the server so the server can verify that the client is allowed to connect and so that the server can keep count of how many times a particular user has connected to the server and for how long. Adding code to check the user's ID is simple enough that you should easily be able to figure out how to do it without seeing an example, so I'll leave it as an exercise for you.

# Index